THE MARKET MEETS ITS MATCH

THE MARKET
MEETS
ITS MATCH

Restructuring the Economies of Eastern Europe

ALICE H. AMSDEN

JACEK KOCHANOWICZ

LANCE TAYLOR

HARVARD UNIVERSITY PRESS
Cambridge, Massachusetts · London, England · 1994

Library of Congress Cataloging-in-Publication Data

Amsden, Alice H.
    The market meets its match : restructuring the economies of Eastern
Europe / Alice H. Amsden, Jacek Kochanowicz, Lance Taylor.
        p.   cm.
    Includes bibliographical references (p.   ) and index.
    ISBN 0-674-54983-X (acid-free paper)
    1. Europe, Eastern—Economic policy—1989–   2. Mixed economy—
Europe, Eastern.   3. Post-communism—Economic aspects—Europe,
Eastern.   4. Europe, Eastern—Economic conditions—1989–
I. Kochanowicz, Jacek. II. Taylor, Lance. III. Title.
HC244.A629   1994
338.947—dc20

94-18600
    CIP

Contents

Preface   vii

1   From Pseudo-Socialism to Pseudo-Capitalism   1

2   Transition Macroeconomics   17

3   The Black Box of State-Owned Enterprises   52

4   Overloading the Market Mechanism   79

5   Pseudo-Privatization and the World Bank   113

6   Enterprise and the State   129

7   Challenges Facing the State   158

8   Reconstructing the State   181

9   Economy, Society, and the State   206

Notes   213

References   225

Index   243

Preface

In Eastern Europe of the mid-1990s, enthusiasm for change and excitement over the coming capitalist future are long gone. After five years of transition economics, a gloom has spread over the region reminiscent of the grimness that gripped it in the interwar period. The popular mood is one of anger over rising unemployment, inflation, deteriorating living standards, the collapse of social services, and soaring crime.

Frustration is understandable, yet there are also grounds for optimism. Eastern Europe has a highly educated population, well trained in mathematics and science. It also has the remnants of an exceptionally equal income distribution. These characteristics were critical in the postwar industrialization of East Asia's rapidly growing economies, and provided a promising structural foundation for the re-industrialization of Eastern Europe in the post-socialist transition after 1989.

What has inhibited the harnessing of Eastern Europe's energies for the purposes of economic growth has been a dogged determination to stick with a fixed set of economic policies that pays little attention to the shape, form, and substance of the region's existing economic institutions and ignores the realities of constructive government intervention in the postwar rebuilding of Germany, Italy, and Japan; the economic transformation of South Korea and Taiwan; and the recent restructuring of China and Vietnam. The transition policies that have been adopted in Eastern Europe have varied across countries, but they have been generally unsuited both to the region's semi-industrialized status and to the oligopolistic market structures of the global economy of the 1990s. In particular, "shock therapy" has been excessively inflationary, has promoted stagnation, and has had the further effect of de-industrializing large segments of Eastern Europe's economies.

In part, these economic transition policies have been involuntary. They are largely a consequence of the conditions attached to the loans of the Bretton Woods institutions—the World Bank and the International Monetary Fund. In the 1980s these two institutions promoted an extreme form of neoliberalism in the assistance they offered around the globe. In doing so they followed prevailing opinion in Washington, D.C., where the Republican administrations then in power—for reasons of ideology and foreign competition rather than theory or empirical data—espoused a mythologized version of eighteenth-century laissez-faire. Indeed, most of the theoretical work done in economics in these years weakened rather than strengthened the free market paradigm. The models of economists such as Joseph Stiglitz show that the assumption of imperfect information seriously undermines the core of traditional neoclassical theory. "New Growth Economics" demonstrates the need for more public investment in education than the market might determine. The "New Trade Theories" show that free trade is not always optimal, given the market structures and product development modes of mature capitalist economies. Yet for political reasons, a virulent form of neoliberalism spread from Washington throughout the world, reinforced by the collapse of its opposite extreme, central planning.

The neoliberalism that set the stage for Eastern Europe's primitive capitalist policies was thus not grounded in new insights or fresh empirical evidence about economic development. In reality, views about government intervention vary with the political winds. Thus in 1943 Joseph Schumpeter wrote about the United States: "The public mind has renounced allegiance to the capitalist scheme of values . . . Political forces strong enough to liquidate the organs of the war economy as they were liquidated in 1919 are not in sight" (pp. 121–122). But by 1953, with the United States in the throes of McCarthyism, public opinion had reversed. Evidently popular feelings about the role of the market and state in economic development are subject to fairly swift change, for better or for worse.

Despite dire results, the persistent reliance on shock therapy in Eastern Europe has also been voluntary. Its use is a reflection of the opinions of the local intelligentsia, whose views carry much greater weight than in other countries. Since the Meiji era in Japan, for instance, the faction within the middle class with substantial power over economic decision making has been the bureaucracy. In the United States, it has always been private business. In Eastern Europe, it was and remains the intelligentsia. East European nations experienced a natural swing of the pendulum from tight state control before the transition to textbook laissez-faire immediately afterward. Ironically, it also became an article of faith for most intellectuals that rapid, radical economic reform was imperative to avoid a reversal of change at the voting polls. According to Leszek Balcerowicz, Poland's premier shock therapist and former minister of finance: "Radical economic reform creates safeguards to make the transition process *irreversible*. It rapidly introduces a number of economic and institutional changes that act as policy constraints on any new government taking over, whatever their basic ideology and value system" (1993, p. 2, emphasis added).

In the Polish, Czech, and Russian parliaments, any member suggesting the use of even moderate government planning to abet restructuring risked being labeled a Red. Just as McCarthyism in the United States regulated the public mood after World War II, economists in Eastern Europe after the transition were pressured to commit themselves to radical reform or gain a reputation—not least among the Western press and Western advisers—for being "crypto-Stalinists."

In practice, extremist economic policies have bred extremist political responses, thereby undermining the entire reform effort. Even radical reforms have proved reversible. Instead of openly and systematically restructuring only the best state-owned enterprises, even the most ardent free market governments (say, that of Vaclav Klaus in the Czech Republic) have been forced surreptitiously to continue subsidizing public enterprises willy-nilly in order to prevent economic collapse. Instead of nurturing financial systems that intermediated savings and investment flows among households, the public sector, and productive enterprises, the authorities have sanctioned unregulated financial speculation and pyramid schemes such as the ill-fated MMM operation that crashed in Russia, destroying the wealth of millions of shareholders. So while one might sympathize with the intelligentsia's fears—of a resurgence of the old system if radical reforms were not introduced or if minimalist government long-run investment planning were tolerated—this does not mean that it is productive for fear to carry the day.

As Franklin Delano Roosevelt observed in 1933, during the height of the Great Depression, fear can lead to a fatal paralysis.

This book seeks to explain why economic transition policies have failed. Further, we argue for the necessity of restructuring the states of Eastern Europe in order to introduce the institutions essential for long-term capital accumulation and employment growth. It is toward sensible economic transition policies that this volume is dedicated.

We approach the subject of the East European transition from diverse backgrounds and occasionally different perspectives.

Alice H. Amsden, who is primarily responsible for Chapters 3, 4, and 5, became familiar with the managerial, technological, and competitive problems of twenty state-owned enterprises in Hungary and especially Poland after conducting field work for the OECD (1992a) on a project to develop an industrial policy for Poland and participating in a pilot project for the OECD on industrial restructuring in Hungary. She is grateful for support from Daniel F. Malkin, Head of the Economic Analysis and Statistics Division, Directorate for Science, Technology, and Industry at the OECD, as well as for encouragement from Luca Barbone, Jean Guinet, Andrzej Koźmiński, Jan Kulig, Anthony Levitas, Adam Lipowski, Marcin Święcicki, and Graham Vickery.

Jacek Kochanowicz, who contributed Chapters 7 and 8, came to this project after many years of studying the historical origins and nature of economic backwardness in Eastern Europe (Kochanowicz, 1989), and more recently, the historical and political aspects of market transformation (Kochanowicz 1991, 1993, 1994). He has been engaged in a comparative project on the transformation to market and democracy in Eastern Europe and Latin America sponsored by the Overseas Development Council in Washington, D.C., under the leadership of Joan Nelson. He acknowledges the immense though often unconscious help of many members of this project in formulating his ideas.

Lance Taylor, who is primarily responsible for Chapters 2 and 6, has worked over the years as a researcher and/or policy adviser in two dozen developing countries. These include Chile and Nicaragua, which have had their own versions of post-socialist transitions. He has also coordinated a series of policy studies on stabilization and adjustment in less-developed countries through the World Institute for Development Economics Research (WIDER) in Helsinki. Through WIDER, Taylor began in 1990 to collaborate with Alexander Vorobyov (Ministry for Foreign Economic Affairs, Moscow) and Stanislav Zhukov (Institute of World Economics and International Relations, Moscow) in studying the transition in Russia. Early products of this research were Taylor (1994, written and circulated in 1991) and Zhukov and Vorobyov (1991), which are virtually unique in anticipating the inflationary stagnation of post-socialist economies described in this volume. Taylor has benefited from the comments of Michael Ellman and János Kornai.

All three authors wish to thank the following people for valuable help in various capacities: Herbert Addison (who suggested the book's title), Yilmaz Akyuz, Andrew Arato, Michael Aronson, Olivier Blanchard, Emily Gallagher, Elizabeth Gretz, Joel Gwynn, Takashi Hikino, Eric Hobsbawm, Helga Hoffmann, Margaret Jacob, Robert Kuttner, Robert MacIntyre, Seymour Melman, Herman Muegge, Edward Nell, Mario Nuti, Minxin Pei, Brian Pinto, David Plotke, Louis Putterman, Wolfgang Reinike, Dariusz Rosati, Andres Solimano, Signe Taylor, Charles Tilly, Leila Webster, and Andrew Zimbalist.

July 1994

THE MARKET MEETS ITS MATCH

From Pseudo-Socialism to Pseudo-Capitalism

In sharp contrast to the high expectations of 1989, when Eastern Europe's "socialist" experiment ground to a halt, in the mid-1990s the world holds its breath over the region's capitalist future. One of the most problematic countries, Russia, is in danger of economic collapse and renewed civil war. Even in the nation with the most promising prospects, Hungary, with its high degree of market activity and disproportionately large share of the region's foreign investment inflows, industrial output has fallen by almost 40 percent, unemployment has reached double-digit levels and continues to rise, and the government has increasingly violated the freedom of the press and other civil rights. After an initial period of euphoria, the transition to capitalism is proving an unparalleled challenge to the market mechanism.

Eastern Europe's earlier experience with a command economy, despite its idealistic goal of human fulfillment, produced only "pseudo-socialism." The institutions necessary for effective and democratic decision making were never successfully put in place, and the system that was created was inefficient, dictatorial, and incapable of achieving sustained growth. Nevertheless, pseudo-socialism was not an unmitigated failure. Throughout Eastern Europe high levels of education and human skill were achieved, basic human needs were satisfied, and essential physical infrastructure was constructed. In some countries, certain state-owned enterprises—even civilian ones—had accumulated technical know-how and skills roughly comparable to those of capitalist firms operating at the world technological frontier. Yet the architects of Eastern Europe's transition to a market economy generally regarded socialism's legacies as uniform liabilities. For ideological reasons, these post–

Cold War policymakers rejected the entire socialist inheritance. In so doing their approach differed from that of Italy, Germany, and Japan after World War II, when those nations pragmatically made use of any possible inheritance from their own previously oppressive regimes that could be mobilized for reconstruction.

There is a danger in generalizing about Eastern Europe's economies, of course, given their diverse histories, demographics, and physical resources.[1] Certainly their record of economic reform in the first five years after (and before) the transition to a market economy has varied greatly. At the same time, however, it can be said that not a single East European country has put a new institutional system into place that can achieve a level of re-industrialization or macroeconomic growth anywhere near the economy's potential. This failure can be attributed both to the blanket rejection of any remnant of the immediate socialist past and, further, to the embrace by almost every country in the region of a simplistic capitalist experiment dating from the eighteenth century. This laissez-faire model may have succeeded in overthrowing mercantilism and creating cottage industry in rural England, but it has incurred high social costs and low rates of return when applied to the project of reconstructing industrial Eastern Europe under the competitive conditions of technologically advanced, twentieth-century capitalism.

In the first years of transition even the most successful East European economies have managed to establish only a system of "pseudo-capitalism," so-called because, again for ideological reasons, few of the institutions essential for long-term capital accumulation have been introduced.

The nature of Eastern Europe's 1989 "revolution" contained the seeds of its own early distress. History's other major revolutions, by definition, left an old order abruptly behind, but did so through a process of striving to create what by world standards was something radically new—modern capitalism in the case of the first industrial revolution, egalitarian democracy in the French Revolution, and socialism in the Bolshevik Revolution. By contrast, although Eastern Europe's overthrow of its ancien régime circa 1989 qualifies as "revolutionary," what it has tried to create in its stead is by historical standards already outdated. True, the transition has been as unique as it has been unprecedented; nowhere in the world has capitalism been created *after* pseudo-socialism. But instead of lurching toward a new economic and political system in order to catch up with the world's richest countries, Eastern Europe's societies have searched for the mores, methods, and models to help them catch up in ways congruent with their own highly selective historical memory and with the mythologized histories of the most advanced capitalist countries, particularly the free market paragons, Britain and the United States.

No revolution is ever completely successful in coming to terms with its own past, but few revolutionary societies have dipped into history so indiscriminately, or abused the past so wastefully, as Eastern Europe's. Perhaps the most tragic exemplar to date has been the former Yugoslavia's "return of the repressed," as Freud would call it, which has unleashed a horrific war of revenge and "ethnic cleansing." "Restitution," or the return of property to whoever owned it before nationalization, by contrast, has proved to be a mere legal nuisance that aggravated the slow pace of privatization. But allowing first-rate firms to go bankrupt and world-scale research and development laboratories to deteriorate has delayed not just catching up with the world's richest countries but recovering pretransition income levels by several years. Most important, the choice of a capitalist model that dates back to the eighteenth century and that represents an extreme, primitive form of market economy has failed in five years to lay the groundwork for the modern capitalist development Eastern Europeans so desperately desire.

Elsewhere in the world compelling examples can be found of countries that have succeeded or are succeeding in their economic transitions—Japan, South Korea, Taiwan, and, within the post-socialist camp, increasingly China and Vietnam. These nations, too, became capitalist in their orientation, emphasizing private property and the use of the market to acquire inputs and sell outputs. But the specific capitalist model these late-industrializers have used was, in fact, new by world standards, and therefore different from the historical relic Eastern Europe has worshiped in its first years of transition. The Eastern Europeans have faithfully followed a model that would have been familiar to Adam Smith. The approach of the successful late-industrializers, however, represents something distinct: it has been capitalist in orientation yet a significant departure from either textbook theory or eighteenth- and nineteenth-century Anglo-American capitalist norms. This late-industrializing model has been successful not because reforms were introduced gradually (as in China and Vietnam) rather than in a great "shock" (reforms in Hungary were also quite gradual), but because it represented an attempt to customize a capitalism to suit the realities and exigencies of having to catch up with technologically advanced countries in a world economy that espoused free competition but exhibited pervasive oligopolistic business practices.

It is the contention of this book that Eastern Europe's below-potential performance (and thus political instability) has stemmed from copying the wrong capitalist model—voluntarily or otherwise. Until post-socialist countries learn from both their own past and from successful late-industrializers and piece together their own sensible growth model specifically geared to their semi-industrialized status, their efforts to restructure will continue to sputter.

The Moral Crusade of Market Fundamentalism

A critical difference between the classic capitalism that the Eastern Europeans have tried to promote and the late-industrial capitalism that the East Asians have pioneered lies in the role of institutions in shaping the form, substance, direction, and pace of economic expansion. In the East European case, the role of institutions has been minimal; resource allocation has been left almost entirely to the market mechanism. When advocates of this "market fundamentalism" refer to "institutions" and the necessity of "institution building" in order to foster capitalism, they have in mind a strictly limited agenda: the specification of property rights, contract law enforcement, and the removal of impediments to private enterprise. The market mechanism in the East Asian case, by contrast, has been relied on instrumentally rather than as a matter of ideological conviction; institutions—including a bureaucratic, "developmental" state—assume a major role in allocating investment resources. Institution building in this context refers not just to the establishment of clear property rights and contract law but also to the creation of private and public organizations capable of carrying out expansionary macroeconomic policies as well as investment, trade, competition, and technology policies, all operating under the umbrella of what has loosely come to be called industrial policy.

Victims of their own immediate history, the East European countries in the early years of transition have rejected the approach taken in East Asia. The pseudo-socialism that became ensconced after World War I in Russia and after World War II in the remainder of Eastern

Europe was a caricature of capitalism in its most modern form: the size of business enterprise was not simply large, it was rigidly bureaucratic; the role of the state was not just developmental, it was all-determining. Out of this dismal past and out of considerable naiveté about how markets truly work (as opposed to how they are supposed to work in theory), Eastern Europe's chosen brand of capitalism has been strongly biased toward small firms and weak states. This preference has been uncritically endorsed by most East European intellectuals, fearful that a strong state would stifle democracy (although history has proved that a weak state does not necessarily stimulate it) and hopeful that small firms would nurture a middle class (although the professional, as opposed to property-owning, middle class was already substantial).

Such a bias toward conservatism has been rigidly reinforced in Eastern Europe by its bankers, the Bretton Woods institutions, the World Bank and International Monetary Fund, set up after World War II to advance credits—with policy strings attached—to countries with economic problems. At the time the East European transition began, these organizations were themselves in the grips of a strong neoconservatism stemming from the United States's crisis of self-confidence. In reaction to the rise of the East Asian late-industrializers, American and hence Bretton Woods policies exaggerated the virtues of free markets and, by means of the conditions that the World Bank and IMF attached to their loans, limited Eastern Europe's policy menu. Eastern Europe has thus been assigned a place in the international economy roughly comparable to what it occupied in earlier centuries: that of a poor cousin in the division of labor with the rest of Europe (Kochanowicz, 1989). From the sixteenth to the eighteenth centuries, "the eastern regions of the European Continent became an agrarian reserve of the increasingly industrialized West," a pattern of specialization that did not, contrary to the predictions of classic trade theory, result in a convergence in income and productivity levels (Berend and Ránki, 1974, p. 3). In the post-socialist era, the eastern regions of Europe have been encouraged to specialize in low-end goods, despite equally gloomy prospects for success.

In analyzing the dire consequences of Eastern Europe's choice of the wrong model, we focus on what can be learned from this costly error in order to develop a more sensible alternative for post-socialist late comers, who must not so much industrialize as *re*-industrialize and create the macroeconomic structure suitable for the task.

Contractionary Macroeconomic Policies

Although there have been some differences across countries, Eastern Europe's transitional macroeconomic policies, examined in Chapter 2, have borne a strong family resemblance. In effect they have been a celebration of Say's Law, that supply creates its own demand and that markets automatically maintain equilibrium *if* wages are low enough. A pillar of transition economics, therefore, has been the reduction of real wages. One consequence of declining real wages, however, has proved to be a sharp and sustained fall in economic activity, more contractionary than either transition economists anticipated or the final collapse of a command economy could explain.

With their own hypothetical model in mind, the economists who designed the global shocks and big bangs of the early 1990s did not take into account the mechanisms for output determination that emerged on the eve of the post-socialist era. Assuming the validity of Say's Law, planners thought that production would remain at the level of potential supply, just as it had been under the repressed inflation and soft budget constraints of socialism. The dynamic changes that the reformers did not foresee hinged on the effects on aggregate demand of the massive income redistributions induced by price liberalizations. As real incomes were cut, domestic demand fell to unforeseen depths.

Shock therapy suddenly removed all price and other administrative controls in the presence of the latent excess demand that had built up under planning—queues and shortages vanished almost overnight. But the only way that the resulting surge in attempted spending could be held down to available supply was by price increases; in most countries, enterprises raised their selling prices several-fold in the wake of liberalization. Real wages dropped almost in proportion, forcing consumer spending to collapse at the same time that exports within the formerly socialist trading bloc imploded in a chain reaction. With no stimulus from consumer demand or exports, capital formation—the driving force of the planning system—also collapsed. For all the talk of creating a market economy, the irony was that with plunging real incomes there were no effective markets in which firms could sell their goods. Total output consequently dropped well below potential supply.

Meanwhile, workers tried to recover the purchasing power that price increases had taken away. Their attempts were frustrated by policies aimed at holding money wages in check, but they still led to nominal labor cost increases that fed through enterprises' markups into an on-going price spiral. Credit crunches and high interest rates along with increases in raw materials prices aimed at getting their levels "right" also contributed to cost-push, or rising inflation in response to higher production costs.

The resulting combination of wage/price inflation and production stagnation is almost certain to persist over time, while complex supply-side linkages, built up over decades of planning, unravel further. This macroeconomic situation can be expected to continue to deteriorate until post-socialist policymakers create the means (and gather the courage) to control prices and encourage production through measures affecting both aggregate demand and supply, as do all modern capitalist nations. Yet in so doing, transition planners must thereby go against the advice of—and perhaps endanger credits from—Western sources of funds.

Do-Nothing Microeconomic Policies

One of the highest costs of the noninstitutional approach to catching up has been a failure to grasp the potential of the institutions that actually existed in the early stages of transition, especially a significant number of inherently viable state-owned enterprises (SOEs). Their numbers far exceeded the ranks of reasonable buyers interested in privatization, while their responsibility for producing the lion's share of industrial output and exports outstripped the instruments and resources made available to them for restructuring. At best, Eastern Europe's futile reliance on privatization and market forces to restructure has resulted in lost time and missed market opportunities, particularly those associated with sustaining the growth of the public sector exports that boomed in the very early transition years. At worst, doing nothing has contributed to the erosion of skills and the deterioration of promising enterprises, thereby worsening unemployment and balance of payments disequilibria.

Eastern Europe's skill base at the time the transition began was one of its potential assets (see Table 1.1). In terms of educational indicators, Eastern Europe and the Soviet Union ranked below the industrialized countries but well above the developing countries. The levels of education in the USSR and Eastern Europe even slightly exceeded those of semi-industrialized countries in East Asia and Latin America. The

Table 1.1 Semi-industrialized countries: International human capital
comparisons

Country group	Mean years of schooling (age 25+) (1990)	Tertiary graduates[a] (1987–1990)	Science graduates[b] (1987–1990)
Industrialized	10.0	9.4	36
Semi-industrialized			
East Asia and Latin America[c]	7.2	5.2[d]	36[e]
Eastern Europe and the USSR	7.7	5.6	44
Developing	3.7	1.2	31

Source: Compiled from UNDP (1992), tables 5 and 31.

a. As percent of corresponding age group. For East Asia and Latin America,
1986–1988. "Tertiary" refers to college, professional, and other forms of post-secondary
education.

b. As percent of total graduates. For East Asia and Latin America, 1986–1988.

c. Hong Kong, Republic of Korea, Chile, Singapore, and Argentina.

d. Data not available for Korea and Argentina.

e. Data not available for Hong Kong.

quality of Eastern Europe's educational system was also good, at least
in the physical sciences. In international chemistry competitions for
high school students, for instance, Eastern Europe placed close to the
top: in 1992, China ranked first, followed by Hungary and Poland
(the United States ranked fourth). A year earlier, China had ranked
first, Romania second, Hungary third, and Poland fourth (Browne,
1992).

The industrial strategy in the first years of the transition implicitly
amounted to "getting the prices right" (reducing real wages and increasing capital and raw material costs) and specializing according to
"comparative advantage," or manufacturing a bundle of goods whose
production techniques favored the relatively cheapest available domestic factor inputs (land, labor, or capital). Such a competitive approach
may have made sense, at least logically, under *de novo* conditions of
underdevelopment, where lowering wages and liberalizing imports
might be expected to create a competitive edge for labor-intensive
industries, with minimal negative spillover on the (nonexistent) re-

maining industries. But the idea of specializing based on a factor-price comparative advantage makes no sense at all in a semideveloped country, defined as already having a broad base of industries, especially mid-tech industries, and a stock of accumulated human skills.

At the time of the transition a wide array of industries and a diverse assortment of skills already existed in Eastern Europe, and relying on lowering real wages and abruptly liberalizing imports to boost growth and efficiency has therefore left a large segment of industries out in the cold. For this segment, transition policies have resulted in *de*-industrialization rather than *re*-industrialization. Just after the transition began Eastern Europe's heavy goods producers and large engineering sector, for example, tended to be internationally cost competitive, at least in terms of labor costs. Still, they were unable to compete in world markets, due to low-quality and out-dated technology. Lowering real wages did not address their problems and inflicted real injury by widely lowering domestic demand. Rather than following comparative advantage, a more sensible industrial strategy would have been to focus on restructuring the most promising enterprises, whatever their industry.

Some labor-intensive industries have benefited from real wage cuts, such as garment making in Poland and Estonia, whose low-wage workers engaged in cutting, sewing, and finishing cloth supplied to them by German and Swedish merchants. Such activity could be considered part of either the rise of capitalism or the return of the "putting out" system. At the same time, the initially larger domestic cotton spinning and weaving industry in Poland died for lack of resources to redress its quality problems. Overall, then, these developments are likely to have left total employment unchanged.

To resolve the pervasive bottlenecks of low quality and out-dated technology required time and money (substantial or modest, depending on the firm). Yet few private capitalists—certainly few local ones—were interested in tackling these long-term problems. Amid the transition's political uncertainties and erratic inflation rates, the objective of most capitalists was understandably a fast payback and a high rate of return, both of which were possible in many segments of the service sector. Without government intervention in the form of long-term restructuring of promising industrial enterprises, the threat of wholesale bankruptcy was very real. The failure of large state-owned enterprises also seriously endangered the health of small, new private manufacturing firms. The latter were typically dependent on the public sector for their inputs or final demand (Webster, 1993a, b; Webster and Swanson, 1993).

Resolution of the firm-size problem in Eastern Europe, moreover, could not simply be left to spontaneous market forces to rationalize whole industries or subdivide large-scale firms. The firm-size configuration that transition economists inherited was not only distorted in terms of too few small firms and too many large ones; it tended to be wrong in *every* direction. In a substantial number of leading industries firm (and plant) size was *too small,* requiring the hand of government (or some other long-term planning agent) to nourish enterprises to a scale sufficient to compete against the world's leading oligopolies.

Finally, for the defense industries of Russia and to a lesser extent those of other East European countries even to begin the process of "conversion" was inconceivable without long-term rationalization; restructuring would be unavoidably time-consuming given the specialized technology of this sector and its lack of commercial products. We do not discuss the defense industries here—they warrant a book in themselves—but it is worth stressing that unemployment in this sector, given the high skill level of its employees, involves huge opportunity costs, while the chances for mass redundancy and political dislocation are enormous.

An active role for the state in Eastern Europe's industrial restructuring is thus inevitable. The more this is openly acknowledged, the more rational and systematic government involvement can be. Instead, transition economists have shifted the entire burden of restructuring onto the shoulders of privatization.

Foreign Investment

If "getting the prices right" and pursuing comparative advantage have been the pillars of Eastern Europe's otiose capitalist model, privatization has been its foundation. For transition economists and the World Bank, restructuring state-owned enterprises became identical to privatizing them.

There was no consideration of restructuring *before* privatization, or providing inherently viable enterprises with resourses and a finite breathing spell to reach international competitive standards. It became an article of faith that state-owned enterprises were run either by crooks or by incompetents, and therefore providing them with the means to restructure before a change in ownership was assumed to be a waste of money. In any event, this sequence was out of the question because the conditions the World Bank attached to its structural adjustment loans effectively prohibited lending to public sector manufacturing firms.

In reality, however, to transfer ownership of state-owned enterprises (other than those engaged in petty manufacturing or small-scale services) to genuine capitalists—buyers with "capital," broadly defined to embody technology and human skills as well as financial resources—has been virtually impossible. Pseudo-socialism did not allow private accumulation on a scale large enough to enable even modestly capitalized enterprises to be privately bought at politically acceptable prices. As for foreign investors, expectations about their enthusiasm for investment in Eastern Europe in the first years of its transition to a market economy have proved highly exaggerated, and conditions attached to World Bank loans prevented Eastern Europe from offering incentives to foreign investors comparable to those available to them in, for instance, China's special economic zones.

The history of direct foreign investment in other late-industrializing countries suggests that typically such investment lags rather than leads growth; it enters when growth has already gained momentum and then accelerates it. And with few exceptions (such as Malaysia, which was very rich in natural resources, or Brazil, which enjoyed a huge domestic market), foreign manufacturing investment amounts to a marginal fraction of total gross domestic capital formation (for East Asia, see Amsden, 1992).

The foreign capital that has flowed into Eastern Europe in the early stages of transition, particularly in the manufacturing sector, has tended to be tiny (a grand total of $14 billion at the end of 1992) and unevenly distributed among a few countries (Hungary ranked first, followed at a distance by the Czech Republic and Poland). The major motive of foreign investors in Eastern Europe has been to exploit domestic markets, and thus real wage reductions, perversely, may have been more of a discouragement (in terms of reducing total demand and political stability) than an encouragement (in terms of lowering production costs) (OECD, 1993). Large investors such as General Motors in Poland, Suzuki and Samsung in Hungary, and Volkswagen in the Czech Republic have also demanded protective tariffs or quotas against competitive imports as a precondition for investing (UNIDO, 1992). Although a subsidy-free environment has been the goal of transition economists, make-shift incentives have become the reality.

Pseudo-Privatization

The recognition that foreign investors are not bringing to Eastern Europe the requisite credit, expertise, and skills for capitalist development has necessitated a thorough policy reassessment. In a study sponsored by the European Commission of the United Nations two eminent economists, more candid than most other policy advisers, observed:

> Why has output fallen so quickly and sharply in Eastern Europe, and why has the fall persisted? Such a deep contraction and its persistence were not predicted. That may reflect either misunderstanding of the microfoundations or unforeseen external shocks. But there is a good case for the cock-up hypothesis: that those devising policies and forecasting their outcomes simply got the policies wrong. (Nuti and Portes, 1993, p. 8)

A reappraisal took place around 1993, but has not thus far resulted in a major policy shift on the part of either the Bretton Woods institutions or the East European governments. Despite the mounting evidence that most state-owned managers were honestly trying to restructure but with their hands tied[2] and that trade unions and employees' councils were not obstructing either privatization or enterprise reform (see Dąbrowski, Fedorowicz, and Levitas, 1991), there was still no question of restructuring before privatization. Instead, a grand experiment was launched in many East European countries that was as significant for its omissions as for its commissions, or for what it suggested could be done to restructure as for what it actually accomplished in privatization.

Guided by the ideological conviction that virtually any means were justified to achieve privatization, the privatization method finally resorted to in desperation was one of "giveaways"—shares in state-owned enterprises were distributed to adult citizens virtually free of charge. This amounted to "pseudo-privatization"; it represented an attempt to create capitalism without any capital, or without the credit, skills, and expertise necessary to restructure now "private" enterprises hindered by long-term bottlenecks.

Just as privatization has been the foundation of the transition's capitalist model, so, too, has pseudo-privatization been emblematic of the pseudo-capitalism that has characterized the first years of transitional orthodoxy. The success of capitalism depends on the emergence of institutions to support long-term investment and risk taking. Yet even the most optimistic reading of the deep recession years of the early 1990s did not find serious institution building along these lines throughout most of Eastern Europe. To relieve pent-up consumer demand, the early transition was notable for small investments in services (such as retail stores, restaurants, and home-improvement construction). Just as the historian Fernand Braudel observed about early European capitalism, however, a distinction must be drawn between using the market for exchanging goods between family-owned firms and creating the institutions necessary for large-scale capitalist ventures (which took Europe, with minimal state intervention by late-industrializing standards, centuries to achieve). The transition economies of Eastern Europe have largely succeeded only in inducing simple market exchange. They have also succeeded in creating substantial wealth for a few amid rising poverty for many, but that wealth was generated more as a consequence of "buying cheap and selling dear" than of saving and investing. As the Hungarian economist János Kornai notes: "The most important factor [in transformational recession] is the dwindling propensity to invest" (1993, p. 1).

The first five years have been too brief a period to determine whether "pseudo-privatization" will ultimately succeed in concentrating capital for buying the machinery, skills, and technology necessary for major restructuring (a task for which mutual funds and holding companies are being primed) or whether it will simply succeed in financial swindle on a massive scale. Given the political instability and the opportunities for short-term gain characteristic of the early transition period, the progressive face of capitalism seems unlikely to appear until a government willing and able to induce long-term investments in new plant and equipment is reconstructed.

Nevertheless, the dogged determination of post-socialist governments to privatize, with generous financial assistance from the Bretton Woods institutions and technocratic support from a well-paid, elite bureaucracy (such as the Ministry of Ownership Change in Poland, the State Property Agency in Hungary, and the Committee for the Management of State Property in Russia), is evidence of what Eastern Europe's educated societies are capable of achieving. In the name of privatization, these government agencies have accomplished what was assumed to be impossible in the name of restructuring: they ranked state-owned enterprises according to their future promise based on information provided by professional management consultants. In the case of Poland, they have even created state-owned banks (which, of course, they intended to privatize) to serve as the coordinating agents of further financial reform.

The ideological flexibility to begin reforming the government itself, however, is still lacking. The process of reconstructing the state is a step that is crucial in order to restructure industrial enterprises on the basis of a carefully considered, systematic, and clear set of policies.

The Late-Industrializing Model

What Eastern Europe and other late-industrializers elsewhere share in common is the need to catch up without original technology, which could have made their entry into world markets far easier. Radically new technology was the basis for the economic development of both England and the United States, and even aided "backward" continental countries such as Sweden in catching up with world income leaders (Hikino and Amsden, 1994). But in the late twentieth century technological differences are a primary reason making Anglo-American and even Western European development patterns quintessentially inappropriate for Eastern Europe to try to follow. Late-industrializers have had to grow exclusively through learning or borrowing foreign technology that has already been commercialized elsewhere. With entry barriers to modern industry rising in the form of high research and development expenditures in advanced capitalist countries, it has become impossible for late comers to leapfrog to the world technological frontier, as the economic historian Alexander Gerschenkron had imagined (1952). Without the competitive advantage of radically new products and processes to determine the pace and direction of industrial development, the need for government guidance is much greater than in the past (Amsden, 1989).

Eastern Europe, however, has made few efforts to learn about the successes or failures of other regions' late-industrializing experience. This neglect is in part due to Eastern Europe's cultural identity with Western Europe and in part due to a lack of information. The economic doctrines that penetrated the Iron Curtain stopped short even of

Keynesianism, let alone East Asian developmentalism. Because the East Asian experience—which has involved rapid growth *and* dirigisme—so contradicted Western economic philosophy, it has tended to be misrepresented as laissez-faire (see World Bank, 1993, and a symposium in *World Development,* 1994). The late-industrializing model has also understandably been ignored because it has been associated with dictatorship or authoritarianism, and because not all dirigiste late-industrializing regions have performed well; memories of the debt crisis that ravaged Latin America (and Eastern Europe) in the 1980s are still vivid in the 1990s.

Eastern Europe's dismissal of the late-industrializing model, however, is costly in terms of the lessons foregone. If the post-socialist economies could actually succeed in matching, say, the growth rates of Brazil and Turkey from 1965 to 1980 (around 9 and 6 percent per annum), or even the steady "Hindu" growth rate of India (about 4 percent per annum), they would be doing rather well. As for democracy, though it is unclear whether East Asia's spectacular growth rates could have been achieved under more democratic conditions, it is absolutely clear that Eastern Europe's primitive capitalism has undermined political democracy by failing to achieve even minimal rates of broad-based growth. Ironically, infringements on political liberties in the early transition period (Hungary's free press violations, for example) have been justified by pragmatists as necessary for rapid economic development.

At the same time, two key ingredients in East Asia's success have been strongly represented in Eastern Europe in the early stages of transition: high levels of education and income equality. In Japan, South Korea, and Taiwan, high levels of education have underscored the efficiency of the bureaucracies in both the private and the public sectors. Equal income distribution (owing to land reform) has prevented self-interested private concentrations of economic power from dictating economic policy. Government intervention in East Asia has been relatively effective partly because the government is powerful enough to impose performance standards on business in exchange for financial support (Amsden, 1989).

Unfortunately, the economic policies of the early transition have severely underutilized Eastern Europe's human capital and either fatalistically accepted or deliberately provoked rising income inequality as a badge of the arrival of capitalism. One objective of this book is to juxtapose the East European and East Asian experiences and to examine the conditions in Eastern Europe that were conducive to re-industrialization before time ran out and opportunities vanished.

Blurry Blueprint

Influential economists insisted early in the East European transition that there was a broad theoretical and policy consensus regarding market reform.[3] Yet a complete tableau of transition economics was never fully specified, and precisely what policy instruments were supposed to achieve which specific growth targets was not made absolutely clear (the account by Jeffrey Sachs [1993a], a leader among "shock therapists," is remarkably brief). Reading between the lines, however, it appears that a four-part policy was operative.

First, the application of standard macroeconomic policy packages of the sort recommended by the Bretton Woods institutions to late-industrializing countries (with highly dubious success rates) was expected to set the stage for sustained market-driven economic growth.

Second, concessionary capital inflows and direct foreign investment were expected to provide the foundation for privatization and the means of infusing good management, new capital, and modern technology into business enterprise.

Third, the emergence of private small-scale enterprise in services and manufacturing was expected to absorb much of the labor shed by the withering state sector and provide the political nucleus for an indigenous middle class.

Fourth, market forces were expected to discipline all firms—private, privatized, and still publicly owned, if any. Simultaneously, lower wages, stemming from anti-inflationary policies, devaluation, and "shock therapy," were expected to provide hearty entrepreneurial survivors with low costs in international markets (export and import-competing). Low wages were expected to be the transition's competitive weapon.

Some of this logic proved to be sound. Most of it proved to be faulty. The chapters that follow seek to explain why this was so, and why the transition to capitalism required a more visible hand than neoliberalism envisioned. As Karl Polanyi observed about Western Europe: "The road to the free market was opened and kept open by an enormous increase in continuous, centrally organized and controlled interventionism" (1944, p. 140).

2

Transition Macroeconomics

The design was ultra-orthodox, but the blueprints for macroeconomic policy were blurry. Despite reformers' best-drawn plans, the economywide disorders that plagued the nations of Eastern Europe and the former Soviet Union under decaying socialism turned sharply worse as they embarked upon their transition to the market.

Throughout the late 1980s, the disintegration of the planning system had been associated with rising inflation rates and declining output levels in economies all across the region.[1] The situation deteriorated dramatically during the transition years of 1990–1992, as many countries' real income and output fell by between 20 and 40 percent of gross domestic product (GDP) while price increases accelerated to triple-digit annual percentage rates (Åslund, 1994). Although inflation slowed into double digits and income stabilized in some countries in 1992–93, output levels continued to decline or scarcely grew (the 3–4 percent and slightly positive 1993 GDP growth rates projected for Poland and the Czech Republic appear to be isolated exceptions).

Shocks of this magnitude had not been experienced in industrial economies since the Great Depression or in the wake of World War II; they were large even in comparison with the dismal record in developing countries over the previous fifteen years. Output losses and price spirals were extreme because the economic policies pursued by new, democratic governments in the region substantially exacerbated other, more fundamental, obstacles to change.

Early post-socialist reform programs bore a strong resemblance to each other for several reasons. They were largely designed by economists sharing a free market ideology who came into power as communism disappeared. Although such free market doctrines have ultimately proved destructive, they initially motivated reformers to push change through the system. Even observers who knew that the packages were likely to fail viewed them as an inevitable catharsis or *rite de passage*. Few, perhaps because of well-founded disgust with the socialist state, were willing to point out that public economic interventions are ubiquitous under modern capitalism.

The local true believers in the market were fortified by advisers from Western universities, the World Bank, and the International Monetary Fund. They pushed the reforms in predictable directions, minimizing the role of the state and postulating that uncontrolled markets are an infallible guarantee for robust output growth. These ideas follow from a fundamentalist reading of mainstream, neoclassical economic theory, which flourished during the administrations of Presidents Reagan and Bush. By the late 1980s this approach had become the "Washington consensus."[2]

For political leaders committed to reform, the best Western conventional wisdom dovetailed with universal political hopes for miracles from a wonderfully hypostatized capitalism. The problem was that free market logic did not fit the economic realities at hand. It foundered on inappropriate abstractions: instantly liberalizing prices was supposed to lead to rapid adjustment to a full employment, inflation-free macroeconomic equilibria while the invisible hand would painlessly reshape preexisting industry along Western lines. As Kornai (1993) observes, no "forecast of . . . serious recession [can] be found in the early theoretical writings to outline the program for the transition." More realistic theory does—and did—predict such an outcome, by taking the demand-limiting distributional effects of price increases plus their tendencies to overshoot toward inflation into account.[3]

The history of interventions by Bretton Woods institutions in the Third World, moreover, suggests that prospects for future growth are bleak if present post-socialist policies are maintained (Taylor, 1993). Developing countries have a long history of both success and failure to achieve industrial progress and economic growth, with the successes universally relying upon a degree of state intervention. These outcomes have stimulated much thought on the ways in which inherited economic and social structures constrain the possibilities for change, and this knowledge and nonmainstream economic theory are indispensable for understanding how poor policy design and structural barriers derailed the post-socialist transition. The macroeconomic side of the story is presented here and in Chapter 6.

The Administrative System

A natural place to begin is with a description of the economic order that market reformers tried to supplant. We sketch it as an ideal type, but attempt to bring in some of the complicating details as we go along.

The planning or administrative system of Leninist "socialism," despite its manifest failings, managed to hold per capita incomes in Eastern Europe roughly stable during the decades after World War II (Solimano, 1991) and permitted the Soviet Union to become a military if not an economic superpower. In its cumbersome way, planning was able to handle the myriad decisions for the coordination of economic actions that modern-day production entails. The system differed fundamentally from capitalism, however.

One major divergence lay in the interface between economics and politics. Especially in the Soviet Union, economic reform was hindered by the political structure. At the top of the Communist Party and state was a leader named by the Central Committee; his charisma and administrative ability were vital factors in keeping (or not keeping, as under Brezhnev) the system going. Yet although the leader had a large say in picking the committee's members, his power was not absolute. Both in the Soviet Union and in the nations of Eastern Europe, slots on the committee were assigned to representatives of functional groups—the military, the military-industrial complex, other industry, agriculture, labor, and so on. Coalitions within the committee could block reform, which is one reason change proved so difficult under Soviet socialism. In China, by contrast, Central Committee membership changed in less mechanical fashion, which gave economic reformers freedom of action as long as they were supported by the highest authorities.

Subject to the leadership's political direction, economic planning in principle functioned in physical terms, with Gosplan (the Soviet central planning agency) and its equivalents in other nations assigning output goals for enterprises along with targets for intermediate deliveries among them as well as for final sales for consumption, export, investment, and the government itself. Legal market transactions were mainly for personal consumption, subject to supply limitations imposed by productive capacity and the plan.

In practice, plan targets were geared toward rapid growth of the physical capital stock without much concern for its productivity. Demand for goods on the part of the military were given even more priority. Administered public purchases (augmented by enterprises' diversions of sales to the black market) were set high enough to drive the economy close to its potential output; when these ceilings began to be surpassed, household purchases were the first claims on commodity supplies to be crowded out.

As a financial counterpart to physical planning, flows of cash money were largely restricted to wage payments. These in turn cycled back to the fiscal budget via taxes and markups on state outlets' sales to workers (who had to purchase only part of what American consumers did, since transport, health, education, housing, and other benefits and services were provided by the state at nominal out-of-pocket costs). Money thus "served as a means of exchange and store of wealth at best in consumption. In exchanges between enterprises, it was only an auxiliary planning instrument used to reduce physical flows to the same denominator. Imbalances resulting from resource allocation by the center were corrected in physical terms by barter transactions among enterprises and flows through the black market, and in financial terms by frozen accounts in the banking system" (Zhukov and Vorobyov, 1991). All monetary flows took place in a highly centralized system, or in Western terminology, a "monobank." Separation of the central bank and commercial banks (an institutional feature central to Western monetary theory) was rudimentary at best.

In Soviet usage, household and enterprise moneys became "cash" and (mostly frozen) "noncash" rubles, respectively. Balances of the latter sort were enormous, because the planning system was unable to specify interenterprise commodity flows with any precision. Noncash transactions mediated customary trade linkages, which became established among firms; these commodity flows continued through their familiar channels even after the planning system that had called them into existence had disappeared.

Prices of goods and services played a secondary role under socialism. For consumers, prices were set to penalize certain purchases and subsidize others. The subsidized items included household essentials, for which queues and rations were used to hold demand to available supply. Among firms, prices were rigged to stimulate certain lines of investment. Both enterprises and households were provided energy cheaply in comparison with international standards (although not in comparison with Persian Gulf or even Soviet production costs). In effect, the state as an overarching producer-*cum*-distributor chose to take its profits in such forms as taxes on vodka turnover rather than as markups on energy sales. As a consequence, the socialist productive apparatus used energy very intensively. It also paid scant heed to the social costs of degrading the environment.

Especially in the USSR and to some extent in Eastern Europe, enterprises became highly vertically integrated and large—planners found it expedient to deal with only a few behemoths at one time. There was a dearth of small, innovative production units. This enterprise structure led to extensive bilateral bargaining over transactions that crossed firms' boundaries; within them bureaucratic decision making guided intermediate input flows. There was no scope for competition in markets for services (with supplies typically restricted under socialism, in any case) or goods. In particular, socialist plant managers had no incentives to hold down their use of production inputs manufactured elsewhere; at least through the 1970s, the physical quantity of goods processed was a positive goal in the plans. In comparison with Western norms, shares of intermediate input purchases in total manufacturing costs were high prior to the post-socialist transition. They rose thereafter, as price increases for energy and raw materials far exceeded increments in labor costs.[4]

Because the state "owned" most enterprises in the name of the people, it also avoided discipline in markets for corporate liabilities such as bonds and equities; nor was the banking system likely to use its lending powers to push them toward efficiency, as we have seen. Just as competition in markets for commodities was lacking, capital market pressures on firms to improve their performance did not exist (although it is fair to say that their beneficial effects in Western economies can be overrated[5]).

All these market failures were rampant. Their ill effects on economic performance were somewhat mitigated, but not fully eased, by successive waves of economic reform after the 1960s. But the basic problems in production stemmed from another cause—a lack of technological dynamism. Socialist enterprise and financial structures provided scant means for generating new production processes and innovative products from the usual sources: corporate research labs, new entrepreneurs, or foreign borrowing. The labs serviced existing commodity flows; the planners to whom they reported were tied up in the operational minutiae of managing existing technologies and goods, and had little time for new endeavors. The innovations that the system did come up with typically took the form of new processes and not new products, which did not help the consumer backwardness that pervaded late socialism.

Even worse, entrepreneurs hatching ideas in attics or garages could not flourish with the help of infusions of credit from investment banks or venture capitalists—the critically missing agents in the capital market. Only in the scientific-military complexes were incentives consistently rigged to favor technological innovations or reverse engineering of Western products, but high-tech weaponry did consumers little good. Although technological borrowing was directed toward export industries in Hungary and Poland after 1970, it never dominated industrial strategy as it did in South Korea and Taiwan.

Finally, socialist economies were egalitarian, and equality was politically prized. The productive apparatus was harnessed to this social goal, as enterprises provided housing, schooling, and other services to the families of their workers. Because of the absence of capital markets and because firms often had strong employees' councils, Western-style distinctions between management and labor tended to blur.

Yet despite this overall leveling, income and class differences remained. The major one was the gulf between the *nomenklatura* of party and state officials and the rest of the population. This division generated social discomfort over differences in levels of living and, more important, in life chances. In reality, compared with Western, especially American, practices, the income distinctions were not great. Almost everyone in harsh climates had enough to eat and a roof over his or her head, in obvious contrast to many residents of New York City, for example. At the other end of the scale, the *nomenklatura* had houses with extra bedrooms, and their bathrooms were more modern. Such contrasts have been widening rapidly in the first years after socialism and are a potential new source of political discord.

Leninist socialism broke down for many reasons. It squandered resources and lost political clout as the *nomenklatura* protected itself from reprisal by gradually abandoning ideology and terror as means for disciplining the masses. Socialist elites began to travel abroad during the 1960s and saw a lifestyle that they could not begin to enjoy at home. Mass media subsequently transmitted the message of relative consumer impoverishment to the populace at large. Consumption standards inevitably began to rise, while by the 1970s planning control had already faltered and investment fell sharply from its historical peaks (with slower capacity growth leading to faster inflation).

These failings and the much more serious lapse of not incorporating technical advance into goods circulating outside the military-industrial complex doomed the administrative system. But it is important to recognize that on its own terms socialism *did* function. Commodities were produced and military might projected; originally overwhelming popular aspirations for a more than subsistence standard of living with relative social and economic equality were fulfilled.

To an extent, planning was even a self-regenerating system, although the attempts at reform that began in the 1960s ultimately fell short. Even in the Soviet Union, the "treadmill of reform" moved enterprise incentives and behavior in rationally defensible directions. Prices were substantially freed in Hungary, and Poland's partial liberalization efforts of the 1980s may ultimately bear fruit. Despite all these efforts, however, socialism built up a durable set of institutions—an inflexible political structure tightly interlinked with the economic system; primitive financial awareness; frequently monopolistic, vertically integrated firms with established transaction flows among them; technical excellence in the military-industrial complex in contrast to shabby state provision of consumer goods and services; and a set of relative prices "distorted" from those of the West—which were functional to the system but obeyed their own laws and dynamics. Under post-socialism's initial years of transition, these institutions are proving impossible to replace.

Modes of Macroeconomic Adjustment

In Eastern Europe and Russia, economists initially tried to reconstruct socialist institutions overnight, in "big bangs" or "global shocks." These programs, despite their violent names, aimed at the humane ends of political liberty supported by rapid economic growth. Their means were market liberalization, macroeconomic stabilization, and enterprise privatization, three "izations" that recall the slogans of Mao Zedong. The reformers' radical intent did not fall short of the Chinese visionary's wildest dreams. The promises made by national political leaders and foreign advisers during the first months about how rapidly socialism would be dismantled and how large would be the output and consumption gains that the market would provide, were both unrealistic and unworkable.

The predictions failed for both aggregate and microeconomic reasons; we begin here with the former. A useful point of entry is to contrast the means by which aggregate demand is limited to (or falls short of) the potential supply of commodities in socialist and capitalist economic systems. Along lines laid out by the Polish theorist Michał Kalecki (1971) and elaborated in Taylor (1991), one can distinguish three ways in which excess aggregate demand can be erased.

First, administrative methods can be used to limit demand to available supply. The traditional socialist preference for rapid capital accumulation and acquisition of goods by the military led to a "shortage economy" due to "soft budget constraints" for favored sectors (Kornai, 1981). Consumers found their available supplies and budgets limited, leading to "repressed inflation" in their economic sphere (Malinvaud, 1977).

Second, more or less autonomous demand "injections" such as exports, investment, and public outlays can decrease in exogenous fashion. Along with breakdowns in supply linkages, such reductions help explain the dramatic declines in output during the first years of the transition. They were worsened by increased demand "leakages" such as higher taxes or import costs. Production losses were arrested in some countries in 1992, in part due to lower leakages. Tax receipts from state enterprises had previously made up a large part of the government's revenue base, but diminished as profits shrank. The ensuing fiscal deficits partly offset other reductions in overall demand.

Third, changes in national distributions of income and wealth can contribute to output loss. In any economic system, wage cuts and other forms of regressive income redistribution will restrain consumption. But they may stimulate exports via lower production costs, or spark investment by raising the share of profits in the GDP. If the first effect is stronger, consumption will fall by more than exports and investment rise so that total aggregate demand will decline. "Wage-led" macroeconomic adjustment of this form is a familiar characteristic of semi-industrialized economies all over the world (Taylor, 1993).

Inflation helps lubricate the real spending reductions, through two channels underplayed by orthodox economic theory. One is "forced saving," or a demand-cutting shift in the income distribution from low- to high-saving groups, for example, from workers whose money wages are not fully indexed to price increases toward profit recipients and/or the state.[6] The other is the "inflation tax," whereby price increases erode real money balances and induce people to save more.

Such income and wealth redistributions do hold down demand, but at high social cost. In the 1980s, developing countries had to reduce real spending to meet supply contraction caused by scarce foreign exchange. African and Latin American economies ended up with inflations at double- or triple-digit annual rates and real wage reductions of 50 percent or more. The post-socialist experience is depressingly similar, even to the extent to which inflationary processes are becoming institutionalized or "inertial," as economic actors learn to use whatever market power they possess to raise their "own" prices in self-protection against generalized price increases. An enhanced inertial component in the price spiral is one fundamental reason why it will be very difficult to reduce post-socialist inflations toward single-digit annual rates.

Taking into account these three modes of adjustment plus their inflationary implications, we can say something about the macroeconomic imbalances that post-socialist economies face. Figure 2.1 illustrates the

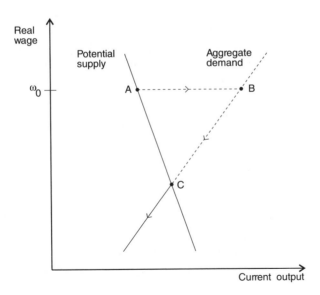

Figure 2.1 Macroeconomic adjustment to a global shock.

implications of relaxing the administrative system, with the real wage and the output level as the variables that adjust toward schedules for aggregate demand and supply. These schedules themselves were shifting during the transition, a complication addressed below.

The "potential supply" curve in Figure 2.1 shows the maximum amount that firms are willing to produce at a given real wage. Potential output does not go up very much as the wage declines, in a shorthand description of the weak "supply response" that has characterized post-socialism. The curve is steep (indicating a small response to wage changes) in the wake of economic reform for several practical reasons.

Wage cuts did not give strong incentives to boost production, because labor payments were a small proportion of total costs (profits and taxes plus costs of intermediate inputs and labor). Owing to the supply biases built into the planning system, intermediate purchases dominated firms' variable costs; rising energy and other input prices drove their cost shares higher during the transition. Meanwhile, profits rose as a proportion of value added (the total value of output less intermediate input costs). Both shifts have sharply reduced the already low wage share and the leverage of labor cost changes in influencing firms' decisions. Real wages fell because prices rose; enterprise cash flows were also adversely affected. High interest rates on loans for working capital exacerbated this problem. Moreover, as demand collapsed after the big bangs, there were few nonprice signals to raise output in any case. Finally, insofar as real wage cuts are a metaphor for price adjustment more generally, the lack of an entrepreneurial tradition and entrenched monopoly positions helped make potential output inelastic in post-socialist systems.

The economy of Figure 2.1 is assumed to be wage-led, but the "aggregate demand" schedule is also steep; demand reductions require substantial price increases and wage cuts in forced saving/inflation tax regimes.[7] The curve is dashed to show its "virtual" nature to the right of the potential supply schedule. At the real wage ω_0, for example, unrestricted demand would be at point B, but under socialism the observed level was held down to point A by the administrative mechanisms already discussed.

When constraints in all markets were suddenly lifted in a global shock incorporating near total price liberalization, demand surged from A toward B. Because demand at point B exceeded potential supply, some new limiting mechanism had to appear. Price jumps were the only possible outcome, as in, for example, the triple-digit inflation in Poland in 1990 and the many-fold price jumps in Russia after decontrol in January 1992. The inflation tax and forced saving kicked in, driving the economy toward point C. As demand fell, inflationary pressure abated, but there was no reason for real wage reductions to stop at full capacity use. Under macro policies aimed at wage restraint (certainly the case under post-socialism) and with increasingly inertial inflation, demand followed the arrows down the observable or solid schedule below point C.

Demand reduction via inflationary wage cuts was an essential aspect of the early transition, played down by orthodox theory, which posits inverse and not direct linkages between real wages and output. (The standard argument is that cheaper labor induces firms to hire more workers who produce more goods—regardless of whether or not there is any chance to sell them.) As discussed in the next two sections, however, other factors are important as well. One is an inward shift in supply schedules, as traditional linkages among producers fell apart; another is the inward shift in demand schedules.

In the Soviet Union, for example, the number of centrally allocated products was sharply cut in the late 1980s, reducing the efficiency of the planning system (Ellman and Kontorovich, 1992). Meanwhile, the state procurement committee (Gossnab) continued to handle interfirm trade; most enterprises had neither sales nor purchasing departments. When Gossnab itself was abolished, the resulting breakdown of commodity transactions further reduced potential supply, forcing still more inflation to drive demand downward. Such disorder was less in the smaller, more internationally open Eastern European economies such as Hungary and Poland. They had previously begun to replace the centralized supply system, and they were better able to bring in imports to widen supply bottlenecks in any case.

Demand schedules also shifted inward, for several additional reasons besides the fiscal adjustments just noted. As part of the forced saving process, profit flows rose early in the transition process. In the face of output stagnation and extreme uncertainty, however, firms did not undertake new capital formation. Fixed investment was cut back dramatically, worsening the output declines in economies that had been investment-led. Exports among the members of the socialist trade-clearing authority (CMEA) collapsed in a chain reaction, but these losses were partly offset by sales to new markets in the West. Imports fell but trade balances improved early in most transitions. The implication, as we shall see, is that post-socialist economies are constrained by aggregate demand, not scarcity of foreign exchange.

Shock therapists hoped for more pacific outcomes. Figure 2.2 illustrates the sort of global adjustment based on relative price changes (wage-cutting, in particular) that they had in mind. For low levels of the real wage, the potential supply curve is assumed to become less steep as its elasticity rises. Also at the wage level ω_1, the demand curve changes slope, presumably as exports become cheap enough to make them competitive in world trade. Further wage reductions stimulate sales abroad as the economy becomes "profit-led." It can converge through point D to a new low wage/high output equilibrium at point E.

Even if price movements alone could induce such a dynamic process (see Chapters 3 and 4 for micro-level arguments why not), there is no obvious institutional reason why it should occur. In Yevgeny Kuznetsov's (1991) phrase, there could be cycling or chaotic fluctuations in the "Bermuda triangle" defined by an administered equilibrium point C, stagnation at D, and the market optimists' solution E.

Moreover, no time scale can be inferred from the diagram. The experi-

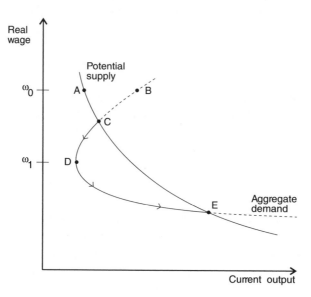

Figure 2.2 Hypothetical long-term response to a global shock.

ence of developing countries suggests that one has to think in terms of decades for transitions of the sort illustrated to transpire. Even with unstinting support from official aid donors, Chile required almost a dozen years to return to sustained economic growth after its "post-socialist" transition began in 1973; by 1990 its per capita GDP still had not reached the level of twenty years before. In 1993 Mexico, after a decade of orthodox intensive care in the wake of its debt crisis and recent annual inflows of foreign resources of more than 5 percent of its GDP, had virtually no private saving and negative growth of output per head.

With hindsight, from a mainstream perspective, the Chilean transition could have been shorter, had policymakers seen through the veils of ignorance and misunderstanding. It is hard to imagine that post-socialist authorities will be any less maladroit than the Chileans with their ample advice from American scholars, the World Bank, and the International Monetary Fund. Perhaps a more relevant observation is that Turkish, South Korean, Chinese, and other developing countries successful in their adjustments have not been led by the invisible hand; substantial state intervention over decades sowed the seeds of their sustained output growth.

In considering modes of macroadjustment, two lines of thought are worth sketching out. First, the obvious way to avoid the overshooting of Figure 2.1 is not to undertake a global shock. Stanislav Zhukov and Alexander Vorobyov (1991) point out that a messy "multifaceted price system" (or MPS) with diverse values and rationing for the "same" commodity in different markets may be a necessary crutch for the transition from an administered toward a market regime, as monopoly structures are gradually broken down and entrepreneurship is nurtured. The Polish multifaceted price system of the 1980s has been roundly condemned, but its homely virtues are perhaps becoming more evident in light of the crash of 1990–1992. The gradual Hungarian reforms that began in the late 1960s or the pragmatic Chinese movements toward the market after the 1970s look even better.[8]

The second observation is that designing policy for stabilization and growth is trickier in wage-led than in profit-led systems. Both the real wage and inflation usually respond positively to output, for example. But then a wage reduction will cut demand, reducing wage growth further still even if inflation slows down. This is one mechanism behind the overshooting below point C in Figure 2.1.

Similarly, a positive wage/output linkage complicates the adjustment to increases in labor productivity. If unemployed labor is present, a productivity gain (or a fall in the labor/output ratio) is not likely to be accompanied by a higher real wage. At the initial level of output, total wage payments will decline, reducing consumption demand and ultimately investment and potential output growth via the accelerator. If exports are sensitive to local production costs, however, they may jump up enough to raise total output in profit-led fashion. The price elasticity of exports becomes a crucial parameter, key to absorbing productivity growth as well as the pleasant outcome of Figure 2.2. In practice, market mechanisms alone are not likely to make export demand responsiveness rise. A government agency or publicly backed large enterprise such as a Korean *chaebol* or a transnational corporation has to search out buyers and pressure local producers into making goods and services that sell.

Transition in Eastern Europe

Even including Hungary, with its far earlier entry into reform, the economies of Eastern Europe have followed the pattern of Figures 2.1 and 2.2, traveling via rapid increases and then slow declines in price inflation from administered equilibria as at point A toward low-wage stagnation at D. Inflations were set off by sudden price liberalizations combined with nominal maxi-devaluations (of hundreds of percentage points, in some cases), followed by partial or complete exchange rate freezes.

These policies had the joint goals of eliminating differentials or "distortions" of local relative prices from their international counterparts and getting rid of "monetary overhangs," the putative excess supply of currency and deposits inherited from socialism. After the initial policy shocks, "nominal anchors" in the form of stable exchange rates and money wages were supposed to fix prices. Via inflation stabilization, liberalization was supposed to segue into sustained output growth. Yet after several years, these pleasant outcomes have not transpired.

Fiscal and monetary austerity has played a role in each country's package. Along with the initial devaluations (which typically reduce aggregate demand in wage-led economies), austerity contributed to the output loss. Although wage controls have been prominent, no additional heterodox moves such as setting up multifaceted prices or pushing public investment to restructure the productive apparatus have been attempted.

This flight from planning has led to depressingly similar outcomes across the region, as the data in Table 2.1 make clear.[9] Although all countries initially were at broadly similar levels of per capita income, other conditions varied. Hungary had kept up gradual reforms after the political unrest of the 1960s; about 80 percent of consumer goods were free from price controls by 1990, and 90 percent by 1991 (Bruno, 1993). Like Poland, Hungary engaged in massive foreign borrowing (compare the columns for dollar debt and GDP level in Table 2.1), but its ratio of broad money (currency plus easily accessible bank deposits, or M_2) to GDP was only 40 percent. Compared with the other countries, Hungary had no monetary overhang.[10]

The Czechoslovak Federal Republic (CSFR) and Romania were politically repressive and orthodox in planning; both had relatively modest overhangs and low foreign debt. Bulgaria had specialized in industrial exports to the Soviet Union while Poland was much more populous and presumably closer to being self-sufficient; both had run up large overhangs and external debts.

Initial conditions in Yugoslavia were somewhat different, in that the Federation had never been a member of the CMEA and had gotten away from the monobanking system. The economy was highly dependent on remittances sent home by emigrant workers. There was also a complex structure of cross-subsidization among the central bank, commercial banks, and state enterprises as well as among regions (richer Slovenia and Croatia made transfers to the republics lying to the southeast). Despite all this machinery, regional inequality continued to increase, as did unemployment in the poorer republics.

Creation of money to finance the subsidies became worrisome in the 1980s, reaching 4 or 5 percent of GDP each year after the middle of the decade, and 11 percent in 1989.[11] Driven by increasing social disorder and facilitated by innovations such as wage indexation and rising monetary emission (enforced lending by the banking system to the government), inflation began to speed up. The annual rate went from 50 percent in 1984 to 194 percent in 1988; it spiked in 1989, with the monthly rate reaching 40 percent (or 5,600 percent annually) in November.

Table 2.1 Macroeconomic developments in post-socialist economies

Country and Year	Pop. (mill.)	GDP per cap. (1980 US$)	GDP (mill. 1980 US$)	Percentage change in				
				GDP	Consumer prices	Real wages	Nominal wages	Broad money
Yugoslavia								
1989	23.7[a]	3050[b]	72234.0[b]	0.6[c]	1252.0[c]	25.3[c]	1585.9[e]	2347.0[e]
1990	23.8	2787[h]	66094.1[h]	−8.5	580.0	−4.7	420.6	39.3
1991	23.9	2351	56180.0	−15.0	118.0	−5.8		
1992						−50.0	4547.3[d]	
Poland								
1989	38.0	1603[b]	61240.0[b]	0.2	259.5	8.3	283.0[f]	514.6
1990	38.1	1382[b]	54136.2[h]	−11.6	558.4	−24.4	397.6[d]	166.0
1991	38.2	1310	50022.0	−7.6	70.3	−0.3	70.5	45.0
1992				−0.5 to 2.0	43.0	−3.6	40.4	
Hungary								
1989	10.4	2376[b]	25114.0[b]	0.4	18.8	0.7	17.0[e]	15.2
1990	10.4	2336	24285.0[h]	−3.3	28.9	−3.7	27.4[d]	29.3
1991	10.3	2077[h]	21395.0	−11.9	35.0	−4.0	33.5	
1992				−4 to −6	23.0	3.9	27.8	
CSFR								
1989	15.6	3970[b]	62060.0[b]	1.4	2.2	0.1	2.2[e]	4.7
1990	15.7	3898[h]	61191.2[h]	−1.4	9.9	−5.4	5.2[d]	−0.7
1991	15.6	3299	51462.0	−15.9	57.9	−25.2	15.2	26.7
1992				−7 to −8		10.1	20.0	
Bulgaria								
1989	9.0	2863[b]	25776.0[b]	−0.3	6.2	3.0		
1990	9.0	2524	21265.2[h]	−17.5	19.3	7.3	31.6	
1991	8.9	1775[h]	15800.0	−25.7	338.5	−43.0	158.5	
1992				−22.0	79.3	22.5	119.7	
Romania								
1989	23.2	2193[b]	50782.0[b]	−5.8	0.9	2.7	3.9[e]	5.3
1990	23.2	2027[h]	47024.0[h]	−7.4	5.7	6.0	10.5	25.2
1991	23.2	1763	40911.0	−13.7	165.5	−16.6	121.3	100.9
1992				−15.4	210.4	−15.1	163.8	
Russian Federation								
1989	147.7	4232[b*]	625066.0[h]	1.6	3.2		9.0[d]	13.1
1990	148.3	3923[b]	622566.0	−4.0	6.9	9.0	14.7[e]	14.3
1991			554084.0	−11.0	91.8	−10.5	95.0	19.5
1992				−20.0	1110.0	−46.5	891.0	80.7

Sources: In each column, each note refers to all items below until another note is given.

a. United Nations Department of International Economic and Social Affairs, *Monthly Bulletin of Statistics* (Feb. 1993).

b. United Nations Industrial Development Organization, *Industry and Development Global Report,* various years.

b*. Former Soviet Union, from source b.

c. United Nations Economic Commission for Europe, *Economic Survey of Europe,* various years.

Table 2.1 (*continued*)

Percentage of GDP			Convertible curr. ext. debt (bill. 1980 US$)	Trade balance (bill. 1980 US$)	Total exports (bill. 1980 US$)	Annual % change in exports
Budget balance	Conv. curr. acct.	Broad money				
0.2[g]	2.5[f]	87.8[e]			13.4[a]	4.8[c]
−5.7[c]			16.5[c]	−4.6[c]	14.3	7.1
−9.6			14.5	−1.4	9.6[a] to 14.0[b]	−3.9
	−1.7				13.2[a]	0.2
0.4[c]	4.8	62.9	48.5	5.7	14.3	24.7
−3.8		32.6	48.4	−0.6	14.5	−18.5
−6.0			49.4	−2.6		9.7
−1.9[g]	−2.0				9.6	0.3
−0.1[c]	1.1		21.3	0.9	9.7	0.6
−4.9			22.7	−1.2	10.3	5.1
−7.4			21.4	−0.4		4.1
−3.8[g]	1.9	73.0			14.4	−2.0
0.5[c]	−2.7	67.2	8.1	−1.1	11.9	−10.5
−1.8	2.7	71.4	9.3	0.4	11.3	5.6
−1.8			9.5	−0.9		3.2
	−1.6				16.0	−2.3
−4.9			10.0	−0.4	13.4	−21.3
−3.6			11.4	0.7		−34.2
−3.1			12.0			1.6
8.2[g]	4.7	51.4			10.5	−10.8
1.0[c]	−8.6	60.8	0.4	−2.3	5.9	−43.4
1.9			1.9	−1.4	4.1	−17.1
−2.0			3.5	−0.8		0.9
					80.9	
			61.1	−5.9	54.7	−5.2
			65.3	1.3		−24.6
			75.8	3.0		−25.2

d. Calculated on basis of average monthly wages in national currency units (*Economic Survey of Europe,* various years).

e. Calculated on the basis of *International Financial Statistics* (International Monetary Fund, various years, 1985 = 100).

f. Calculated current account balance as percentage of GDP (IMF *Handbook 1992,* p. 141).

g. Calculated from government deficits/surpluses (IMF *Handbook 1992,* p. 92).

h. Calculated from base year GDP, GDP growth rates, and GDP per capita.

With advice from the Bretton Woods institutions and Western academics, the central Yugoslav government reacted to this incipient hyperinflation[12] with a big bang in mid-December 1989, which served as a model for transition packages elsewhere in the region. The main elements were fiscal stringency, a freeze on nominal wages, a freeze on the exchange rate after an initial maxi-devaluation, and ensured convertibility for foreign exchange inflows to attract remittances. The inflation rate dropped to 2 percent per month by May 1990, real tax revenues rose, and real wages fell by over 20 percent. Over all of 1990, the official unemployment rate rose by 1 percent and the national product fell by 8.5 percent.

Although they were modest in comparison with those that were to occur elsewhere in the region, the real wage and output reductions were an economic straw on the back of a political camel that already limped badly. The central government's failure to combine an acceptable output and employment performance with inflation stabilization was a large component of its ultimate indictment. Spurred in part by the failing economy, separatist movements in the republics pushed the Federation into a brutal war.

The political aftermath of the Yugoslav experiment did not carry over to the rest of Eastern Europe in the first years of transition, but its economic sequelae certainly did. The reform packages (except, to some extent, Hungary's) adopted Belgrade's policy blend: economy-wide removal of price controls and production subsidies, and proclamations of fiscal and monetary rectitude. After initial devaluations, exchange rates were pegged as "nominal anchors" on prices in Poland and the CSFR (which had enough foreign currency on hand to maintain fixed exchange rates by buying up the local currency when it was subject to a speculative run), and allowed to float in Bulgaria and Romania (where dollars and deutschemarks were scarce). Hungary went in a similar direction, but followed its gradualist inclination by devaluing by only 15 percent and liberalizing a bit more of the price system. The Polish package was put in place early in 1990, and the others a year thereafter.

Prices were expected to jump after liberalization, in proportion to the degree of monetary overhang as calculated from the equation of exchange.[13] Except in Hungary, observed price increases far outstripped the jumps that were anticipated in the first year after stabilization (UNECE, 1992; Bruno, 1993):

	Expected annual inflation rate (%)	Actual annual inflation rate (%)
Poland (1990)	90–100	249
Hungary (1991)	34	32
CSFR (1991)	30	54
Bulgaria (1991)	288	339
Romania (1991)	120	223

Underestimation of inflation rates is a common feature of IMF stabilization packages in developing countries (Taylor, 1988), but the errors in the case of Eastern Europe are striking. Two reasons are usually advanced to explain why price forecasts under post-socialism have been so wrong. First, the monopoly power of state enterprises was not taken into account in the initial price calculations (but as argued in Chapter 4, this factor may have been exaggerated in any case). Second, the devaluations that initiated the programs sent clear messages to all sellers, from dentists up to the largest state-owned firms, to raise their own prices in the same proportion as the exchange rate hike.[14]

Both observations make sense, especially in economies previously bereft of normal market information apart from the value of the official or parallel value of foreign currency. But they miss the fundamental point that after liberalization, price increases are the only means available to move the economy from the infeasible point B in Figure 2.1 toward the schedule for potential supply. Each country's initial price jump stemmed from an unrealizable increase in effective demand due to decontrol, not violation of the equation of exchange.

After the initial price surge, monthly inflation rates in Eastern Europe began to fall (see Table 2.2). Except in the successor states to the CSFR (the Czech and Slovak Republics had 11 percent and 10 percent yearly inflation respectively in 1992), however, price increases did not decline to Western European norms. Incomplete indexation of money wage to rising prices as an aspect of nominal anchoring was a premeditated component of the packages, and standard practice for the IMF. Such "income policies" ratify the reductions in the inflation rate that tight money is supposed to ensure. More pointedly, they contribute directly to slowing price inflation by braking rises in costs. In the process, real wages necessarily fall.[15]

Table 2.2 Inflation and liberalization shocks (percentage change in consumer price index)

	Poland (1990)	Bulgaria (1991)	CSFR (1991)	Romania (1991)	Russia (1992)
Year before shock[a]	260	19	10	6	92
Year of shock					
January	80	14	26	9	250
February	24	123	7	7	24
March	4	51	5	7	21
April	8	3	2	26	14
May	5	1	2	5	11
June	3	6	2	2	13
July	4	8		10	8
August	2	8		11	8
September	5	4		7	11
October	6	3		10	21
November	5	5	2	11	25
December	6	5	1	14	26
Within year[a]	249	474	54	223	1,653
1st year after shock[a]	70	79	10	210	
2nd year after shock[a]	43				

Source: UNECE (1993).

a. Annual rate.

Following Andrew Glyn (1992), we draw three main conclusions about wage cuts in Eastern Europe from the data in Table 2.3. First, income compression can be pushed only so far; the data suggest that reductions of more than 30–40 percent were all that post-socialist civil societies would endure. How well this generalization will carry over to Russia—where real wages fell by close to 50 percent in 1992 and continued downward in 1993—is a politically loaded question.

Second, the relative real wage stability of 1992 meant that money wages had started to rise at about the same speed as prices (as also became true of nominal exchange rates, as more and more countries switched toward "crawling peg" regimes, in which the nominal exchange rate is devalued at the same pace as the general price level rises). The presence of such inertial price increases, especially when

Table 2.3 Components of changes in income (percentage change over previous year)

	Bulgaria				CSFR				Hungary				Poland			
	89	90	91	92	89	90	91	92	89	90	91	92	89	90	91	92
Total	-1	11	-42	18	1	-2	-27	8	-2	1	-9	-1	6	-15	6	
Wages	3	3	-53		0	-8	-34	-2	-2	-4	-10	-8	6	-32	-7	-12
Social transfers	0	3	-28		4	-5	-22	4	3	1	-5	0	8	-14	29	-3
Farm	-5	30	-20		2	-8	-52	-16	-6	-6	-34	-12	14	-50	-19	
Other	-6	24	-45		2	27	-3	41		10	17	-5	5	19	17	
Private consumption	3	-9	ld	sd	2	3	-32	5	2	-5	-6	si	1	-16	7	si

Source: The table is based on UNECE (1993), tables 3.1.5 and 3.2.8, and surrounding text.
Note: In the row for private consumption, ld = large decrease, sd = small decrease, si = small increase.

the core inflation rate exceeds 2 percent per month, means that reducing them will be difficult. Ominous experience with inertial inflations in developing countries shows that a plateau with much more than 2 percent monthly rates is unstable—prices can easily take off in response to adverse shocks to output, the income distribution, or aggregate demand.

Finally, we note that real consumer spending dropped more or less in step with falling purchasing power (less strongly in Poland, more in the CSFR), along Kaleckian lines. These declines were important contributing factors to the observed output slumps. Despite the apparent stabilization of real wages in 1992 (and a likely reduction in private savings rates as desires for imported consumer goods continued to rise), there has been a long-term fall in effective demand, which will not be offset by the modest export growth and rising fiscal deficits observed in that year.

In addition to the reductions in consumption, other components of final demand contributed to the output slumps. Relative prices shifted toward producers during the inflations, so that profits initially surged but then dropped off as the output reductions set in. Because they were faced with output stagnation and extreme uncertainty, enterprises did not take advantage of their early high profit flows to undertake capital formation. Fixed investment was cut back dramatically, worsening the output declines in economies that historically had been investment-led.[16]

Fiscal revenues, derived in large measure from taxes on state enterprises' profits, also followed an inverted U pattern. During the initial phase of the transition, spending cuts (reduced injections) magnified the contractionary effects of higher public revenues (or increased leakages). Rather than increasing their outlays to offset the demand gaps created by investment and real wage reductions, governments chose to rein in. Infrastructure investment was cut back, imperiling the modernization of the capital stock that will be required for successful production reform. Later in the process, fiscal deficits widened as tax revenues from state enterprise profits declined in 1992 (see Table 2.1). A fiscal crisis was in the making, but it did help offset some of the contraction caused by stagnant consumer demand.

Alongside household and government consumption and gross capital formation, exports are the third important component of final demand. Orthodox explanations of the output slumps in Eastern Europe emphasize the collapse of CMEA trade in 1990–91 (IMF, 1992)—a chain reaction that steadily worsened as more and more countries dropped out of the payments union. Because they had to start purchasing raw materials at world rather than subsidized Soviet prices (a deterioration in the external "terms of trade") and also lost export volume in the region, the East European economies suffered adverse external shocks. Output contracted as the demand injection from exports was suddenly curtailed, while higher import costs had the same effect as would a higher indirect tax or an increased leakage.

One should not gainsay the significance of these misadventures. As Glyn (1992) emphasizes, however, export markets opened up in the West, especially for Poland, Hungary, and the CSFR. Firms hard hit by domestic demand contraction searched for foreign outlets more aggressively than they might otherwise have done. Despite the fact that imports of consumer goods were encouraged as an anti-inflationary measure (with devastating effects on national enterprises producing "inferior" substitutes for foreign goods), domestic recessions made import volumes decline, *not* the other way around, as the orthodox argument would imply. A question about the direction of macroeconomic causality necessarily arises, as in the Reagan-era debate over whether the U.S. fiscal deficit caused the "twin" trade deficit to widen, or vice versa.

Evidence to disentangle the causal question is not readily available, in part because of the difficulties of converting CMEA trade flows to Western prices. Typically external balances improved after the reform packages were imposed (see Table 2.1). Indeed, the gain was greater than anticipated, as the data for expected and observed trade surpluses in billions of dollars make clear (UNECE, 1992):

	Expected trade balance	Actual trade balance
Poland (1990)	−0.8	+3.8
CSFR (1991)	−2.5	+0.9
Bulgaria (1991)	−2.0	+2.0

The simplest explanation is that output losses caused imports to decline enough to lead trade surpluses to rise despite the disappearance of CMEA exports. Falling exports were not the main source of contracting demand. Countries that experience export declines and adverse shifts in the terms of trade typically see their trade balances deteriorate, not improve as they did in Eastern Europe.

Table 2.4 illustrates the output and other changes that Eastern European countries may have suffered in the wake of reform, based on a simple demand-driven macroeconomic model (summarized in this chapter's appendix). The model's main implication is that real wage reductions and export losses of the magnitudes observed in Eastern Europe are consistent with recorded falls in output, with the wage cuts being the more important source of contraction. Although such a simple model cannot deal with the full complexity of each country's history, it suggests that one factor underlying improvements in observed trade balances after shock therapy was plummeting aggregate demand.

When real wage reductions leveled off and demand began to stabilize in years subsequent to the policy shocks, external balances swung back toward deficits (Table 2.1). Arguably, bringing extra imports into small open economies helped produce the stabilization of inflation rates pointed out in connection with Table 2.2. These foreign currency outlays were in part offset by the modest export growth shown in the last column of Table 2.1. Despite this favorable sign, however, external balance in Eastern Europe is by no means assured, for at least two reasons.

First, using the exchange rate as a nominal anchor inevitably led to real appreciation, which encourages imports and makes marginal exports unprofitable. As their initial devaluations were eroded by on-

Table 2.4 Effects of macroeconomic shocks: An illustration

	Real output	Real wage	Real consumption	Real exports	Real imports	Trade surplus[a]
Initial levels	100	1	65	25	25	0
30% real wage reduction	84.7	0.7	38.6	25	13.8	11.2
Export reduction[b]	76.6	0.7	34.9	19	12.2	6.8
50% rise in import prices	68.1	0.7	31	19	11.2	2.1

a. Changes reflect shifts in both import and export volumes and import price movements.

b. Initial exports are 25. There is a loss of 10 because of the disappearance of the CMEA, and a gain of 4 because of new exports to the West.

going inflation, all the East European economies except Romania saw their currencies strengthen in the range of 15–30 percent in dollar terms in comparison with levels in late 1990 (UNECE, 1993).

Second, any substantial increases in output or investment could draw in enough imports to raise trade deficits to several percent or more of GDP. Consumer preferences have shifted toward imports, perhaps with a reduction in overall savings rates as noted earlier. More ominously, as post-socialist economies begin to use Western technologies, they will become increasingly dependent on imports of intermediate and capital goods. Without massive foreign aid or an export boom, growth and/or output could be held down by inadequate supplies of hard currency in traditional developing country fashion (Taylor, 1993).

Apart from the CMEA export collapse, other orthodox explanations for production losses are based on the tacit assumption that post-socialist economies remained on the potential output schedules of Figures 2.1 and 2.2. Yet the collapse of socialist institutions surely pushed these schedules to the left; mainstream economists emphasize market-based mechanisms.

Guillermo Calvo and Fabrizio Coricelli (1992) of the IMF, for example, pick up the old structuralist observation concerning the adverse effects of high interest rates. They argue that dear and/or tightened credit worsened stagflation by shifting supply schedules inward. In Russia, where in comparison with Eastern Europe the economy is large and less open to price stabilization via foreign trade, supply restrictions in certain sectors clearly did bind. Zhukov and Vorobyov (1991) argue that Russian enterprises are likely to raise prices in response to higher interest rates on loans for working capital, in a form of cost-push. Inflation stabilization relying on tight money and high interest rates becomes that much more difficult.

Using a mainstream rational expectations model, Wojciech Charemza (1992) argues that substantial supply failures emerged under the extreme negative correlations of prices and quantities observed in Poland after liberalization. His model also rationalizes the collapse of enterprises' investment demands.

With regard to real wages, recall that orthodox theory postulates that they have an inverse relationship with output. The implication for the post-socialist transition is that wages did not fall *enough* (IMF, 1992). The idea is that more draconian wage repression could have led the economy to a position like point E in Figure 2.2, with high exports permitting production and employment to rise. As already observed, the low share of wages in total costs as well as a host of other technological and institutional factors influencing supply make the strong response underlying point E improbable. On the demand side, real wages and output run together. Both dropped sharply during the first years of transition, despite a rise in exports to the West. It is hard to give the Bretton Woods institutions' argument for further wage cutting much credence.

Finally, there is the question of unemployment. In developing countries, lower total real wage payments during economic contractions have shown up both as wage reductions per unit of labor and in job destruction per se. The unemployment rate in Chile (counting people on the dole), for example, rose from 5 percent to over 25 percent as both real wages and output fell by about 15 percent under an orthodox stabilization package in the mid-1970s. More typical, perhaps, was Mexico's experience, in which unemployment scarcely increased but the average real wage fell by a third between 1983 and 1988.

As will be discussed in Chapter 4, post-socialist economies initially followed the Mexican (decreasing labor productivity) rather than the Chilean (open unemployment) pattern. As state firms began to go under, however, unemployment rates reached double-digit levels in most countries by 1992 (UNECE, 1993). Because "safety nets" were in tatters due to budget cuts, another source of social tension appeared to be on the rise.

The Transition in Russia

At this writing, it is too early to draw strong conclusions about Russia's post-socialist transition. So far, it bears a striking resemblance to the experience in Eastern Europe. The principal difference is that the macroeconomic dislocations caused by the global shock of January 1992 in Russia were even worse than in the other countries.

As pointed out by Vorobyov (1993) and Zhukov (1993), the economy of the USSR had already begun to falter by the 1970s, but found a convenient crutch in raw material (especially oil and gas) exports. The resulting hard currency inflows permitted imports of consumer and intermediate goods to rise, pushing a reckoning with the weaknesses of the planning system into the future. The situation worsened in the mid-1980s for several reasons. The fiscal position deteriorated under *perestroika,* owing to an ill-planned and ill-executed investment push and a decline in tax revenues (for example, from the vodka turnover tax during Gorbachev's anti-alcoholism campaign). State control over enterprises was weakened, permitting them to engage in massive (but frequently uncompleted) capital investment projects and to raise wages. Output began to decline, and inflation to speed up (see Table 2.5).

The political turmoil that went along with the deteriorating economy ultimately led to the break-up of the Soviet Union at the end of 1991. Meanwhile, several economic reform proposals were floated, typically long on rhetoric but short on specifics about exactly how the planning system was to be replaced by the "market" (with no discussion of how the latter was to be regulated). Fears of inflation and a money overhang grew, fanned in part by decontrol of the noncash ruble balances that made up about a third of the total money supply. Prior to that, cash money had risen by 170 percent between 1979 and 1990 while real GDP only grew by 40 percent as a consequence of the fiscal exuberance of *perestroika.*[17] Demand was strong enough to push the economy onto Figure 2.1's potential supply curve, which itself was shifting inward as the capital stock deteriorated and the effectiveness of the planning system declined.

The first policy shock was orchestrated by the Pavlov government in April 1991, when enough prices were liberalized to lead to an increase of the overall index by 170 percent (see Table 2.6). Pavlov adopted an old Soviet ploy of confiscating "excess" money balances by sudden price

Table 2.5 Macroeconomic indicators for Russia (before 1992, USSR)

	1986	1987	1988	1989	1990	1991	1992
Real income							
Official	102	104	106	125	140	133	53
Independent	100	102	100	120	115	49	37
GNP	98	93	88	84	80	61	47
Inflation (annual rate)	4%	5%	11%	14%	17%	529%	1,650%
Nominal money (January 1)[a]	639	593	614	703	781	945	1,744

Source: Zhukov (1993).

a. In billions of rubles.

Table 2.6 Monthly inflation rates (%) and exchange rates in Russia

	1991		1992		1993	
	Inflation	Exchange rate	Inflation	Exchange rate	Inflation	Exchange rate
Jan.	4.5		227.0	199	25.8	489
Feb.	14.2		5.2	176	24.7	580
Mar.	15.0		17.7	148	20.1	668
Apr.	170.0		11.6	153	23.2	776
May	2.5		13.1	122	18.5	908
June	2.2		21.9	124	19.9	1,078
July	2.2		5.9	143	22.0	1,018
Aug.	2.6		9.2	170	28.0	986
Sept.	3.7		17.1	225	21.0	1,073
Oct.	12.8		25.1	353	25.0	1,188
Nov.	24.1		33.3	427	11.5	
Dec.	32.4	149	24.2	415		

Sources: Zhukov (1993) and Russian economic periodicals.

increases (Zhukov, 1993). This act of political suicide caused inflation to slow down temporarily.

These operations set the stage for a very big bang in January 1992, undertaken with at least the tacit cooperation of the Bretton Woods institutions. The aim was to use liberalization and a maxi-devaluation to induce a price jump by a factor of about 3.5; thereafter, inflation was to slow down to about 5–10 percent per month by April. As usual, fiscal and monetary austerity was to be imposed. The ruble exchange rate was to be stabilized by central bank operations in the foreign currency market (which had been consolidated from several parallel transaction channels into the Moscow International Currency Exchange, or MICE, at the end of 1991).

Not one of these three goals was attained, and each of the failures substantially worsened the economy's prospects for the future. Prices initially jumped by a factor somewhere between 3 and 6, depending on which indexes one uses (the numbers in Table 2.6 are based on the official consumer price index, which generates the lowest rates of inflation). Soon after, the monthly rate took on values in the double digits, reaching the 30 percent range by the year's end.

Fiscal and monetary control likewise proved elusive. With a proliferation of spending initiatives and the sequestration of revenues by local governments and other fiscal drains, it is impossible to put a number on the consolidated deficit of all levels of government, but it was large. The money supply was also expanded by two peculiarly Russian factors.

First, central banks of the other former Soviet Republics in the Commonwealth of Independent States (CIS) could create rubles at will and refinance them with the Russian central bank. Second, there was a so-called insolvency crisis—a much more acute version of a stabilization problem present in Eastern Europe and the developing world. Enterprises kept up the interindustry delivery patterns that had prevailed under the planned economy. The old system of noncash ruble finance had been curtailed, so they hit on the expedient of issuing credits to one another. The volume of this interfirm lending skyrocketed, from about 39 billion rubles in January 1992 to more than 3,000 billion in July. Ultimately many of these credits were absorbed, that is, monetized, by the central bank. Part of the acceleration of inflation in the second part of 1992 can be explained by these manipulations; at the same time, they probably prevented real GDP from falling by more than the officially estimated 22 percent.

In nominal terms, the exchange rate depreciated by a factor of about 3, a number that might have been larger if the central bank had not sporadically supported the market (in the face of capital flight of at least hundreds of millions of dollars per month). Because prices increased over 1992 by a factor of 15 to 20, the year ended with real appreciation far greater than that observed in Eastern Europe, another headache for the future. In 1993, the ruble appreciated further in real terms (see Table 2.6).

The inflation inevitably led to real wage reductions and a collapse in consumption (on the order of 40 or 50 percent). Investment fell precipitously as the "plan whip" for accumulation previously cracked by Gosplan and Gossnab fell into disuse; emerging proto-capitalist enterprises were unwilling to invest in an increasingly insecure economic regime. Exports also fell. Only the support of interindustry transactions via the interfirm loans and a good agricultural year prevented the loss in GDP from being far greater. The Russian economy moved rapidly toward a position similar to point D in Figure 2.2, with output as a whole falling short of potential supply. Meanwhile, specific sectoral bottlenecks emerged and added to price pressure, owing to the breakdown of the geographically diversified production web of the former Soviet Union.

By late 1993 inflation had temporarily settled at about 10–20 percent per month, and output continued to decline (the projections were for a 16 percent loss in industrial output, and 10 percent in GDP). Along with the overall political situation, policy design turned erratic, leading to comic opera maneuvers over demonetization of old, low denomination rubles in July. In October, Boris Yeltsin's coup against the former Supreme Soviet was ostensibly provoked by its desire to approve a budget deficit of 22 trillion rubles. Six weeks later, the government itself adopted almost the same deficit figure. By early 1994, in turn, most reformers were left out of power in the wake of Yeltsin's defeat in the elections of December 1993.

Even if further economic and political faux pas can be minimized and inflation follows the East European pattern of slowing to single-digit monthly percentage rates, after its first few years of transition Russia seems doomed to continued stagnation with increasing unemployment over time. As the existing economic structure turns into a shambles that the market system is unable to replace, grave political consequences may not be far behind. The events of late 1993 were perhaps only the first of many post-socialist political temblors.

The Lessons of Transition

Orthodox policy during the first years of the transition went together with the socialist institutional inheritance to lead to massive output and income losses and rapid inflation all over Eastern Europe and the former Soviet Union. In 1992 and 1993 trade and fiscal deficits were rising, along with growing unemployment in countries without adequate social safety nets. All in all, the situation was a sad denouement to the high hopes of the late 1980s, with no better prospects for the future.

To observers familiar with the experience of developing countries with reform packages embodying the Washington consensus, this unraveling came as no surprise. Orthodox packages at times clear the ground for better economic performance by getting rid of highly distorted prices and pushing governments toward fiscal rectitude. But they are not a sufficient condition for halting inflation or ensuring output growth, let alone growth with an equitable income distribution and external self-reliance. Much more needs to be done in all policy fields.

A first issue is the choice of economic strategy. The bottom line of the

Washington consensus is that government market intervention should be renounced, while external and internal liberalization and internationalization should be pursued with vigor. Taken to the desired extremes of the Bretton Woods institutions, such actions are a leap into the void. Adam Przeworski (1992) observes: "This strategy appears to be without precedent in history. All previous attempts at modernization conceived of development as a project linked to national, economic, and political independence. All previous modernizing leaders asserted the importance of national cultures, called for political institutions consistent with national traditions, and envisaged growth led by national industries and oriented toward local markets."

The only such goal visible in the Bretton Woods institutions' strategy is the idea that the state should become a "night watchman," monitoring a liberalized market in which local private enterprises can maximize the size of the national "pie." As Przeworski implies, no economy in history has attained sustained output growth under such a policy regime. On the contrary, intelligent state intervention in markets will be needed during the transition, for many reasons.

Inflation is a key macro problem. Especially in economies in which sharp distributional conflicts exist and inertia sustains price spirals, inflation is a riddle that economists have been conspicuously unable to resolve. There are only a few methods that governments can use to attack steady price increases: fiscal and monetary austerity aimed at reducing the growth of the money supply; income policies such as forcing the money wage rate or the nominal exchange rate to increase less rapidly than the price level (thereby inducing a real wage cut or currency appreciation); income policies combined with price controls aimed at stifling inertial processes; and bringing in imports to reduce excess demand (at least in markets for traded goods).

All these moves were attempted at one point or another in the East European and Russian transition—except widespread price controls, because of the reformers' liberalization fetish. Most emphasis was placed on austerity, which usually can stop an inertial inflation only at unacceptably high costs in terms of wage reductions and/or unemployment. If price increases at double- or triple-digit annual rates are to be slowed in the future (especially in Russia, a large country in which the option of massive imports is not available), austerity will have to be complemented by measures such as price controls, going against World Bank and IMF prejudices in favor of laissez-faire.[18]

With regard to output determination, orthodox models rely on Say's Law. The Washington consensus obsession with "getting the prices right" follows from this postulate. Cutting wages and eliminating price distortions are the only means that mainstream theory has in hand for driving the economy toward Figure 2.2's high employment point E.[19]

The arguments in this chapter suggest that forces of both demand and supply influenced the level of production in the first years of the transition, with real wage cuts, leading to falling household purchases, being the most important. Now that wages have dropped by 30–40 percent and net investment is close to zero, new sources of effective demand will have to emerge if output in post-socialist economies is to expand.

Gradual wage increases supporting noninflationary expansion in consumer demand are one possibility; along with a general backing away from shock therapy beginning in 1992, rising household purchases help explain Poland's output increase in 1993. Exports also add to demand, but even with massive wage cuts and devaluation they are not likely to support sustained output growth. The implication is that capital formation will have to take up the slack—both by creating demand and by adding to potential supply.

Given the almost universal observation that public investment stimulates or "crowds in" private capital formation (Taylor, 1993), this form of recovery is unlikely in the absence of activist investment policy on the part of the state. The other side of the coin is that long-term accumulation will be hindered by low private savings rates resulting from the massive intrusion of imported goods into household consumption baskets that followed the liberalization of external trade.

The public sector will probably have to pick up the savings shortfall, if macroeconomically balanced growth is to take place. Providentially, the resources may be at hand in the form of the income flows of the nouveaux riches conceived by forced saving and born from financial speculation. Tapping this new wealth—and putting down the Mafia elements that control it—will be a challenge for post-reform states.

Policy sequencing is another contentious issue. The conventional wisdom is that countries should "stabilize" inflation and/or balance of payments problems, and then "adjust" toward balanced output growth (World Bank, 1991). In practice, the two areas blend together: reducing inflation may be impossible unless and until output starts to increase (as was the case in Chile in the mid-1980s), while supply responses are likely to be weak under uncertainty about the future caused by macroeconomic disequilibrium.

The experience of developing countries indicates that few economies successfully reform without ample access to foreign exchange (from external assistance or, preferably, exports) to support the effort. Hard currency inflows, however, are not a sufficient condition for growth. Bangladesh's per capita income stagnated throughout the 1980s, despite Bretton Woods institutions' advice and financing for trade deficits of up to 10 percent of GDP; and as already noted, more affluent Mexico's growth record with 5 percent trade deficits in the 1990s was no better.

In both Bangladesh and Mexico, the private sector proved incapable of transforming foreign resource transfers into a motor of output growth. It generated neither investment demand nor an adequate saving supply, so that foreign capital in effect financed public and private consumption demands. Such failures can be critical in large nations for which the billions of dollars required to support a trade deficit of several percent of GDP are not likely to be forthcoming: it will be much cheaper for the West to "save" Estonia or Slovenia than Russia or the other populous successor states of the USSR. Growth strategies for the large, closed economies will necessarily have to be inward-looking, based upon the utilization of resource endowments and national demand.

Historically, even relatively open economies that have created conditions for private sectors to save, invest, absorb new technologies, and grow have not done so in an unregulated market regime. From England of two hundred years ago, in which public action formed and soon thereafter regulated the market in Polanyi's (1944) famous "double movement," to South Korea from 1950 to 1980, in which the government first underwrote the conglomerate *chaebol* trading/industrial companies and then invested in a heavy industrial base for them to utilize (Amsden, 1989), all successful industrialization experiences have rested on state intervention.

Such actions will be necessary under post-socialism, both macroeconomically and at the level of firms. The industrial strategy riddle for post-socialist governments will be how to nurture state-owned enterprises while gradually transforming some of them into privately owned enterprises (POEs) that can be tutored to support economic growth. If historical experience is any guide, new privately owned enterprises will not become innovative and dynamic by themselves.

APPENDIX

The Model Underlying Table 2.4

There are five equations in the model used to generate the numbers in Table 2-4. One says that

$$X = C + E + A,$$

or national output (X) equals consumption of goods produced at home (C) plus exports (E) and autonomous spending (A).

The second is

$$PX = wbX + \pi PX,$$

or the value of output (P is the price level) equals the wage bill wbX (w is the nominal wage and b is the labor-output ratio) plus profits (π is the share of profits in the value of output).

The third equation is

$$D = (1 - s)wbX,$$

or the value of consumption (D) is a share $1 - s$ of the wage bill (where s is a saving rate). All profits revert to the state, and are assumed to be saved.

The last two equations embody a simple model of consumer demand for national goods (C) and imports (M). It is known as the linear expenditure system:

$$PC = P\theta_c + \alpha(D - P\theta_c - P^*\theta_m),$$

$$P^*M = P^*\theta_m + (1 - \alpha)(D - P\theta_c - P^*\theta_m),$$

where P^* is the price of imports, and α, θ_c, and θ_m are parameters. It is straightforward to verify that $PC + P^*M = D$, or purchases of national goods and imports exhaust consumer demand.

The model can easily be solved for X as a function of the demand injections E and A, the distributional variables w and π, the import price P^*, and the parameters b, s, α, θ_c, and θ_m. The national price is implicitly determined according to the markup rule $P = wb/(1 - \pi)$.

Initial values assumed for the variables are in line with output proportions in Eastern Europe in the late 1980s: $C = 40$, $E = M = 25$, $A = 35$, $\pi = 0.25$, and $s = 0.1333$. The consumer demand parameters were set to make the income elasticity of demand for imports equal to 1.1, and the own-price elasticity equal to -0.5.

The three perturbations summarized in Table 2.4 are

1. A reduction in the real wage w/P from an initial value of 1.0 to 0.7, with a corresponding increase in π from 0.25 to 0.475;
2. A reduction in exports E from 25 to 19 (representing a loss of 10 to CMEA partners and a gain of 4 to the West); and
3. An increase in the import price P^* from 1.0 to 1.5.

The Black Box of State-Owned Enterprises

A state of deep crisis [is] traceable largely to the SOE [state-owned enterprise] sector . . . Enterprises have reputedly failed to adjust, stalling growth and delaying the "supply response," thereby calling into question a fundamental point of design in the Economic Transformation Program: that macro stringency alone would suffice to press firms into spontaneous adjustment measures . . . Macroeconomic stringency and price liberalization, while necessary, are insufficient to induce firm-level change.

—*Report of the World Bank Resident Mission, Warsaw*

The collapse of Eastern Europe's information system left the status of the state-owned enterprise sector largely unknown, thereby complicating the crafting of effective policies for enterprise restructuring. Here we rely on our own enterprise-level case studies to learn more about SOEs.[1] Because these enterprises have remained central in post-socialist economies, especially in the industrial sector (including industrial exports), they are key to the level of employment and recovery. This chapter is a first step toward analyzing whether the free market approach to enterprise restructuring, which reigned in the early transition and featured privatization and full exposure to free market forces, was the appropriate one in light of the actual problems SOEs were encountering.

Under central planning, an SOE's founding ministry (usually the ministry of industry) and the research and development institutes with which it collaborated were fairly knowledgeable about the enterprise's problems and potential. As state-owned enterprises became more autonomous in the 1980s, that knowledge became more vague. It faded almost entirely in the process of transition, with the diaspora of the *nomenklatura* from the state to the private sector, the decimation of research institutes, and the destruction of ministries of industry (or their equivalent) as a deliberate post-socialist policy to reduce government influence.[2]

Ignorance about what was happening at the enterprise level in transition economies was only partially corrected by an influx of Western "experts." For the purposes of promoting privatization, the World Bank and other international lenders commissioned expensive studies of enterprises and industries from international consulting companies such as Bain and Company and the Boston Consulting Group. Some of these studies were excellent in their coverage, but their conclusions were kept confidential so as not to frighten off foreign buyers. The reports often belonged to particular ministries and were not even generally shared among policymakers, who tended to be much more influenced by macroeconomists, with little knowledge of enterprises or industries, than consultants in the field.

"Supply Inertia": Bad Policies or Bad Managers?

The state-owned enterprise sector in early post-socialism was vast, still producing the lion's share of manufacturing output and often determining the fate of private manufacturers by supplying them their inputs and demanding their final output. The sector's enterprises varied widely in quality—some were clearly hopeless, with little chance of becoming viable, while others, though experiencing losses (in part due to transitional turbulence), were likely to become profitable at world prices after being restructured. The potential of inherently viable enterprises had to be ascertained by examining eclectic pieces of information, including their pretransition performance in export markets, the quality of their existing management, and their product and process technology. Identifying inherently viable enterprises was no easy matter (see the proposals in OECD, 1992a). But by following the indicators in consultants' reports, privatization ministries had no trouble in selecting the best state-owned enterprises for the first round of offerings to private buyers.[3] The identification problem was nontrivial but not insuperable.

The state sector after the transition was also mixed in terms of enterprise requirements. All firms were short of working and investment capital, but in addition, some firms needed to be "converted" from being suppliers of military hardware to suppliers of commercial products; others needed to be "restructured." Restructuring here refers to the process of relieving enterprises of the single or multiple structural bottlenecks that impeded their becoming profitable at world prices: product quality bottlenecks (constraining sales due to a product poor in quality by world standards); technology bottlenecks (constraining sales due to obsolete technology); and equipment bottlenecks (constraining sales due to inferior pieces of capital equipment).

We focus here on two pervasive types of structural bottlenecks in representative settings—one involving the product quality problems of a Polish textile company, and the other the obsolete technology of a Hungarian metalworking firm. These firms were not only "promising" but also operated in industries that could reasonably be expected to prosper given the cost structure and skills of post-socialist Eastern Europe. The two particular firms in question might not pass the acid test (if it were practically possible to conduct one) of having lower restructuring costs than expected post-restructuring benefits (even taking social costs and benefits into account). But both firms were similar to other promising firms in their industry, and if the best firms in these industries were not restructured, it is hard to imagine how post-transition economies intended to employ their working-age populations.

We argue in this chapter and in Chapters 4 and 5 that even the best state-owned enterprises have been unable to restructure because the tasks of restructuring could not be accomplished by full exposure to free market forces or by "pseudo-privatization" (the transfer of public assets to private owners without an exchange of money and technological expertise). Typically the transition literature blames the inertial "supply response" of SOEs on poor managerial motivation, politicized employees' councils, and general indiscipline. Policymakers' concern over "firm governance," or the control system within the firm to motivate managers and monitor their performance, was legitimate in the long run. In the early transition period, however, many managers were strongly motivated by the objective, both altruistic and egoistic, of preventing their own firm's imminent collapse. We argue that the "supply inertia" of such managers has been due to inappropriate transition policies.

Exposure to free market forces largely meant cutting real wages, whereas most state-owned enterprises were constrained by noncost problems that could not be redressed by lowering labor costs, a very small fraction of total costs in any event. Real privatization was rare, and what little there was did not bring sufficient foreign capital, technology, and know-how necessary for mass restructuring. Pseudo-privatization agents such as commercial banks and mutual funds showed little likelihood of providing the interfirm coordination and long-term investment necessary for successful transformation—particularly amid the political instability of the transition. Yet our case studies indicate that even promising state-owned enterprises require a period of subsidization to become competitive. During that time, the state's participation in restructuring is inevitable. Such participation, therefore, needs to be systematically planned and carefully devised.

Product Quality Bottlenecks

State-owned enterprises with a product constraint were particularly ill equipped by the legacy of central planning to adapt to new circumstances. The minimal attention paid to corporate marketing in the past was especially damaging in product-differentiated industries. Moreover, technology activity under central planning tended to be oriented more toward process than toward product innovation. In Poland, for example, "A 1977 study of 164 innovations in several Polish industries indicated that new processes clearly dominated technological change in the economy. In contrast, market enterprises are preoccupied mostly with new products" (Poznański, 1987, p. 160).

The importance of the product bottleneck is suggested by the responses from a sample of seventy-five large Polish SOEs to the question of what they wanted from a foreign partner (in a survey undertaken in 1991 by the Warsaw Mission of the World Bank). If we assume that what the seventy-five were seeking in a foreign partner reflected what they themselves lacked, we find that "help in sales abroad," a proxy for product-related problems, was important in those industries with highly differentiated products—light industry (which includes textiles) and electro-machinery (which includes metalworking) (see Table 3.1). In the case of light industry, almost 30 percent of all responses emphasized a need in this category.

The problem of out-of-date equipment did not seem of overwhelming concern to the enterprises that produced light and electro-mechanical products. For both industries "help in sales abroad," along with "technology and licenses," were much more important than the need for "modern machinery." Such survey responses suggest that the major problems of these industries lay in "software" rather than in "hardware," a case in point being the textile sector.

Table 3.1 Major problems of seventy-five large Polish SOEs (as proxied by what they seek from foreign partners)

Problems	Importance (%)				
	All industries	Light	Electro-mech.	Chemicals	Food
Finance	27.4	32.6	27.8	29.5	15.8
Modern machinery	19.8	16.8	7.6	17.6	36.8
Technology and licenses	25.2	13.5	32.9	28.2	19.1
Modern management	8.1	6.7	10.1	7.1	15.8
Help in sales abroad	16.5	27.0	21.6	14.1	7.9
Personnel	3.0	3.4	0.0	3.5	2.6

Source: Pinto, Belka, and Krajewski (1992).

The Polish textile industry did, in fact, suffer from obsolete equipment in certain stages of its production. Generally, however, at the outset of the transition, it was using more modern equipment than textile industries in many other countries, as assessed by the Boston Consulting Group (BCG) in its study of the Polish textile and clothing industries. According to the BCG: "There is a high penetration of new technology in Poland compared with the rest of the world. In terms of open-end spinning, this high penetration can be explained by the fact that this technology was initially developed in Czechoslovakia" (1991, pp. 2–4). Poland's installed capacity of shuttleless looms (a more modern technology than shuttle looms) was also relatively high (see Table 3.2). In restructuring, therefore, Poland's textile industry did not face the costly burden of introducing altogether new technologies or buying completely new systems of machinery. Other problems, however, abounded, as the case of the Uniontex Company suggests.

The Uniontex Company (Cotton Textiles)

Uniontex, a typical East European cotton spinning and weaving company located in Łódź, the Polish textile center, employed about 3,500 workers as the transition began. This number of employees was somewhat large by world and Polish standards, but not exceptionally so (at the end of 1989 the top twenty Polish textile mills had an average size of around 2,800). Uniontex was especially large, however, in terms of its plant area, which covered a site of seventy hectares. Like many other post-socialist SOEs that were constrained by the quality of their product, Uniontex had to restructure under conditions of financial distress and intense competition from abroad and, more often than not, at home. Domestic competition in Poland's textile industry, for example, took the form of thirty-two medium- to large-scale mills producing roughly the same mix of products.

Most textile companies in Poland were also at a disadvantage in not having begun their restructuring before the transition period; unlike other Polish enterprises that had modernized in the 1980s, Uniontex only began this process in 1990, with the arrival of a team of foreign experts. The team determined that the prospects for Uniontex to restructure were fair, provided it made some internal changes and received external technical and commercial assistance: "There are reasonable prospects for restructuring at Uniontex, but the enterprise management needs technical and commercial assistance in order to prepare a focused strategic development plan, and a programme for the

Table 3.2 Penetration of shuttleless looms and international comparisons with Poland, 1988

Country	Number of shuttleless looms	Percentage of total capacity
West Germany	14,100	90.2
Italy	18,148	89.4
United States	64,181	74.7
Spain	6,511	70.4
United Kingdom	5,257	69.5
Taiwan	27,009	63.3
POLAND	9,400	62.8
Japan	34,434	38.4
Turkey	5,700	29.0
India	2,213	3.3
Pakistan	0	0.0

Source: Adapted from International Textile Machinery Federation data.

implementation of this plan" (IDI, 1991b, pp. 1-8, 1-9). A comprehensive follow-up report on Uniontex by the consultant, International Development Ireland (IDI), predicted the outcome (correctly, it turns out) if nothing were done to help Uniontex restructure in light of the conditions unleashed by "shock therapy": "The catastrophic impact of the events since 1989 is all too evident, with falls in annual volume of output between 1989 and 1990 of 30–40%, continuing at the same rate in the first quarter of 1991" (IDI, 1991a, p. 1-21). IDI noted: "The total loss of export markets could not have caused by itself a slump of the scale that the textile industry has suffered. The state of the Polish economy is such that real incomes have fallen drastically since the beginning of 1990, leading to a severe fall in domestic demand for textiles" (IDI, 1991a, pp. 1-7, 1-25). A collapse in demand created a liquidity crisis for Uniontex that required immediate redress:

> Despite [its] best endeavors, the company is experiencing a major liquidity crisis and is in a very weak financial position which needs immediate remedial attention. An urgent restructuring proposal is required covering Marketing and Sales, Finance, Production, and Organization and Management areas. A "no change" strategy will not secure the viability of the enterprise. In the short term liquidation will be the outcome (IDI, 1991a, pp. 1-1, 1-41).

The major long-term problems of Uniontex were judged by the consultants to be "non–cost related," in the sense of being unrelated to factor prices. Instead, long-term problems centered on a too-narrow product line, weak management cost and information systems, overly hierarchical channels of communication, and poor product quality for both direct and indirect exports (through sales to local garment exporters).

LABOR COSTS AND PRODUCT QUALITY

How did market reform work in practice for product-constrained companies? Did Uniontex get its own house sufficiently in order, or did it demonstrate "supply inertia"?

In the transition period falling demand was supposed to induce market-driven firms to lower their costs and reduce their prices. In what is generally considered to be a labor-intensive industry such as cotton textiles, laying off workers (and thereby raising productivity) and/or lowering wages were presumed to be the best ways to reduce costs. In the first twenty-four months of the transition, however, Uniontex and most other textile companies in Poland did neither.

An analysis of early movements in employment provided by Uniontex suggests that despite the company's expressed wish to cut employment, there were almost no retrenchments for economic reasons (see Table 3.3). The most important motives for separation were natural attrition (worker's age), mutual agreement, absenteeism, and worker's request (allegedly because workers either preferred self-employment or considered wages at Uniontex too low). Nevertheless, Uniontex's de facto no layoff policy may have been quite rational. First, even in the absence of economic layoffs, Uniontex managed to shed roughly 2,300 jobs in sixteen months, or more than half of its total employment. Attrition proved to be a much cheaper way to cut the work force than mass layoffs, which, by Polish law, obliged firms to provide high severance pay. Second, in firms with large fixed investments (including Uniontex, which had long runs of the same product), underutilized capacity increased unit costs. At the beginning of the transition many Polish companies, therefore, were reluctant to shed workers if doing so left machinery idle.

The costs of idle capacity were a major factor in the textile industry's

Table 3.3 Reasons behind employment reductions, Uniontex Company, January 1990–April 1991

Reason for employment reduction	Proportion of total (%)	Number of employees
Dismissal		
Firm's request	7.5	173
Worker's request	12.5	289
Retirement		
Age	30.9	714
Mutual agreement	12.6	292
Unjustified absence	12.6	292
Other[a]	23.9	549
Total	100.0	2,309

Source: Uniontex Company.

a. Death, contract transfer, maternity leave, unpaid leave, military, other.

poor competitiveness. Cost per unit of output increased exponentially with a fall in machine hours worked (see Figure 3.1, utilization panel).

Reduction in employment in the textile industry in 1990–91 was sufficient to lead to a small increase in labor productivity (turnover per employee). The real increase in average monthly earnings, however, was greater, such that unit labor costs rose slightly (GUS, various months). But to attribute the absence of restructuring in Poland's textile industry to higher unit labor costs is to misunderstand the industry's cost structure and to ignore more important noncost factors at play.

Because wages were so low in the Polish textile industry—less than half the all-industry average, which itself was low even by developing country standards (about $200 per month)—labor costs were a small fraction of total costs in virtually all stages of the textile value chain. Consider the international cost structure of spinning, according to calculations of the Boston Consulting Group (see Figure 3.2). Total costs are defined to include raw cotton, working capital, spare parts, energy, and labor. Labor's share in total costs is minuscule, and lower in Poland than in Brazil, Turkey, South Korea, and even India. Further, Poland appears to have already had a labor cost advantage over competitors in 1990 and 1991. According to the estimates of Werner International, labor costs in the spinning and weaving industry in Poland in the summer of 1990 ranged from only $0.45 to $0.50, compared with $0.72 in India (see Table 3.4). The failure of Poland's textile industry to navigate the transition's treacherous waters, therefore, cannot be attributed to wage behavior.

The Boston Consulting Group's analysis of the sensitivity of cotton process spinning in Poland to various factors influencing costs (Figure 3.1) further substantiates the relative unimportance of labor cost increases to total costs. The BCG found that labor-related parameters had almost no bearing on total costs. Total costs were found to be highly sensitive to changes in machine productivity (grams per spindle hour); utilization (machine hours worked per annum); and real interest rates (to a slightly less extent). They were not at all responsive to changes in total operator hours per unit of output or average wages (including benefits) for all employees per hour.

Considering all cost factors, total costs were not what impeded Polish textile companies from becoming internationally competitive. The BCG observed that the short-term cost position in spinning was "favorable,"

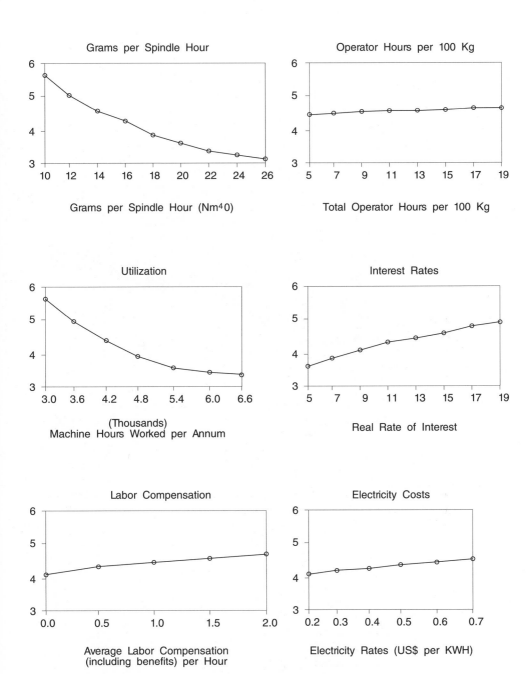

Figure 3.1 Sensitivity analysis of cotton spinning: Total cost (US$ per kilogram) as a function of changes in key parameters. From BCG (1991), by permission of The Boston Consulting Group.

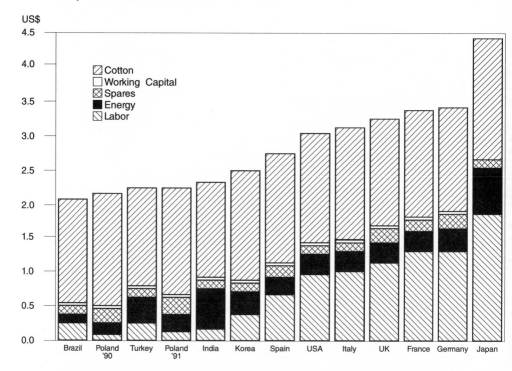

Figure 3.2   The short-term cost position of the spinning industry: International comparisons with Poland, 1990, 1991. From BCG (1991), by permission of The Boston Consulting Group.

Table 3.4   Labor costs in spinning and weaving, international comparisons with Poland, summer 1990

Country	US$/hour
India	0.72
Philippines	0.67
Kenya	0.63
POLAND	0.45–0.50 (estimate)
Egypt	0.45
Pakistan	0.39
China	0.37
Indonesia	0.25

Source: For Poland: Calculated from Uniontex data using existing exchange rate. For other countries: Data from Werner International.

and even more favorable in weaving (1991, p. 4). Emphasis by free market reformers on reducing employment and lowering wages thus made little sense in terms of either politics or microeconomics. To restructure, the best firms in the Polish textile industry needed to pay immediate attention to their liquidity problems and long-run attention to improving their product quality and reducing costs by raising capital productivity (output per machine hour).

INDEBTEDNESS AND EFFECTIVE (PENALTY) INTEREST RATES

When producers first enter into market relationships, they tend to have inadequate financial reserves to protect them against demand fluctuations. Given that they must usually borrow working capital in the early phase of the production cycle, there is a tendency for them to fall into debt. Such has been the fate of most post-communist enterprises, whose demand did not so much fluctuate as collapse. Indebtedness acted as a barrier to borrowing in order to finance restructuring.

Uniontex became indebted to its suppliers, to the banks (Uniontex typically borrowed dollars at the start of its production cycle to import raw cotton), and especially to the government (in the form of tax arrears). (See Table 3.5 for a breakdown of Uniontex's debt.) The government's overwhelming role in Uniontex's debt position, whether in the form of money owed to the central government, the social security system, or the research and development fund, was one of several reasons why any restructuring plan had to include some form of government involvement.

Uniontex's indebtedness restricted its access to working capital, which created a vicious circle of further indebtedness and decline. Without working capital, purchases were dictated by what inputs Uniontex could afford to buy rather than by what inputs it needed to ensure process quality and continuity. Routine maintenance and spare-part replacement were frozen, creating inefficiencies and raising unit costs. Most serious of all, a lack of working capital led to a loss of customer and supplier confidence and further declines in demand.

As was true for many other firms, Uniontex's indebtedness was aggravated by tax increases. The Ministry of Finance levied two special taxes on state-owned enterprises to pressure them to privatize (and to dampen inflation): a surtax on wage increases above a specified maximum *(pobiwec);* and a dividend tax on assets *(diwendwa)*. The inadvertent effect of the former was to unlink changes in wages and productiv-

Table 3.5 Debt structure of Uniontex, April 30, 1991

Type of indebtedness	Percentage of total (%)
Money owed for deliveries of materials and services	
for 1990	24
for 1991	13
Interest not paid on overdue money	11
Debt toward central government and social security system, together with outstanding penal interest	33
Bank credits with outstanding interest	8
Other debts (investments, research and development fund, etc.)	12
Total	100[a]
Total debt in billions of zloty	298
Accounts receivable as of April 30, 1991	66

Source: Uniontex Company.
a. May not add to 100 due to rounding.

ity, while that of the latter was to penalize state-owned enterprises which borrowed to modernize their capital stock. The wage tax amounted to about 14 percent of Uniontex's total tax liabilities as of April 1991. The dividend tax amounted to about 16 percent (these shares are somewhat higher than those computed for the sample of seventy-five Polish enterprises by the World Bank [Pinto, Belka, and Krajewski, 1992]).

Enterprise indebtedness was worsened by penalty interest rates imposed on tax or loan payments in default. These penalties were set on a monthly basis by the Ministry of Finance, and hence the government had discretionary power over the indebtedness of state-owned enterprises. Penalties were applied to arrears in government tax payments, interest and principal payments to banks, and even credit extended in the interfirm credit market (although firms in this market could negotiate among themselves to dispense with late payment penalties).

The compound effect of interest rate penalties on Uniontex's costs is suggested in Table 3.6. Because Uniontex failed to pay 65 percent of its taxes, it incurred extra penalties amounting to 45 percent of its total tax liability. Table 3.7 provides data on penalty interest rates in Poland for the period 1988–1991 with respect to overdue taxes. In January 1990 the annualized interest rate on unpaid taxes amounted to as much as 828 percent.

Increases in tax penalties and bank servicing charges, more than wage increases, drove up Uniontex's costs immediately after the transition began. In 1988 the share of wages in Uniontex's overhead was 20 percent. This share rose to 24 percent in 1989 and 26 percent in 1990. By contrast, the share of bank servicing rose from 8 percent to 25 percent to 27 percent over the same period.

Because of penalties, the real "effective" *ex post* interest rate was even higher than the real interest rate net of penalty payments. Given the economic and political uncertainties of the transition, effective interest rates discouraged firms *ex ante* from borrowing to restructure, contributing to an excess supply of credit in the banking system and capital-starved public enterprises.

The Ministry of Finance, working closely with the International Monetary Fund in devising Poland's taxation policies, was thus directly responsible for a significant share of the financial difficulties of public sector enterprises immediately after the transition. The government's tax policies toward such enterprises were designed with multiple objec-

Table 3.6 Taxes owed and penalty tax payments, Uniontex, January–April 1991

| Obligation | Taxes on[a] | | | | |
	Sales	NHI[b]	Assets	Wages	Total
Taxes due	25.7	22.7	14.4	12.5	91.5
Tax arrears	18.7	15.3	6.5	9.8	58.9
Tax penalties	12.6	6.4	1.4	5.6	41.1
Tax penalties as a percentage of taxes due	49%	28%	10%	45%	45%

Source: Uniontex Company.
a. In millions of zloty.
b. National health insurance.

Table 3.7 Penalty interest rates in Poland, 1989–1991 (imposed by the Ministry of Finance on overdue taxes and national health insurance payments)

Date from . . . to	Interest per year (%)
April 25, 1989	18.0
September 30, 1989	60.0
October 1, 1989	115.2
November 18, 1989	180.0
January 1, 1990	828.0
February 1, 1990	468.0
March 1, 1990	216.0
April 1, 1990	180.0
May 1, 1990	126.0
June 1, 1990	90.0
August 1, 1990	64.8
October 16, 1990	82.8
December 1, 1990	110.0
February 1, 1991	142.0

Source: Promasz, Inc.

tives, including curbing their wage increases as a way to dampen inflation and induce them to privatize. An inadvertent effect was to weaken severely the financial structures of the great majority of inherently viable state-owned enterprises that were unable to find private buyers.

POOR QUALITY

Quality problems in Poland's textile industry were endemic throughout the production chain for a variety of reasons, including defective raw materials (synthetic fibers) and out-dated, unspecialized machinery at particular stages of production (although machinery tended to be well maintained). In the case of Uniontex, quality was poor along four dimensions (not counting measurable physical characteristics such as tensile strength, crease resistance, abrasion resistance, and so on). First, the construction of Uniontex's fabric was unsatisfactory. The market in apparel applications was generally demanding fabrics with finer yarns and greater numbers of threads per centimeter than Uniontex was supplying. Second, the "handle" of its cloth was considered inferior; it was rather stiff and harsh to the touch. Third,

Uniontex's designs were considered to be old-fashioned. Fourth, packaging was poor. The consultant reported: "The current system of packaging poorly lapped or rolled fabric in poor quality brown paper which often does not completely enclose the bolt or roll and which becomes torn in handling even before it leaves the firm's premises is quite unacceptable. Improvements in rolling lapping, wrapping, ticketing and handling procedures are urgently required" (IDI, 1991a, p. 3-2). The consultants recommended that product quality, not labor costs or employment levels, become Uniontex's "essential business goal."

AUTONOMOUS RESTRUCTURING

In the early transition period, Uniontex tried to restructure itself: "The management [has] taken decisive action to try to minimize the impact of the large reductions in sales" (IDI, 1991, p. 1-1). In its endeavors it had the support of both its employees' council and its trade unions, whose representatives emphasized the importance of modernizing. According to the consultants: "The company operates a positive policy towards employees, workers' representatives and the union. It appears to have a good relationship with all" (IDI, 1991a, p. 5-11).

Uniontex introduced new organizational changes to improve decision making by top management. To raise money, it attempted to sell some of its land and to terminate certain social services unconnected with production (a fire brigade, nursery school, and cafeteria). Most of all, Uniontex attempted to privatize and improve its quality and its marketing. The company petitioned the Ministry of Finance to allow it to "commercialize," the first step in privatization. If approved, Uniontex would become a joint stock company wholly owned by the Treasury. The governing employees' council would be disbanded, replaced by an advisory board with one-third employee and two-thirds government representation. After nearly a year's delay by the ministry, Uniontex achieved commercialization.

To become more market-oriented, Uniontex hired a marketing manager (with experience in the Netherlands with Phillips, the electronics giant). It also opened a prize-winning booth at the Interfashion Fair in Łodz.

To upgrade its products, Uniontex tried to improve its production management and quality control incrementally. Many of its production managers were highly experienced. If in the past they had been too concerned with quantity rather than quality, some now made strenuous attempts to adjust. Incrementalism made headway, but not enough. The consultant's report observed: "According to respondents in the marketplace, both at retail level and garment manufacturing, the quality of Uniontex's fabric has improved over the last few months[,] but much more work in this area still needs to be done to reach acceptable quality levels across the whole range of products" (IDI, 1991a, p. 3-2).

As part of its efforts, Uniontex also took the initiative to find a foreign partner. Late in 1991 Uniontex negotiated with a Finnish company to form a joint venture. Each partner was supposed to invest $50,000, then raise outside financing to buy modern machinery and ultimately produce fabrics in one of Uniontex's plants.

In the end neither full privatization nor the joint venture materialized; the Finnish firm terminated negotiations. In theory, privatization was confounded by a claim for re-privatization or restitution by Uniontex's prewar owner. In practice, privatization failed because no one wanted to buy Uniontex, certainly not in its indebted state, which the government made no effort in the early transition to renegotiate, and not in the globally depressed market for textiles in the early 1990s (although foreign investors in the same period did acquire two major Hungarian textile companies, Gyor Textile Works and Cantoni-Kobanyai Textiles Ltd.). Hindered by the multiple tasks involved in restructuring as well as by the macroeconomic stringency and indifference or hostility toward SOEs on the part of the post-socialist state, Uniontex's autonomous restructuring efforts failed.

COLLECTIVE RESTRUCTURING

To achieve a thorough transformation in quality, Uniontex needed not only to get its own house in order, which it seriously endeavored to do, but to work collectively to restructure with other agents, not least of all the government. A restructuring plan for a product-constrained company such as Uniontex was estimated by consultants to cost about $10 million (including working capital) over a five-year period. Four components were judged to be essential.

1. *Financial restructuring,* involving, inter alia, (a) conversion of government (tax) debt into equity; (b) conversion of current bank loans into long-term loans (40,000 million zlotys at 14,000 zl. to the dollar); (c) access to working capital (90,000 mill. zl.); a long-term loan to finance capital investment and restructuring, with a

moratorium of principal for the first eighteen months (80,000 mill. zl.) or so. The financial restructuring plan recommended by foreign consultants thus contained elements of subsidy, which, realistically, only the government could provide.

2. *Product restructuring* as part of an overall marketing strategy, involving the introduction of new products and the optimization of certain existing ones to act as "cash cows" in the short term.

3. *Production rationalization and consolidation,* involving closing certain plants, subcontracting specific tasks, retrofitting existing machinery, investing in selected new equipment, and other similar procedures.

4. *Management restructuring,* involving the introduction of quality, accounting, information, and other control systems.

These collective restructuring tasks were well beyond Uniontex's capabilities. They required coordination among many institutions to be effective; loans from the private banking system were required, for example, but with government guarantees to secure easier than commercial terms regarding short-term repayment. Restructuring also relied on institutions that were in a position to take a long-term view toward profitability, necessary in Uniontex's case if only because many endogenous components of restructuring had to be achieved simultaneously. For example, it was difficult for management to decide which product offerings to add or subtract in the absence of an accounting system that provided accurate information about each product's costs. Introducing a management information system was not insuperably difficult, but it took time that Uniontex, with its cash flow problems, did not have.

Product-Constrained Firms: Conclusion

Suffice it to say that the invisible hand failed to marshall the resources Uniontex required for restructuring, and no visible hand (in the form of a foreign buyer or the government) came into view. By 1992 Uniontex (and much of the Polish spinning and weaving industry) was not yet liquidated but was technically bankrupt. This loss was a major blow to the economy. In 1989 textiles had made up Poland's second-largest industry in terms of output (and Hungary's eighth largest), and a competitive domestic textile sector had had the potential to save foreign exchange by supplying inputs to a small but growing garment export trade.

Product-constrained companies like Uniontex, which in the early years of transition stood in a long queue to be privatized (having been "commercialized" or "transformed" into joint stock companies), provide little evidence that either worker militance or managerial myopia lay behind their "supply inertia."[4] Uniontex itself initiated privatization and searched (albeit unsuccessfully) for a foreign partner. Uniontex may not have resorted to economic layoffs, but its work force declined by over half nonetheless. It did not cut wages, but the problems that bankrupted it had nothing to do with rising labor costs and could not be cured by cutting wages and employment. Uniontex tried to restructure on its own, on the basis of the market mechanism, but the solution to its problems required a collective restructuring approach, involving the government and private agents such as the banks and professional consultants.

Uniontex's restructuring requirements were straightforward and their estimated costs were not prohibitive (at about $10 million). Nevertheless, there is no denying that the tasks involved in restructuring Uniontex would take time (estimated at five years), and for at least part of that time Uniontex could not be expected to make a profit. Some institution would have therefore had to underwrite it. Moreover, certain elements of Uniontex's restructuring plan involved subsidies (such as debt forgiveness by the government and deferred payments on new loans). The only realistic restructuring agent (however indirect or invisible a role) was thus one with a long-term profit-maximizing horizon. Amid post-socialism's political instability and ample opportunities for quick profit making in the service sector, such an agent, if any, was increasingly likely to be the government.

Technology Bottlenecks

To study a representative firm suffering from a technology bottleneck in the transition, it is appropriate to investigate a Hungarian example, because machinery and transport equipment manufacture was one of Hungary's major industries, and technology bottlenecks tend to be constraining in the engineering field. At the time the transition began, the engineering sector accounted for more than 25 percent of Hungary's manufacturing value-added. Exports of machinery and transport equipment were a slightly rising share of total hard currency exports, increasing from 8.7 percent in 1989 to 11.8 percent in 1991 (MIT, 1991).

Rising exports suggest that not all Hungarian engineering firms faced a binding technological bottleneck, although exports more often than not were undertaken to offset drastic declines in demand, and were not necessarily an indicator of sustainable growth (Amsden, 1994a). A large number of engineering firms in Hungary and elsewhere did, in fact, suffer from out-dated technology, and the question addressed below is what set of policies were required to transform the most promising enterprises into world-class competitors.

MMG Automatika Muvek (Machine Engineering)

Like some other multiproduct engineering firms, MMG managed to stay afloat in the early transition period by milking a "cash cow." It continued to export its major product, process controls, to its most important customer, the Russian government, which paid for parts to maintain oil and gas operations. MMG expected this arrangement to last for a few years until American oil companies moved into Russia and began obtaining their process controls from American suppliers.

MMG's competitive advantage lay in its low labor costs and experienced engineers, who were willing to work long stints in Siberia installing MMG's turn-key (ready to use) plant exports. The social calculation behind restructuring MMG came down to whether to allow these engineers to disperse (many had already gone abroad or into private, higher-paying service jobs in Hungary) or whether to invest in the resources and especially the time necessary to upgrade MMG's technology and its commercial capabilities.

Restructuring a technology-intensive, differentiated product manufacturer like MMG was more difficult than restructuring a quality-constrained producer like Uniontex. The collective effort necessary to revive MMG involved not only MMG's own employees, the government, and possibly Hungarian banks (or mutual fund managers) but also foreign technology suppliers.

TECHNOLOGICAL OBSOLESCENCE
MMG employed 4,491 people in 1988 (down to 3,492 in 1991) and was one of Hungary's leading machine engineering companies, with a his-

tory of low debt, focused product diversification, and quality in strict conformance with specified standards. Conformance quality had become a strength of MMG's as it competed successfully against other companies for contracts to supply process control systems to Hungary's electricity industry, nuclear power station, and railways and to the former USSR's oil and gas industries. The standards of these industries, though not necessarily as technologically exacting as those of the defense sector, were nonetheless rigorous enough to raise MMG's conformance quality to a relatively high level.

The design, manufacture, installation, and maintenance of complete control systems was historically MMG's main source of revenue, typically accounting for more than 20 percent of direct sales (over 60 percent of which had gone to the Soviet Union). MMG's systems were large and usually turn-key and they integrated many of MMG's own manufactured products (for example, transmitters and industrial microcomputers).

MMG functioned with numerous foreign licenses—from the Italian company Nuovo Pignone, for an eight-bit industrial microcomputer system; from the Finnish company ESMI, for a range of safety devices; from the German company Festo, for pneumatic components; from the Swedish company AGA, for welding equipment; and so forth. Foreign licenses are not necessarily evidence of high-quality products, but in MMG's case, many foreign technology transfers were accompanied by in-house technological effort, and these investments did reflect MMG's own technological capabilities. For example, MMG manufactured a "coriolis effect" mass-flow meter from patented technology originally designed by MMG in the context of a cross-licensing agreement with K-Flow of the United States. K-Flow considered the product first class, with MMG making several improvements to the original design. MMG manufactured one microcomputer system under license from Nuovo Pignone, but also manufactured another similar system it had developed in-house.

MMG supplied instrument panels to Maruti-Suzuki (India) and the major East European car manufacturers that produced cars of Fiat origin (in all cases MMG was a second, albeit sometimes larger, source for instrumentation). It sold mass-flow meters to the United States, castings to Sweden and Germany, pneumatic and cash register components to Germany, and heat pressure sensors to Belgium. By 1988 MMG's hard currency exports equaled about 10 percent of its sales, which was roughly the same percentage achieved by the Hungarian machinery and equipment engineering sector at large.

MMG's main structural problem early in the transition period was the obsolescence of its control systems designs by about five years. The obsolescence was attributable to the general decline of the Hungarian economic system: MMG had once spent 8–10 percent of its sales revenues on research and development, which was subcontracted to a government research division dedicated to large flow meters, but over the years this percentage had fallen to barely 2 percent. By 1990 MMG had lost many of its talented software developers and had no money to develop new products, buy foreign licenses, or hire the marketing expertise necessary for commercialization. MMG considered loans to finance new product development out of the question—given the large number of unknowns in its transitional business environment, such debts were viewed as both too risky and too expensive. (In fact, by 1992 real interest rates in Hungary were more variable than high—they were very high in the early part of the year but negative in the late part.)

AUTONOMOUS RESTRUCTURING

Privatization. In April 1991, when it became obvious that MMG's sales were in a free fall, its employees' council voted unanimously to approach the State Property Agency (SPA) for approval to participate in the Hungarian government's privatization program. On December 31, 1991, MMG was transformed into a joint stock company owned by the SPA and governed by a supervisory board of six persons, only two of whom were chosen by employees. (On the former employees' council, by law, half the representatives had been appointed by employees.) MMG's trade unions remained in existence, but relations between union and management at MMG were good, with no history of strikes.

The SPA looked for a privatization adviser and found one in a consortium that included Barclays de Zoete Wedd and Coopers & Lybrand Deloitte, two international investment banks. The consortium worked on a contingency fee and had one year to find a buyer for either the whole or parts of MMG.

MMG's management was eager for a foreign buy-out to gain capital to invest in new technology, expertise, and market access.[5] Moreover, the tax benefits derived from obtaining a foreign partner in Hungary were overwhelming. According to the Foreign Investment Act, (a) if a company's equity exceeded a rather small minimum investment, and (b) if at least 30 percent of its equity was owned by foreigners, and (c) if more than 50 percent of its sales came from manufacturing, then that company could receive a 60 percent reduction in taxable profits in the first five years and a 40 percent reduction for the next five. If the company's sales were derived from activities deemed "particularly important" (as was the case with many of MMG's activities), then no profit taxes were payable for the first five years, and profit tax obligations for the next five were reduced by 60 percent. Value-added tax paid on capital investment was also fully recoverable by companies with foreign participation, and no customs duties were charged on imported equipment that formed part of the foreigner's capital investment. In addition, companies with at least 20 percent foreign equity participation were exempted from wage caps (the Hungarian equivalent of the Polish *pobiwec* tax), which thereby allowed them to compete for the best labor.

These incentives notwithstanding, amid the uncertainties of the early transition and global recession, MMG, like most of the rest of Hungarian state-owned industrial enterprises, was unable to find a foreign partner. In the first two years of the transition, income from privatization accruing to various branches of the Hungarian government amounted to less than 3 percent of the estimated total value of state property to be privatized (Richter, 1992).

Marketing. MMG took steps to improve its marketing capabilities by opening overseas sales offices and forming joint ventures with major customers. Even before the transition, MMG opened a sales office in Moscow, the timing of which (1988) followed the abolition of the monopoly of state trading organizations over exports. In April 1991, the same month in which MMG petitioned the State Property Agency to privatize, it made a 61 percent investment (of about $25,000) in an Austrian joint venture company, Eximtrade GmbH, located in Vienna, to facilitate the development of its products in Western markets. In September of the same year MMG made a 40 percent investment (of about a quarter of a million dollars) in a joint venture with its German customer Festo, which provided MMG with an exclusive five-year manufacturing contract. To improve information about the plans of its customer Suzuki Motors, MMG invested $130,000 in Autokonszern, which was a 39 percent equity partner in a Suzuki joint venture company in Hungary. This investment allowed MMG to attend shareholder meetings of Suzuki Hungary.

Costs and efficiency. MMG took steps to improve quality, reduce costs, and raise efficiency. It hired four Japanese consultants to train key people in its Quality Assurance Department. A major cost reduction was gained by cutting unessential social services for workers, particularly with respect to vacation facilities. The lengthy process of rationalizing production was also begun. MMG operated from six sites that had historically had a high degree of technological interdependence, and now certain production technologies were relocated to encourage production efficiencies. MMG also introduced a program that converted each site from a "cost center" to a "profit center," thereby permitting sites to out-source and subcontract rather than rely solely on each other for components. As a result of all these measures, MMG succeeded in lowering the ratio of overhead costs to sales from 40.5 percent in 1988 to 30.5 percent in 1991.

BARRIERS TO AUTONOMOUS RESTRUCTURING

As was true for Uniontex, autonomous restructuring in MMG failed for reasons that had little to do with worker militance or management myopia. MMG management could probably have been more energetic in undertaking restructuring, but there were no quick fixes to its problems. (If there were, private buyers presumably would have found them.) Even if MMG were cut up into small parts according to product line and production site, each part required time and money to upgrade.[6]

Everything suggested that a company like MMG could prosper after being restructured. In terms of costs—particularly skilled and unskilled labor costs—MMG was highly competitive. It also had the advantage of a staff of experienced employees willing to work under conditions that competitors (in Germany, say) were unwilling to accept. MMG's capital equipment was not uniformly new, but according to the assessment of the investment bankers acting (unsuccessfully) as privatization agents on MMG's behalf, neither was most of MMG's capital stock old. With market contacts, experienced staff, and acceptable capital equipment, there seemed to be no reason why MMG could not become profitable, subject to serious technological upgrading of its best product lines.

MMG, however, could not reasonably be expected to undertake technological upgrading autonomously. The idea of the firm's borrowing large sums of capital to begin the restructuring process alone, without government involvement, was simply unrealistic. Even if property rights had been clarified, and even if MMG had been privatized (except possibly by one of its international competitors), given the uncertainties of the transition on both the demand and the supply sides and the time interval necessary to restructure (five years is probably as good an estimate for MMG as for Uniontex), taking on large financial obligations would have been reckless without government credit guarantees and other forms of support.

The Technology Acquisition Problem of Re-Industrializers

At the end of 1993 MMG continued to limp along by exporting its "cash cow," but with insufficient returns to buy the foreign technology it needed to upgrade. MMG's fate awaited a decision by Hungary's State Property Agency on whether or not to begin restructuring promising state-owned enterprises before they were privatized.

The case of MMG illustrates the extent to which the task of technological upgrading is even harder for East European countries attempting to re-industrialize than for East Asian countries attempting to industrialize de novo. In the case of South Korea and Taiwan, no infant industry was promoted at the outset of industrialization unless foreign technology was available in the form of technical assistance or foreign licenses (for South Korea, see Amsden, 1989). In post-socialist Eastern Europe, by contrast, existing industries need new technology to upgrade, but acquiring that technology has often proved problematic. A strategy different from that adopted for industries in their infancy is therefore required.

Later on in the industrial development of South Korea and Taiwan, when they had reached a semi-industrialized status comparable in terms of industrial breadth to the status of post-socialist Eastern Europe, their attempt to upscale technologically altered from that of the past and involved a two-fold approach. First, their efforts to buy foreign technology often took the form of acquiring small, financially troubled high-tech companies in, for example, the United States (a strategy of small Taiwan machine tool builders), or locating research and development facilities in advanced countries to absorb the expertise of local engineers (as in the case of Korea's Samsung Electronics research facility situated near Matsushita Electronics in Osaka, Japan) (Amsden and Hikino, 1994). Second, their investments in their own research and development increased, often taking the form of joint public-private ventures or, if entirely private, being subsidized by the government. The government provided research and development in the private sector with preferential credit, below-market rental facility sites near major urban areas, tariffs or other forms of protection from imports, and so forth (Hou and Gee, 1993; L. Kim, 1993).

Post-socialist enterprises in Eastern Europe may not have been willing or able to follow this type of late-industrializing strategy to upgrade technology to the letter. Nevertheless, the examples of "promising" state-owned enterprises such as MMG suggest that, as in the case of East Asian enterprises attempting to upgrade technologically, restructuring is unlikely to occur without systematic, long-term government administrative guidance and financial support.

The two case studies we have examined suggest that state-owned enterprises that were "promising" (in part in terms of being cost-effective at market prices) but that suffered from various structural bottlenecks could not reasonably be expected to restructure autonomously on their own, driven by the forces of supply and demand. The reason such firms failed to restructure was due not to "supply inertia" but to the absence of any policies conducive to restructuring.[7] Indeed, the taxation policies of finance ministries exacerbated the structural adjustment problems of such firms. Tax penalties increased such firms' financial burdens at a time when they could least bear them.

The failure of both privatization and autonomous restructuring in inherently viable state-owned enterprises has altered two types of cost calculations that economists made in the early years of the transition. The costs of doing nothing to promote pre-privatization restructuring by the government have risen in tandem with rising unemployment. Earlier, transition economists dismissed pre-privatization restructuring out-of-hand largely for ideological reasons, but rationalized their decision partly on the grounds that the costs of saving a particular firm would surely fall below the benefits of reemploying the firm's resources in alternative uses. Economists assumed that the labor shed by the public sector would be absorbed by the newly emerging private sector. After several years of transition, however, this assumption has proved wrong and the imagined alternative uses appear less positive. Depending on the grade of labor and type of capital equipment, the alternative to reviving a public sector enterprise involves either unemployment or reemployment in less socially productive uses. In the case of professional employees, they may succeed in finding lucrative work in the private sector, but in activities that do not utilize their professional training.

Given the rising costs of doing nothing, in terms of both opportunities foregone and political instability, the hypothetical costs associated with errors committed by the government in "picking winners," or in allocating restructuring resources to inherently *un*viable enterprises, have also declined. The probability of error could be reduced still further if transition policymakers, instead of romancing the market mechanism, took the time to study actual postwar restructuring experiences. A study of structural adjustment in nine industrialized economies in the Pacific Basin, for instance, finds different degrees of government intervention in restructuring in different countries, but finds no evidence whatsoever of restructuring by market forces alone (Patrick and Meisner, 1991).

4

Overloading the Market Mechanism

An opening of free trade with Western Europe should increase the demand for Poland's skilled workers who are now earning (at around $1) about one-tenth to one-fifteenth of what comparable skilled workers earn just 500 miles to the West.

—*David Lipton and Jeffrey Sachs,*
Brookings Papers on Economic Activity, 1990

The policy of opening the Polish market to all imports (i.e., not subject to quota, etc.) without having time to train and educate local industry as to how to react and the necessary quality requirements has been a high risk strategy and has put the domestic industrial base in great difficulty.

—*Consultant's Report on the Uniontex Textile*
Company, Łódź, August 1991

The case studies of Uniontex and MMG do not, of course, reflect the whole universe of problematic post-socialist enterprises. Neither illustrates a third serious type of bottleneck, related to old capital equipment, that has especially afflicted continuous process industries such as chemicals, iron and steel, and food. Nor have we even touched upon obstacles to restructuring that existed at the industry level, such as excess capacity.

In this chapter, therefore, we argue more generally the proposition that free market forces cannot be relied upon to restructure post-socialist industry. We concentrate on three particular forms of market liberalization. First, we examine the extent to which wage reductions can create profitability. Second, we examine the extent to which anti-monopoly legislation and the withdrawal of subsidies can provide the basis for competitive manufacturing industry. Third, we examine the extent to which liberalizing imports can bring state-owned enterprises the resources they require to compete in world markets.

Supply-Side Growth Momentum

Transition economists expected that the boost of decreasing real wages and the "bang" of free trade and antimonopoly legislation would create a supply-side growth momentum, getting promising state-owned enterprises into shape and encouraging healthy private manufacturers. In practice, these expectations have gone unfulfilled with respect to both state-owned and privately owned enterprises in the industrial sector. Expectations have been disappointed because key transition policies have been either irrelevant or injurious to the restructuring needs of semi-industrialized post-socialist economies.

State-owned enterprises have benefited little from lower real wages because, as mentioned earlier, their labor costs are a small share of their total production costs. Wage ceilings, moreover, have caused SOEs to lose their best people—on whom restructuring depended—to private firms, at home or abroad. (Ideologically, indexing wage increases solely in state-owned enterprises to rates below inflation is designed to convert public sector workers into champions of privatization; only privatization can remove the fetters on their pay.) In addition, as suggested by our case studies, SOEs typically suffer from problems unrelated to factor prices, such as low-quality products and obsolete processes. Until these structural problems are resolved recovery cannot be expected from the supply side, and equilibrium cannot be expected in the external balance of payments.

We also saw in Chapter 2 how monopoly power fans the flames of inflation. Yet concern about monopoly power has blinded policymakers to other problems related to firm size and industry structure. Many mid-tech industries in Eastern Europe, for example, suffer from fragmentation and production units of suboptimal size. Restructuring, therefore, cannot mean single-mindedly downsizing vertically integrated behemoths in every industry.

At the same time the abrupt removal of protection from imports, in conjunction with the World Bank policy of prohibiting export subsidies and making easy trade credits available for imports only, has hurt promising state-owned enterprises in certain import substitution sectors. This action has contributed not only to mounting trade deficits but also to worsening unemployment, given that key import-competing sectors—light industry and engineering—were major domestic employers.

In short, the restructuring requirements of semi-industrialized post-socialist countries have been such that a liberal market mechanism simply cannot handle them. The immediate result of liberal policies was a sharp decline in labor productivity, as output fell faster than employment. As the transition wore on and labor productivity began to stabilize or even rise in certain industries and countries, this was principally due to the fact that output could not fall any further, while employment fell by more than output due to bankruptcy, not restructuring.

Why Didn't Employment Fall Even Further?

During the 1980s Hungary and Poland illustrated a pure "structuralist" rather than "neoclassical" story. That is, real wage declines in both countries were strongly correlated with declining output and declining, not rising, employment (see the appendix to this chapter). The data for this observation are shaky at best, but evidently the market reforms of the 1980s induced Hungarian and Polish enterprises to cut back on their use of labor, and thus there was no increase in overall employment as wages fell. Between 1978 and 1988, the index of total manufacturing employment declined from 100 to 83.5 in Hungary and from 100 to 81.0 in Poland. During the 1980s in the textile industry, the number of workers in Hungary fell from 119,300 to 75,800 while the number of enterprises rose from 52 to 240. In ready-made apparel, Hungarian employment declined from 77,700 to 57,300 and the number of enterprises rose from 125 to 437 (MIT, 1991).

The stagnation in Hungary and Poland during the relatively gentle reforms of the 1980s should have been a warning about the contractionary effects of real wage declines in the early transition period, let alone their paralyzing effects on economies such as those of Russia, Bulgaria, and Romania, which did not have significant prior experience with output and labor cutbacks. Despite earlier reforms, the Hungarian Ministry of Labor made a very rough estimate that overstaffing in the SOE sector remained on the order of 15–20 percent in the early years of transition (OECD, 1991b, p. 54). At issue, however, is why employment was "sticky" and did not fall even further.

The tendency in the early transition for employment to fall less than output (see Table 4.1 for industry estimates) was attributed by the architects of transition policy to nonprivate forms of ownership

Table 4.1 Change in industrial output, industrial employment, and wages
(in percent)

Country	Real wages	Industrial output	Industrial employment
Bulgaria			
1990	7.3	—	—
1991	−43.0	−27.8	−18.8
1992	—	−23.1	−19.2
Czechoslovakia			
1990	−5.4	—	—
1991	−25.2	−24.7	−12.0
1992	10.1	−17.3	−13.1
Hungary			
1990	−3.7	—	—
1991	−3.5	−18.6	−13.0
1992	4.0	−14.2	−16.5
Poland			
1990	−24.4	—	—
1991	−0.3	−15.2	−8.7
1992	−3.6	0.2	−8.1
Romania			
1990	6.0	—	—
1991	−16.6	−18.4	−9.9
1992	−15.1	−20.1	−12.0
Russia			
1990	9.0	—	—
1991	−10.5	−8.0	−4.2
1992	−46.5	−18.8	—

Source: UNECE (1993), tables 3.2.17 and 3.2.3.

(Blanchard, 1992; World Bank, 1992a). Managers in public enterprises (hired and fired in Poland, for instance, by employees' councils) were seen as powerless to prune the work force in line with domestic output declines in the short run or "best practice" foreign production technique in the long run.

This explanation for sticky or persistent levels of employment is inadequate, however, if only because in the 1980s employment tended to fall by less than output in almost all developing countries, and the predominant form of property in these countries was private, not public. Out of a total of thirty-eight non-Asian developing countries, thirty-two experienced either increases or constancy in numbers employed in the 1980s (see Table 4.2). Out of these thirty-two countries, nineteen also experienced stagnating or declining output—often quite steeply declining (Amsden and Van der Hoeven, 1993). Something more than simple property rights was evidently at play in restraining employment declines in Eastern Europe.

Both developed and developing countries typically suffered from declining or stagnating manufacturing output in the 1980s, but the employment response in both cases differed (as Table 4.2 suggests). Developed countries tended to experience declining employment and sticky wages while developing countries tended to experience the reverse, declining wages and sticky employment (Amsden and Van der Hoeven, 1993). That is, if equations (1) and (2) refer to developed (ADV) and developing (LDC) countries respectively, then the elasticity of wages, e_w, and employment, e_n, with respect to output, q, differs systematically between these two cases.[1]

(1) *Developed*

$$e_{wADV} < 1; \quad e_{nADV} > 1$$

(2) *Developing*

$$e_{wLDC} > 1; \quad e_{nLDC} < 1$$

where

$$e_w = \frac{dw}{dq} \cdot \frac{q}{w} \quad \text{and} \quad e_n = \frac{dn}{dq} \cdot \frac{q}{n}.$$

East European countries, being semi-industrialized, fell somewhere in between these two patterns. On the one hand, as indicated in Table 4.1, industrial employment in manufacturing in post-socialist Eastern Europe fell in absolute terms, largely, it seems, as a consequence of natural attrition (see the case studies in Chapter 3; see also R. Freeman, 1993). Whatever employment creation occurred was in services, not manufacturing, much as in developed countries. On the other hand, Eastern Europe's decline in employment was typically not sufficient to offset a decline in labor productivity, and declining productivity was

Table 4.2 Manufacturing employment index, 1980–1990 (1980 = 100)

Decrease	Constant[a]	Increase	
Developed Countries			
Belgium	Australia		
France	Austria		
Luxembourg	Canada		
Ireland	Denmark		
Italy	W. Germany		
N. Zealand	Greece		
Norway	Iceland		
Portugal	Netherlands		
Spain	Japan		
Sweden			
U.K.			
U.S.A.			
Developing Countries (excluding Asia)			
Argentina	Barbados	Bolivia[b]	Kuwait
Brazil	Cameroon	Botswana[b]	Madagascar
El Salvador	Colombia	Chile	Malawi
Mexico	Dom. Rep.	China	Mauritius[b]
Trinidad	Ecuador	Costa Rica[b]	Morocco[b]
Uruguay	Israel	Egypt	Nicaragua
	Peru	Guatemala	Panama
	S. Africa	Honduras	Senegal
	Venezuela	Jamaica	Tanzania
	Zambia	Jordan	Tunisia[b]
		Kenya	Zimbabwe
Asian Developing Countries (including Turkey)			
	Hong Kong	India	S. Korea
	Philippines	Indonesia[b]	Sri Lanka[b]
		Malaysia[b]	Taiwan
		Pakistan	Thailand
		Singapore	Turkey

Source: Calculated from UNIDO (1991).

Note: See Amsden and Van der Hoeven (1993) for countries with different base year or coverage other than 1980–1990 and technical note.

a. Index changes by less than 10.

b. Index changes by 50 or more.

also pervasive in the 1980s in most developing countries but not developed ones, with some exceptions (Amsden and Van der Hoeven, 1993).

Enterprise and Industry Evidence behind Sticky Employment

Enterprise-level studies in Hungary and Poland provide clues about employment rigidities in the early stages of transition. In Uniontex's case, mass layoffs were delayed until the final hour because of their associated penalty tax burden and the rising unit costs associated with idle machinery. In a radio works (which later went bankrupt at the hand of competitive Asian imports), the managing director wanted to determine the company's true costs for different product lines before undertaking selective massive retrenchments, and this entailed delays, given that the company had no cost control system in place. Managers in the Old Lenin Shipyard hoped to lay off certain workers to obtain a better quality work force, hire others in order to expand, and rationalize production overall. Yet they pointed out that rationalization took time (in terms of figuring out which operations to subcontract, what types of skills were in excess, and what types were in short supply), particularly in the absence of a clear government mandate to allow public enterprises to restructure before going private. Top managers said that if they fired roughly 30 percent of their workers overnight, production would collapse due to skill inflexibilities—most workers had a very narrow job description. The managers in a steel mill, Huta Katowice, which had been investing in incremental productivity and quality improvements for over a decade, when asked how they would go about restructuring if they were privatized, said they would not undertake massive retrenchments immediately. What being privately owned would allow them to do (with enthusiasm) was fire incompetent workers and hire good ones.

The same story holds at the industry level. According to a consultant's study of the Polish pulp and paper industry: "At this stage [1991], *high manpower usage is not the most serious problem considering the labour costs.* If anything, it is a problem for effective communication of objectives and accountability. Labour wages in Poland are quite low in comparison to its western neighbors. In relation to the Swedish paper industry, Polish wages are at about 5–10 percent" (NLK-Celpap, 1991, p. 35, emphasis added). Instead, the main problems of Poland's pulp and paper industry were fragmented industry structure, old technology, and poor product quality. The consulting firm emphasized: "*Improving the quality of the paper products has to be a top priority item* which needs immediate attention" (NLK-Celpap, 1991, p. 11, emphasis added).

These cases suggest that, among other factors influencing employment levels in the early transition period, significant retrenchments (above and beyond natural attrition) were difficult for state-owned enterprises to accomplish logistically *before* restructuring (or out-and-out bankruptcy) and generally made little sense in the face of more pressing, life-and-death matters. Ironically, such employment rigidities may have saved the day for Eastern Europe's nascent capitalism on political grounds. At the same time, the whole free market logic of rescuing inherently viable SOEs by means of declining employment and falling real wages was obviously flawed.

The Wag of the Dog by the Wage

A stylized fact about most East European economies in transition, alluded to in Chapters 2 and 3, is the extremely small share of wages in total production costs. Measuring such a statistic is difficult, given different definitions in capitalist and socialist countries of output and costs (net and gross of taxes). Yet again and again, from firm level or aggregate data, a very small share appears in East European manufacturing, on the order of 15 to 25 percent (supposedly around 10 percent in Bulgaria and approximately 20 percent in Czechoslovakia) (World Bank, 1984; MIT, 1991; Pinto, Belka, and Krajewski, 1992). Labor cost reductions, therefore, typically have not had a major impact on any individual firm's production costs or, by extension, its supply decisions (although in aggregate, wage declines could be expected to exert a large negative impact on demand, and also possibly moderate inflation).

The wage share in value added is small in the semi-industrialized economies of Eastern Europe for three reasons. First, for countries with comparable levels of capital assets, labor incomes have been extremely low, having been continuously repressed under central planning. Second, a substantial part of labor's social wage in the past included government-provided services (housing, transportation, and fuels). All these services did not constitute labor costs in the individual business enterprise's calculation of income, and therefore the gap between the social wage and the accounting wage has been especially large in Eastern Europe. Consequently, although shock therapy may have ended consumer queues and thereby increased real income, to the extent that social services were cut after the transition began, the decline in real income was greater than wage data alone indicated. Third, production techniques have tended to be more capital-intensive and raw material–intensive in Eastern Europe than in the typical low-wage capitalist country, and so labor's share in any given individual enterprise's total costs has been correspondingly low.

Transition economists argued that although wages were, indeed, a very small share of the individual enterprise's costs, they were its only variable cost, or the only cost over which it had direct control in the short run. This was probably true to the extent that it took more time to cut other operating costs. The production and operations management of the best enterprises in successful late-industrializing countries have demonstrated the significance for achieving global competitiveness of investing in incremental process modifications to reduce or shift the use of *all* factor inputs (see Amsden, 1989, for South Korea; see also Katz, 1987, for Latin America). But because incremental improvements in productivity and quality take time to achieve, they generally have required some form of government support—protection from imports or subsidized credit, for example.

Given that wages became a less important cost as the transition unfolded because liberalization triggered spectacular jumps in the price of credit, energy, and other raw materials, the rational, profit-maximizing SOE should have put the politically fraught decision of mass layoffs on the back burner and concentrated on cutting other costs and improving long-term product quality and technology. The quick fix of wage cutting was an inadequate solution to the SOE sector's problem and was contractionary in macroeconomic terms (for an analysis of the effect on real wage changes of the exchange rate, see Solimano, 1993).

The orthodox and heterodox stories are depicted in Figure 4.1. Initially socialist firms (at point B) operate with unit labor costs (W/Q) greater than those of competitive (capitalist) firms (at point A). The socialist firm's unit labor costs (whose loci in Figure 4.1 are a rectangular hyperbola, the product of the real wage and labor-output ratio) are relatively high despite lower wages per worker (W/L) because labor productivity in socialist enterprises is extremely low (L/Q is high). In the orthodox scenario, the transition's real wage cuts result in lower unit labor costs and if all goes well, these wage cuts lead to rising total em-

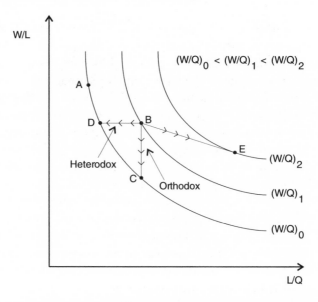

Figure 4.1 Orthodox and heterodox adjustment paths. (L = labor, K = capital, Q = output, W/L = real wage per worker, W/Q = unit labor cost. W/L and W/Q are expressed for countries in a common currency. The unit labor cost loci are rectangular hyperbolas, the product of the real wage and labor-output ratio. Therefore, they are constants.)

ployment and output (from B to C, the rise in total employment and output is proportionate). Heterodox economists, by contrast, prefer to reduce unit labor costs by raising productivity, which usually requires short-term government support and administrative guidance while the productivity- and quality-enhancing investments of business are under way. If all goes well, the firm moves from B to a point such as D, where labor per unit of output is lower than at B but total output and employment are both absolutely greater.

What seems to have happened in the East European and increasingly the Russian transition is that real wages fell, then productivity fell and unit labor costs rose, moving the firm from an initial point such as B to E, with lower absolute levels of both total employment and especially output.

Monopoly Power

Monopoly power has been held responsible by orthodox and heterodox economists alike for the sharp initial contraction in output in Eastern

Europe, though to varying degrees. Instead of lowering prices and raising output, monopolists supposedly raised markups and prices. For the orthodox, antimonopoly policy became one of shock therapy's major weapons (although never used much in practice because of its irrelevance for dying enterprises). In terms of restructuring, the mainstream idea was that the release of market forces and the introduction of antimonopoly legislation would combine to drive beleaguered state-owned firms to privatize the profitable subparts of their monopolistic, vertically integrated operations, thereby holding down prices and creating a nucleus of efficient, small private firms.

There was, in fact, a serious shortfall of output accounted for by small firms in the early transition period. By the late 1980s the percentage of East European employment accounted for by small enterprises (with 10–100 employees) was still minuscule—far too small a number for efficient subcontracting and flexible demand response (see Table 4.3).

Yet if Hungary and Poland are any guide, monopoly power was not the culprit behind the collapse in output that traumatized the early transition. The enterprise survey of the Warsaw Mission of the World Bank, for example, observes: "There is no evidence from the sample [of seventy-five large Polish state-owned enterprises] of the exploitation of monopoly power. Metallurgical firms, which fit the common perception of being monopolistic, actually maintained output . . . despite falling profit margins. Electromachinery firms cut back output, but were heavily burdened by cost increases and rising interest costs" (Pinto, Belka, and Krajewski, 1992, p. 2). Instead, the most aggressive price increases in Poland were accounted for by services, almost all of which were privately owned (see the discussion of the "dentist effect" in Chapter 2, note 14) (OECD, 1992b). In Hungary, price liberalization generally was perceived as responsible for inflation: "The movement in free prices is clearly the dominant factor in explaining the overall price increases" (OECD, 1991a, p. 36).

Consider comparative data on the distribution of Polish and American industrial output by four-firm concentration ratios in 1990 and 1982, respectively (see Table 4.4).[2] In terms of number of industries, Poland is more concentrated than the United States: about 33 percent of all Polish industries (46 out of a total of 138) compared with only 18 percent of all American industries (79 out of a total of 448) had four-firm concentration ratios of 60 percent or more. But these same industries accounted for about the same proportion of total *output* in both countries—roughly 20 percent (see the last two lines of the last two columns

Table 4.3 Average employment and size structure of manufacturing
enterprises

| Country | Year | Average | Percentage employed by firm size | | |
			10–100	10–500	1,000+
Bulgaria[a]	1986	—	—	27.2%	50.1%
Czechoslovakia	1980	2,126	—	1.5	90.8
Poland	1980	901	0.5%	15.2	68.7
	1989	—	1.4[c]	19.6	65.8
GDR	1988	—	1.0[c]	12.2	75.6
Hungary[b]	1955	416	3.8	29.9	45.2
	1970	1,295	0.4	8.1	81.7
	1981	852	0.8	16.1	70.3
	1987	—	1.0	9.1	75.3
Yugoslavia	1955	270	10.7[d]	41.2	35.9
Romania	1959	730	0.8	19.0	59.1
	1965	1,086	0.2	10.1	72.6
	1980	—	0.6	2.9	90.3
USSR[a]	1930	—	5.9	23.3	63.6
	1960	—	5.6	30.9	53.3
	1975	—	2.2	17.5	70.0
	1987	—	1.7	14.9	73.4
Austria	1980	77	29.8	57.5	31.2
France	1980	123	21.8	46.0	—
West Germany	1981	203	15.5	39.6	49.8
Italy	1979	128	24.2	52.2	37.4
Japan	1977	104	31.4	57.0	34.2
Sweden	1980	191	16.4	35.9	52.8
Switzerland	1975	66	35.8	67.0	22.7
United Kingdom	1979	74	17.4	32.3	59.3

Sources: GDR (German Democratic Republic) and Poland 1989: OECD (1992b), table
7; USSR: Yudanov (1995); all others: Ehrlich and Revesz (1991).
  a. 1–100 and 1–500.
  b. State industry only.
  c. 1–100.
  d. 10–125.

Table 4.4 Distribution of Polish and American industrial output by four-firm concentration ratios

Ratio range	Number of industries[a]		Percentage of all industries		Percentage of total output[b]	
	Poland	U.S.	Poland	U.S.	Poland	U.S.
0–19	16	86	12.0%	19.2%	20.8%	21.7%
20–39	40	163	29.0	36.4	29.4	38.8
40–59	36	120	26.0	26.8	29.2	19.7
60–79	26	56	19.0	12.5	14.5	14.9
80–100	20	23	14.0	5.1	5.8	4.9
Total	138	448				

Sources: Poland: Adapted from OECD (1992a), annex 2, table 2.1; United States: adapted from U.S. Bureau of the Census (1986), as cited by Scherer and Ross (1990).

a. Three-digit industries in Poland and four-digit industries in the United States.

b. Output is measured as sales for Poland (1990) and as shipments for the United States (1982).

of Table 4.4). The picture of overall industry concentration in Poland is thus within capitalist-country bounds and consistent with the findings on service sector–led price increases.

In Russia, by contrast, price leadership after the transition came from sectors thought to be heavily monopolized—energy and raw materials (Vorobyov, 1993; Zhukov, 1993). The abuse of monopoly power, therefore, appears to vary among post-socialist countries as well as among industries. Generally, however, monopoly has turned out to be something of a paper tiger in the transition, because policymakers confused economic concentration with inappropriate firm size. After the transition began "monopoly power" was used loosely by transition economists to denote: (a) the percentage of output within each industry accounted for by small firms (those employing fewer than 50 to 200 workers); (b) industry-level concentration; (c) the percentage of aggregate output or employment accounted for by the top hundred or so firms; and (d) large-scale enterprise. Transition economists were correct in stressing that too small a proportion of output was produced by small firms, and that white elephants in certain industries required downsizing and vertical dis-integration. Yet they failed to recognize that in other industries fragmentation and suboptimal plant and enterprise size were the hitch.

Enterprise Size: Too Few Small Ones, Some Not Big Enough

Many of the worst offenders in terms of excessive firm size seem to have been eliminated prior to the transition in those socialist countries that had previously undergone extensive market reforms. In Poland, observers commented: "We do not find evidence of excessive scale inefficiencies for Polish industry in the 1970s and 1980s (with the exception of the coal and gas industries). The elimination of the scale inefficiencies which were evident before the 1970s may be one successful element of the reform/development program initiated in the early 1970s" (Kemme and Neufeld, 1991, p. 54). In Hungary, data prepared by the Ministry of Industry for a subsample of twelve manufacturing branches indicate that, contrary to what Table 4.5 suggests, the average firm size in Hungary fell from 2,163 employees in 1980 to 380 employees in 1990 (see Table 4.5). What is more, the *number* of loss-making companies in 1990 by firm size and industry showed no tendency for large companies to be more subject to losses than small ones. If anything, small firms tended to be more likely to be operating at a loss than large ones in a greater number of sectors (see Table 4.6). The data in these tables are only rough estimates, but they do throw into question Eastern Europe's new article of faith—that "small is always beautiful"—whereas once everything big was great.

The point about post-socialist market structure is not that it has erred necessarily on the side of too much monopoly power or too large a scale. Rather, the little evidence available suggests that before and after the transition it erred in many directions: generally there was an insufficient number of small firms; in some industries firms were too large (especially in terms of employment) and concentration excessive; but in other industries firms were not large enough by world standards (in terms of sales) and plants were below minimum efficient scale. Suboptimality meant that restructuring could not simply take the form of market-driven downsizing.

As post-socialist economies became highly "open," and leading enterprises found themselves having to compete against multinational firms, the problem of suboptimal size became magnified. By 1990 some East European countries exported to convertible currency markets as much as one-fifth of their industrial output (in some cases, however, under conditions of below marginal cost pricing). In Hungary manufactured exports as a share of manufacturing output reached 18.0 percent to hard

Table 4.5 Average size and number of enterprises in Hungary,
1980 and 1990

Industry	Average number of employees per enterprise (number of enterprises in parentheses)	
	1980	1990
Ferrous metals	4,261	461
	(18)	(92)
Aluminum	1,179	443
	(14)	(37)
Machinery	1,194	84
	(108)	(1,444)
Vehicles	2,426	153
	(43)	(416)
Electrical machinery	1,865	161
	(34)	(278)
Telecommunications	4,636	210
	(22)	(297)
Precision instruments	1,289	79
	(46)	(493)
Petrochemicals	1,625	1,180
	(4)	(5)
Organic chemicals	1,328	139
	(32)	(99)
Fertilizers and pesticides	2,138	691
	(8)	(22)
Pharmaceuticals	1,721	647
	(14)	(36)
Textiles	2,294	316
	(52)	(240)
Average enterprise size (unweighted)	2,162	380

Source: Computed from MIT (1991), part VI.

Table 4.6 Number and proportion of loss-making companies by firm size
and industry, Hungary, 1990

	Large companies		Small companies	
Industry	Total number	Loss making (% of total)	Total number	Loss making (% of total)
Mining	20	25.0%	11	63.6%
Electricity	24	—	11	36.4
Metallurgy	61	24.6	83	27.7
Machinery	514	27.6	2,973	32.1
Construction material	87	25.3	172	41.3
Chemicals	126	13.5	509	42.6
Light industry	428	24.8	1,530	36.5
Other industries	44	11.4	219	31.1
All industries	1,304	23.9	5,508	34.5
Construction	217	27.2	2,838	38.3

Source: Adapted from Ministry of Industry and Trade of Hungary, as reported in
OECD (1992c).

currency markets and an additional 6.5 percent to ruble-accounting
markets (MIT, 1991). The comparable 1990 figures for Poland were
20.2 percent and 4.0 percent respectively (Amsden, 1994a). In the case
of Czechoslovakia, the export intensity of most industries in 1991 (ex-
cluding fuel, energy, printing, food, building materials, and nonferrous
metals), was well over 10 percent and rapidly rising (OECD, 1991a).
Because these were fairly "open" economies, their leading enterprises
had to be of a globally competitive scale.

The effect of enterprise and plant size that is suboptimal by world
standards can be illustrated using four specific mid-tech industries, all
of which exhibited long-run growth potential in post-socialist Eastern
Europe.[3]

Steel. In 1991 Czechoslovakia ranked fourteenth and Poland ranked
seventeenth among the top twenty world crude steel producers. Yet on
a *company* basis, neither of these countries ranked high. Among the
top forty major steel-producing companies in the world, VSZ Kosice
(Czechoslovakia) ranked thirtieth and Huta Katowice (Poland) ranked
thirty-second (Nippon Steel of Japan ranked first). Within Poland itself,

Huta Katowice ranked third in sales among the top ten Polish manufacturers in 1988 (*Zycie Gospodarcze,* October 16, 1988). Thus this mill was large by Polish standards (it exported about 30 percent of its output), but not by world steel industry standards. In terms of plant size, "The steel industries of Eastern Europe face certain common problems. These include out-of-date and *undersized* plants" (UNIDO, 1991, p. 318, emphasis added).

Detergents. The detergent industry in Poland was much more fragmented than in either Britain or Germany in the early 1990s. Only two firms, Procter and Gamble (P&G) and Unilever, accounted for about 80 percent of the British market, while three firms, P&G, Henkel, and Unilever, accounted for about the same market share in Germany. By contrast, seven companies divided the same 80 percent market share in Poland. Moreover, in terms of annual capacity, Poland's major detergent producers were estimated to be below minimum efficient scale (Bain and Company, 1991).

Machine tools. Among the world's thirty-three leading machine tool producers in 1991, Yugoslavia ranked thirteenth, Romania fourteenth, Czechoslovakia twentieth, and Poland twenty-first. Despite the fact that the machine tool industry is characterized worldwide by relatively small-scale firms, and despite the reputation of socialist countries for inappropriately elephantine enterprises, no East European company ranked among the world's twenty-five largest machine tool producers in 1990. The four biggest firms were from Japan.

Pulp and paper. Like other industries in Poland, the pulp and paper industry was too fragmented by international standards and operated with too many, not too few, firms. According to a consultant's report: "The past regime has left a legacy of old equipment, inefficiency, low quality products and total disregard for the environment [although the environmental practices of papermakers all over the world were typically also poor]. About 60 percent of production is concentrated in 5 mills out of a total of 42. *With the curtailment of subsidies,* [most of the 42] will not survive" (NLK-Celpap, 1991, p. 25, emphasis added).

As noted earlier, the strategy of transition economists was to restructure state-owned industries simply by cutting subsidies, but this approach usually did not create competitiveness. The Polish pulp and paper industry's five major mills, for example, enjoyed large forest resources and favorable wood and labor costs. Their operating scale was not too far short of world standards. But to compete internationally even the best mills needed further restructuring: "Poland is surrounded by large cost-competitive forest products producers [especially in Sweden and Finland] and domestic producers will have difficulty to face up to the challenge. Considerable capital investment is needed in the future to upgrade neglected mills and to improve the quality of the product, to solve environmental problems and to operate at higher efficiency" (NLK-Celpap, 1991, p. 25). Ending fragmentation by withdrawing subsidies was a necessary but insufficient restructuring move.

Big Business in Late Industrialization

Transition economists have not only ignored the problems of suboptimal firm size but have also tended to exaggerate the share of output accounted for by big business, as is evident from data on aggregate economic concentration. The conventional wisdom (in this case about Czechoslovakia) has been as follows: "Czechoslovak industry is extremely concentrated. The largest 100 companies in 1990 accounted for 26 percent of industrial employment" (Frydman, Rapaczyński, and Earle, 1993, p. 41). Yet this figure is not particularly high by world standards. In the United States, the largest one hundred enterprises in 1982 were estimated to account for 23.8 percent of industrial employment—almost the same share as in former Czechoslovakia despite the United States's being a much bigger country (U.S. Bureau of the Census, 1986).

A general property of late industrialization is big business, typically in the form of large diversified business groups (Hikino and Amsden, 1994). Ironically, such groups characterized prerevolutionary Czechoslovakia and Russia, and appear to be typical of countries—socialist or capitalist—seeking to reach the world technological frontier with no original technology. In 1937, the Bata Works in Czechoslovakia manufactured six-sevenths of domestic shoe consumption and owned a total of twenty-six companies, including mines, transport, building, publishing, and insurance enterprises (Teichova, 1995). In Russia:

> Large enterprises first emerged . . . in the pre-revolutionary period. While Russian industry lagged behind that of the leading European countries and the United States, it still had a high degree of concentration in 1910. Large enterprises were predominantly structured as syn-

dicates operating as joint-stock companies. Had these Russian syndi-cates continued their natural development, they would have, most likely, gradually taken the shape of industrial and trade groups, much like those, say, which emerged in Japan *(zaibatsu)* or South Korea *(chaebol)*. (Yudanov, 1995)

South Korea, with one of the strongest penchants for big conglomer-ates, considered big business essential to realize scale economies in pro-duction and distribution and to invest in the research and development necessary to reach the world technological frontier (Amsden, 1995). (In OECD countries, only 5 percent of small-scale firms were estimated to invest in any R&D [C. Freeman, 1982].) As late as 1993, amid lengthy policy debates on how to nourish small- and medium-size enterprise and limit inequalities in wealth distribution, the Korean government had not lost sight of the importance of scale: "A critical distinction must be made between concentration of ownership, on the one hand, and business rationalization needed for effective competition in the global marketplace, on the other. The latter, which often implies an increase in the scale of business enterprises, is frequently desirable *and should be encouraged*" (MTIE, 1993, p. 7, emphasis added).

Even Taiwan, where a large share of its total output was accounted for by small firms (due to government political opposition to large *private* firms and Chinese entrepreneurship), distinguished itself for its high share of big business (many state-owned) among late-industrializing countries (Amsden, 1993). In 1985, with a population of only 19.3 million people, Taiwan accounted for eighteen of the top two hundred largest domestic industrial enterprises among developing countries, the same number as Brazil, with a population roughly seven times greater. Hong Kong and Singapore did not score high in terms of big industrial enterprises, but they headed the list of developing countries' fifty biggest financial corporations (Hikino and Amsden, 1994, tables 6–7).

The downsizing and demonopolization policies of transition econo-mists are derived from a model of perfect competition. Yet the experi-ence of late industrialization suggests a less simple reality, with large firms having to be bred by deliberate government policies in order to compete internationally against the oligopolies of industrialized coun-tries. The danger of bigness per se (rather than simply an insufficiency of small firms) is inefficiency, as in the coal and gas industries of many pre-transition East European countries. But to re-create an efficient mid-tech economy in the transition from socialism precludes returning to an obsolete model of atomistic competition.

Import-Led Growth

Rising imports induced by market forces initially were a strategic element in transition policy. The logic was that imports of capital and intermediate goods were needed to restructure state-owned firms or, better yet, to enable privatized state-owned firms to grow by exporting. Consequently, several types of policies were established to facilitate imports.

One policy was vigorous import liberalization, which went far beyond the mere rebate of import duties for exporters, a reform introduced in Hungary and Poland even before the transition. Import liberalization in all the post-socialist East European countries (Bulgaria, Hungary, Poland, Czechoslovakia, and Romania) involved drastic across-the-board tariff reductions, the abolition of quotas, and the elimination of other restrictions on trade.[4]

Another policy was the provision of finance for imports by international lenders. World Bank conditions effectively prohibited borrowing countries in the region from offering export subsidies to domestic producers, as will be discussed in the next chapter. Instead, exporters were supposed to benefit from access to overseas credit to cover their costs of importing capital goods and intermediate inputs.

Finally, there was a tendency for transition exchange rate policy, which conceived the exchange rate as a nominal anchor, to encourage imports. Where the exchange rate did not float freely after the transition and where inflation persisted (in East Central Europe, to varying degrees), the real appreciation of the currency made imports relatively cheap, as we saw in Chapter 2.

Thus a de facto policy of import-led growth was introduced into Eastern Europe during the early transition, repeating, we would argue, the fatal import-led growth policies of the 1970s (see, for example, Gomulka, 1976).

Interestingly, massive imports of capital goods were also central to East Asia's development. A reliance on foreign capital goods as a form of technology transfer was much more pronounced in East Asia than in, for example, Latin America or India (Westphal, Kim, and Dahlman,

1985). South Korea in particular ran a balance of payments deficit in almost all years through the early 1990s (unlike the surpluses that Japan and Taiwan began to accumulate) (Amsden, 1989). Easy entry conditions of capital goods imports in Korea's (and Taiwan's) early industrialization were believed to have raised productivity and technological capability (L. Kim, 1993).

Nevertheless, the trade and industrial policy regimes supporting imports differed sharply in the East European and East Asian cases. Import substitutes were selectively protected in East Asia and only certain imports were allowed to enter domestic markets freely. East Asia in the 1960s and Eastern Europe in the 1990s were at different stages of development (unindustrialized as opposed to semi-industrialized, respectively), and so the contractionary impact of imports on the level of domestic economic activity also varied. Complicating matters, by the 1990s world trading conditions had become less favorable to emergent exporters. In addition, East Asian economies in the 1960s were not in the severe depression faced by East European economies in the 1990s. East European enterprises were reluctant to commit themselves to heavy investments in foreign capital goods without risk-reducing government restructuring policies.

Given these differences, Eastern Europe's open-door policy toward imports tended to devastate even promising enterprises in certain import-competing industries. It also threatened to create balance of payments deficits, and was insufficient to sustain export growth.

Pro-Import Policy Bias?

It is one thing to open the door indiscriminately to imports of capital goods and intermediate imports when an economy is starting to industrialize and capital goods or intermediate input suppliers do not exist in large numbers, but quite another matter to do so when an economy is already semi-industrialized and such suppliers not only exist but are in dire need of restructuring, as in post-socialist Eastern Europe. Similarly, it is one thing to introduce neutral policies to enable final users of capital goods and intermediate inputs to choose between domestic or foreign inputs, but another matter to introduce policies biased against domestic suppliers.

Arguably, a bias against domestic suppliers in the early stages of transition did exist. For instance, if a Polish woolen textile exporter wanted to borrow money to finance its purchases of wool, it could only borrow from Poland's Export Development Bank, at 9 percent interest (September 1991), for hard currency credit to import wool. First established in 1988, this bank became a joint stock company, 75 percent owned by the Polish government and capitalized largely with conditional foreign credits. It was committed to grant credit in hard currency only for import expenses. If the firm bought wool in Poland, it would have to borrow from domestic banks, in domestic currency, at 50 percent nominal interest.

It is, of course, real, rather than nominal domestic and foreign interest rates that should be compared for the purposes of assessing any allocative bias, although it is also true that many East European managers apparently suffered from "money illusion" in the early transition period and decided whether or not to borrow credit by comparing nominal interest rate costs with internal profit rates (Pinto, Belka, and Krajewski, 1992). In the presence of money illusion, foreign credit was, indeed, much cheaper than domestic credit. Theoretically foreign and domestic real interest rates should have been equal at the margin, taking into account variables such as average inflation and expected exchange rate changes. Nevertheless, even real interest rates may have been lower abroad than at home in the early transition period from the perspective of individual borrowers, whose relevant domestic inflation rate was not an all-economy average but rather their own industry's price change. In industries suffering from declining demand and price increases (if not decreases) well below the consumer or even the producer price index (in Poland in 1991 such industries included metallurgy, engineering, chemicals, minerals, wood and paper, and textiles and leather), real domestic interest rates most likely were sharply above overseas rates, given extremely high nominal interest rates in the early transition (OECD, 1992a, table 1.7, p. 146). Thus international lending arrangements for imports may well have discriminated against local suppliers catering to industries with below-average price increases, thereby amounting to a policy biased in favor of imports.[5]

The Absence of Export Promotion

Eastern Europe's import regime has differed from that of East Asia in two other critical respects, as well. First, as new industries were established in East Asia, they began to be protected from foreign competition. After the so-called liberalization of the mid-1960s in South Korea, its overall tariff rates *increased,* and quotas became more pervasive (K. Kim, 1993). In 1968 effective rates of protection for industry in Taiwan were even higher than in South Korea (Balassa and associates, 1982). Selective protection, using tariffs and quotas, was energetically monitored by a relatively capable bureaucracy to ensure that wherever possible, producers used local sources (Luedde-Neurath, 1986; Amsden, 1989). Second, not only were imports controlled in East Asia but exports were also strongly promoted. As part of export promotion, local East Asian suppliers of inputs were supported in two ways: they themselves qualified for export incentives if their inputs were incorporated in exports; and direct and indirect exporters received access to preferential credit for working capital that could be used to buy domestic inputs (Rhee, Ross-Larson, and Pursell, 1984). In the 1970s governments offered large incentives to private firms to establish general trading companies as a way to stimulate exports further (Cho, 1987). In other late-industrializing countries that once offered greater incentives to firms producing import-competing products than to firms producing exports, so-called trade liberalization in the 1980s also generally ended discrimination against export activity by raising export subsidies, not by lowering import substitution incentives (Helleiner, 1994).

If export promotion had not been prevented in Eastern Europe by World Bank conditions, it could have been used as a powerful restructuring tool. At a minimum, exporters could have been allocated subsidized working capital such that they could choose neutrally from which companies to buy their inputs—foreign or local. More radically, export incentives could have been introduced that favored domestic purchases over imports. In the case of the textile industry, this would have meant giving domestic clothing makers subsidized working capital to buy locally made fabrics, with freedom to choose the best local supplier (thereby identifying which textile companies were worth further restructuring). This more aggressive policy might have given the best domestic textile enterprises a sufficient breathing spell to improve their quality, without the government having to make the invidious choice between introducing industry-wide textile import controls or letting the textile industry collapse. In Poland the latter occurred, as illustrated by the case of Uniontex.

In the earliest stages of the transition, import liberalization had little effect on the economy because undervaluation of the exchange rate made imports relatively expensive. Initially, the trade balance improved (see Table 2.1). As the transition wore on and pro-import policies took effect, imports increased (although not by as much as they threatened to do if economic growth rebounded). It is most likely that the positive effects of an easy import policy (helping to restructure and buoying the economy) were swamped by its negative effects (hurting specific import-competing industries and reducing output and employment). According to data for 1992, the growth rate of machinery imports was below the growth rate of total imports in almost all East European countries and the former USSR (UNECE, 1993, table 3.3.12). If export incentives had not been prohibited for ideological reasons, a better import-*cum*-export incentive system than the pro-import one that was introduced could almost certainly have been devised.

Trade Deficits

Trade balances worsened over the first years of transition (see Table 2.1). It should be noted that trade data for this period are unreliable, with large discrepancies in the same transactions recorded by importing and exporting countries (UNECE, 1993). Nevertheless, export data seem to be more reliable than import data, and imports were substantially understated: "On the import side, home statistics almost consistently understated the increase in imports from the West, and typically by non-negligible margins . . . For example, while France reported an increase in exports to Czechoslovakia of 180 percent, Czechoslovakia's own statistics suggested an increase of only 2 percent!" (Rodrik, 1992b). Hence the growing real imbalance in trade in the early transition period was probably also understated.

The recorded deterioration in the trade balance partly reflected the fact that once imports were de-controlled, not all of them were channeled toward exports or productive enterprise. An increasing proportion were made up of consumer goods. In the case of Hungary, recorded statistics showed a near doubling of the share of consumer goods in total imports between 1989 and 1991 (see Table 4.7). Consumer goods accounted for only 12.5 percent of total imports in 1989, but rose to 22.7 percent by the first half of 1991. In Poland, in the first eight months of 1991 consumer goods as a share of total imports rose from 18.8 percent to 31.6 percent (OECD, 1992a, p. 44). In terms of growth rate, for

Table 4.7 Hungary's product composition of imports and trade balance (convertible currency trade)

	Imports (percent)			Trade balance (billion US$)		
	1989	1990	1991	1989	1990	1991
Energy	0.8	8.5	13.5	0.17	−0.30	−1.42
Raw materials, components	59.2	50.0	37.7	−0.69	−0.14	−0.51
Machinery	17.3	18.5	20.5	−0.43	−0.44	−1.22
Consumer goods	12.5	13.6	22.7	0.52	0.60	−0.41
Food	10.1	9.4	5.6	1.06	1.24	1.95
Total	100.0	100.0	100.0			

Source: Central Statistical Office, Hungary.

Note: 1991 data are for the first half of the year. Not all columns sum to 100 due to rounding.

Bulgaria, Czechoslovakia, Hungary, Poland, Romania, and the former USSR, consumer goods tended to be the fastest-growing share of total imports in 1992, ahead of technology and capital goods (UNECE, 1993, table 3.3.12).

Not all of what was classified as "consumer goods" went for consumption. Textiles, for example, were classified as a consumer good but were typically used for production (see UNECE, 1993, table 3.3.12, p. 140). In 1992 textiles contributed more to trade imbalances than did clothing (see Table 4.8). This suggests that all of the surge of "consumer goods" imports in the early transition period was not simply related to household purchases. Like imports of other semi-manufactures, which accounted for a substantial share of total manufactured imports in 1992, part of the increase in consumer goods was related to final producers' buying their inputs overseas, probably in reaction to both the "pro-import" policies of international lenders and the absence of restructuring of low-quality domestic import substitutes.

In environments characterized by heavy dependence on foreign credits (foreign aid in South Korea and Taiwan in the 1960s, foreign loans in Eastern Europe in the 1990s), there is a tendency for the balance of payments to deteriorate unless export activity and import substitution are vigorously pursued. One of the specific reasons that South Korea began to encourage exports was to reduce its dependence—economic

Table 4.8 East Central Europe's "consumer" goods trade with the West, 1992[a] (changes, million US$)

Country	Imports		Exports		Net change in trade balance	
	Textiles (A)	Clothing (B)	Textiles (A)	Clothing (B)	(A)	(B)
Czechoslovakia	109	55	29	55	−80	0
Hungary	64	44	−2	24	−66	−20
Poland	149	−5	10	28	−139	33

Source: Compiled from UNECE (1993), table 3.3.12.
a. January–September 1992 relative to same period in 1991.

and political—on assistance from the United States. Nor is it surprising that international lenders to Eastern Europe made credits available in hard currency, for imports only. There would have been little purpose to their lending in a domestic currency, and foreign technology and capital goods were scarce. Yet hard currency credit creates a chronic strain on the balance of payments unless it is deliberately offset with import-substituting or export-promoting policies. What distinguishes Eastern Europe from East Asia as far as exports are concerned is not only differences in financial export incentives. Generally Eastern Europe has failed to start building an economy-wide system incorporating institutions to generate exports, as East Asia did. In the case of the Export Development Bank of Poland, for example, by 1991 the Polish government had disintegrated to the point that it could provide no administrative guidelines except on privatization and fiscal and monetary policy. Whatever guidelines existed with respect to trade policy were set by international lenders. Despite its name, therefore, the Export Development Bank began lending to cover the import component of domestic investors and traders (rather than just export-oriented investors), because that was most profitable. With trade policy strongly oriented toward imports, it is not surprising that the trade balance in many postsocialist countries began to deteriorate.

Export Prospects

Sustained export growth has been intimately linked with restructuring state-owned enterprises because they have accounted for the overwhelming share of exports in the early stages of transition. In Poland it is estimated that in 1991 SOEs accounted for 79.1 percent of total exports and only 51.1 percent of total imports (see OECD, 1992a, table 11). In Hungary, the largest fifty enterprises, most (if not all) of them state-owned (or technically owned by the State Property Agency and awaiting private buyers), accounted for 86 percent of total exports in the first part of 1990 (Gacs, 1991).

With hindsight, one might have expected the surge in exports to convertible currency markets that characterized many post-socialist countries in the early transition period, and not simply because exchange rates tended to be undervalued (though appreciating). After all, hard currency exports had grown rapidly in the 1980s in many such countries, and there was no apparent reason for their growth to decline immediately. Indeed, their immediate growth should have been expected to accelerate, in tandem with the onset of excess domestic capacity.

Hungary borrowed overseas extensively in the 1980s with the specific purpose of increasing its hard currency exports, and with considerable success. Hungarian convertible currency exports (in U.S. dollars) rose from $4.4 billion in 1980 to $7.0 billion in 1990 (MIT, 1991, p. 14). An export development program promoted manufactured exports by means of a series of direct incentives that included profit tax preferences, refunds of value-added tax paid on export-related investments, research and development assistance, and relief from prefinancing of imports used in raw material production of export goods. Agricultural exports were promoted by special production and export subsidies to offset distortions in other countries (Hanel, 1992). Industrial exports in Poland grew at an average annual rate (constant prices) of 6.9 percent between 1983 and 1988, with a set of incentives comparable to Hungary's. In 1989 Poland's export growth rate, compared with the same period of the previous year, was 15 percent. The comparable 1989 figures for the Czech and Slovak Federal Republic and Hungary were 16.1 percent and 18.1 percent, respectively (OECD, 1992a, pp. 154–155).

The jump in exports immediately after the transition began correlated closely with declining domestic profitability. On the basis of econometric results, Dani Rodrik concluded, "Export performance is attributable to exchange-rate policy in part, but the collapse of domestic demand has possibly played an even more important role" (1992b, p. 37). Although reliable profit data in the early transition are difficult to obtain, it is worth noting that a careful enterprise-level study undertaken in Poland by the Resident Mission of the World Bank in Warsaw found that by the fourth quarter of 1990, five out of ten metallurgical firms and one out of twelve chemical firms were incurring losses on exports. Twelve months later, these figures had shot up to a "staggering" eight out of ten and five out of twelve firms, respectively (Pinto, Belka, and Krajewski, 1992).

Given this background, the question to ask about exports is whether market forces alone (easier access to imports, declining wages, rising capital and energy costs, as well as gradually appreciating exchange rates) are sufficient, in the absence of restructuring, to sustain export growth.

Export Product Composition and the Market Mechanism

Compared with East Asia in the infancy of its export growth, post-socialist Eastern Europe had a different export product composition, one that made it more difficult for the market to act as an export trigger.

East Asia's infant exports were concentrated in far fewer products than those of semi-industrialized Eastern Europe, which simplified East Asian export promotion in terms of investment allocation and commercial diplomacy (although, in terms of causality, Japan's export promotion policies may have created its product concentration). Moreover, the products in which East Asia initially tended to specialize—first in textiles and then in clothing (Hong Kong alone displayed the reverse pattern)—created many jobs in a period of high unemployment as well as many investment opportunities for small entrepreneurs. Because textiles had a relatively high labor content, policies designed to contain wages (labor repression, for one) could also be expected to have a large impact on export competitiveness. By contrast, manufactured exports in Eastern Europe's early transition (as in many semi-industrialized countries) were dominated by heavy industry, which required large investments in capital, necessitated significant antipollution controls, and responded little to the real wage cuts that lay at the heart of transition economics.

In 1950 as much as half of Japan's total exports were accounted for by cotton textiles. As late as 1955 cotton textiles still accounted for 37 percent, with steel accounting for another 24 percent (34 percent by 1960) (Nakamura, 1981, pp. 60–61). Textiles in South Korea in 1965 accounted for 41 percent of manufactured exports (Amsden, 1989,

p. 67). As late as 1980, they continued to account for 10 percent (BOK, 1989).

Neither Poland nor Hungary had anything near this concentration in its exports to hard currency countries (although just before the transition began as much as 20 percent of Hungary's exports to ruble currency countries was accounted for by motor vehicles—mainly buses) (OECD, 1992c, table 3.3). The top ten hard currency industrial exports of Hungary in 1990 accounted for only 35.6 percent of total industrial hard currency exports, and were themselves widely dispersed (see Table 4.9).

We must use even rougher export classifications to examine Poland's case, but the same pattern of dispersion manifests itself (see Table 4.10). There is nothing close to East Asia's product concentration in textiles. The largest single relatively homogeneous export item in Poland in 1991 was iron and steel, with a 12.2 percent share of total industrial exports, only a half or a third as much as the share of iron and steel in Japanese exports at the start of Japan's postwar re-industrialization efforts.

The advantage of a diverse export bundle is a lower risk of retaliation by importers, although major exports of both Hungary and Poland tended to feature precisely those products (food and iron and steel, for

Table 4.9 Hungary's top ten industrial exports to convertible currency countries, 1988 and 1990 (percent)

Industry	1988	1990
1. Aluminum fabrications	6.2	6.8
2. Rolled steel plate and wide strip	3.9	4.0
3. Motor vehicles	4.1	3.8
4. Refined oil and gas products	4.5	3.7
5. Plastic granulates	4.0	3.2
6. Textile fabrics	3.6	3.2
7. Pharmaceutical base materials	3.6	3.0
8. Hot rolled bar and steel forms	2.5	2.9
9. Chemical products for agriculture	3.3	2.8
10. Electrical light sources	2.7	2.2
Total of convertible currency exports	38.4	35.6

Source: Adapted from Ministry of Industry and Trade of Hungary, as reported in OECD (1992c).

Table 4.10 Distribution of Poland's convertible currency industrial exports, by industry, 1988–1991 (percent, current prices)

Industry	1988	1989	1990	1991
1. Food products	14.2	15.4	12.6	9.9
2. Light industry	8.7	7.4	7.8	6.4
Textiles	4.3	3.5	2.8	2.0
Clothing	2.7	2.5	2.9	2.8
Leather products	1.6	1.3	2.0	1.6
3. Wood products	4.4	3.7	3.8	4.4
4. Glass products	1.1	1.0	1.2	1.7
5. Metallurgy				
Iron and steel	5.6	6.9	9.7	12.2
Nonferrous metals	10.6	9.2	10.0	10.7
6. Metal products	3.4	4.0	4.3	4.6
7. Shipbuilding	2.3	3.2	1.8	3.5
8. Coal products	10.8	9.4	8.5	8.8
9. Engineering products (including metal products)	27.0	28.4	25.8	22.5
10. Chemicals	13.1	12.6	13.9	15.4
Total	100.0	100.0	100.0	100.0

Source: Amsden (1994a).

Note: Columns may not sum exactly to 100 due to rounding.

example) that OECD countries heavily protected. Whatever the advantage, not having a "leading sector" that could simplify modernization was a serious handicap.

Creating a "Leading (Export) Sector": The Polish Steel Industry

The problems of relying on the market mechanism to create sustained export growth are illustrated by the case of the Polish metallurgical sector, which included the processing of ferrous (iron and steel) and nonferrous (for example, copper and aluminum) metals. The export growth rate of ferrous and nonferrous metals far exceeded the growth rate of Poland's other manufacturing sectors. Total exports grew by 12.3 percent in 1990 and −3.3 percent in 1991 (first eight months); metallurgical exports grew by 44.2 percent and 31.8 percent in the same period.

Despite rapid growth, the chronic problems of Poland's metallurgical sector made it an unlikely candidate to spearhead "laissez-faire" export growth in the early years of transition (even ignoring the issue of job creation, since the employment share of the metallurgical sector in 1990 was only 6 percent). First, metallurgy was generally energy inefficient and polluting. One index, for example, indicated that Poland's steel industry used 4.3 times as much energy as the world average (OECD, 1992a). As energy costs rose in Poland with the abolition of government energy subsidies, costs rose. Poland's metallurgical sector required major investments to meet the environmental standards of the OECD and eventually of Poland itself. It was highly unlikely that the private sector—foreign or local—would be willing or able at market-determined production costs to undertake the necessary clean-up operations (without some form of government guarantee of return on investment). If the metallurgical sector was to become an export leader, therefore, it initially required some government intervention to clear its path.

Second, "getting the prices right" in the form of devaluation might, in theory, boost the metallurgical sector's international competitiveness. In 1992, for example, Poland was not fully using the quota the U.S. government had given it for steel sales to the American market, in part because demand for all imported steels in the United States was soft and in part because the Polish steel industry was not able to compete in terms of price (or quality, perhaps) against either mini-mills at home or integrated steel companies from abroad. Export success in 1990 and 1991 seems to have depended on below–marginal cost pricing. According to managers at the Huta Katowice Steel Company, one of Poland's largest mills and a relatively efficient operation, the European Community had threatened to take it to court for dumping, or charging a lower export than domestic price. Further devaluations could conceivably have improved the Polish steel industry's cost position.

In practice, even if it had been possible to engineer further real devaluations to lower costs, the metallurgical sector suffered from noncost problems that devaluation could not solve. Besides environmental pollution, the Polish steel industry suffered from excess capacity. Observers of the steel industry noted that there were twenty-six steel mills in Poland, all competing against each other, that needed to be consolidated. Some mills needed to be shut down and some needed to be expanded. Within a given mill, subparts needed to be contracted or expanded. These crisscrossing, interenterprise rationalization require-ments made it very difficult to rely simply on subsidy withdrawal *to enterprises* as the weeding out, rationalizing mechanism (as transition economists seemed to imagine). Some steel managers argued that be-fore it was possible to attract foreign investors, it was necessary to know the overall target capacity of Poland's steel industry, and which plants were likely to survive and which to fail. Given all the externali-ties involved in restructuring steel, a government role was inevitable.

In addition, heavy investments were required to sustain exports once excess domestic capacity was exhausted. As in virtually every industry in Poland, the metallurgical sector's exports reflected a diversion of ca-pacity from the severely depressed home market to the export market. This reorientation was not without its price. Huta Katowice managers, for example, stated that their mill was designed to export only about 30–35 percent of its output, which it was doing before 1989, not 70 percent, which it began to do thereafter. Huta Katowice mostly pro-duced by-products that ought to have been further processed by other Polish steel mills to add maximum value, rather than exported directly. The share of exports in total sales of the iron and steel industry rose from 13.2 percent in 1988 to 22.9 percent only two years later. (Compa-rable figures for nonferrous metals were 26.5 percent and 34.7 percent.) Exports in total sales for all industries showed a similar trend, rising from 18.8 percent in 1988 to 24.2 percent in 1990 (Amsden, 1994a).

The danger of an abrupt shift toward exports was that if and when the domestic market recovered, capacity would suddenly be shifted back to home sales. Exports would then collapse at a time when rising domestic income encouraged high import demand. To give stability to export promotion required investments in export capacity, but invest-ment activity in Poland had crashed. Although investments in the iron and steel industry (and in chemicals) were positive in 1990, this re-flected earlier investments that were in the pipeline rather than new ventures (OECD, 1992a). Because investments in the steel industry were lumpy and could not be undertaken in small chunks, steel invest-ments in almost all countries involve some form of government guaran-tee (the U.S. government was the exception, playing almost no role in the investment pattern of the country's integrated steel industry, which ultimately disintegrated for this and other reasons).

Thus while transition economists acted as though import liberalization and investments in foreign machinery and equipment were sufficient to drive enterprise restructuring, the example of the Polish steel industry raised serious questions about the feasibility of such a market-driven approach. This approach assigned the execution of restructuring exclusively to the individual enterprise, whereas the steel industry and other heavy industries like it indicated that restructuring had to be a collective task, involving the government, complex interenterprise transactions, and industry-wide decisions. Given these externalities, the market mechanism could not handle restructuring.

Enterprise restructuring took time, moreover, whereas the import-led vision of transition economists regarded restructuring as instantaneous, co-terminus with importing the technology and capital goods that obsolete production facilities required. East Asia has demonstrated that unlike developed countries, which compete internationally on the basis of research and development, or undeveloped countries, which do so on the exclusive basis of low labor costs, semi-industrialized countries compete on the basis of total costs, borrowing foreign technology and then substantially improving such technology incrementally (Hikino and Amsden, 1994). Making borrowed technology work optimally takes time, however, and in this interval, depending on the industry, some form of government involvement has usually been indispensable.

The fall of central planning reaffirmed the importance of the market in economic development. In terms of supplying products and satisfying certain wants, the market had no proven rival. Yet the early transition to capitalism in Eastern Europe also showed the limitations of the market mechanism to restructure state-owned enterprises and to create a momentum for economic recovery in semi-industrialized countries. In such economies, import liberalization, real wage reductions, relative price changes generally, antimonopoly legislation, and other market-friendly innovations have been insufficient in whole or in part to generate robust capitalist development.

APPENDIX

Real Wage Changes

Real wage changes in manufacturing output and employment in Hungary and Poland, 1978–1988, are estimated as follows.

Variables: MVA = Index of real manufacturing value added.
   EMP = Index of manufacturing employment.
   MWR = Index of real manufacturing wages.

(The value of t statistics is shown in parentheses; n = sample size; *significant at the 0.0002 level.)

Hungary: Structuralist Equation	Hungary: Neoclassical Equation
MVA = 47.4 +0.53 (MWR)	EMP = −28.7 +1.25 (MWR)
(4.83)* (3.86)	(0.54) (2.11)
$R^2 = 0.62.$	$R^2 = 0.33.$
S.E.E. = 7.4.	S.E.E. = 9.91.
$n = 11.$	$n = 11.$
Poland: Structuralist Equation	Poland: Neoclassical Equation
MVA = 14.2 +0.87 (MWR)	EMP = −130 +2.10 (MWR)
(2.10) (7.65)*	(2.90) (4.32)
$R^2 = 0.87.$	$R^2 = 0.68.$
S.E.E. = 6.66.	S.E.E. = 10.4.
$n = 11.$	$n = 11.$

Source: Data from Statistical Office, UNIDO.

Note: Output and wages are in U.S. dollars deflated by the U.S. consumer price index. For technical details, see Amsden and Van der Hoeven (1993), appendix I.

5

Pseudo-Privatization and the World Bank

In Eastern Europe governments have been faced with mounting pressure for protection which has been particularly difficult
to resist, in the case of joint ventures set up with major foreign
partners, or in the case of acquisition of SOEs by foreign investors. In the first half of 1992, the Hungarian government issued
import licenses for only 84,000 cars, a reduction of 44 percent
on the 1991 level, in response to claims for infant industry status by General Motors (United States) and Suzuki Motors Corporation (Japan), both of which have set up car plants in that
country. Similarly, tariffs have increased to 25 percent on
colour televisions locally produced by Samsung (Republic of
Korea).

—United Nations Industrial Development
Organization, 1992

Given the limitations of the market mechanism, an additional agent
has been required to organize and coordinate the restructuring process
in Eastern Europe. A pro-active government role, however, has been
complicated by the conditions attached to World Bank structural adjustment loans. World Bank influence has been far-ranging; its conditions have affected the establishment of genuine development banks,
the subsidization of exports (all subsidies have been off-limits), and the
role in restructuring played by former ministries of industry.

With industrial restructuring at a standstill, by early 1993 Bank conditions in Eastern Europe were extended to choosing the private agents
and the particular procedures to be followed in deliberate attempts at
salvaging state-owned firms. In the case of Poland, for instance, restructuring continued to be equated with privatization; there was never
any opportunity for Poland itself to borrow overseas—which typically
required Bank endorsement—in order to restructure the most promising publicly owned firms.[1] But in addition to the mere equation of privatization and restructuring, which it had insisted on in the past, the
Bank allowed newly founded, inexperienced commercial banks, still

owned by the state but optimistically poised for their own imminent privatization, to take steps similar to those used in U.S. Chapter Eleven proceedings to tackle the serious financial problems of state-owned enterprises: "The Polish Government has developed, with the assistance of the [World] Bank, an ambitious and comprehensive Enterprise and Bank Restructuring and Privatization (EBRP) Program" (GOP, 1993, p. 26).

The loan to recapitalize the state-owned banks was nearly half a billion dollars, and the program included the following innovation:

> To facilitate privatization as an outcome of enterprise restructuring, the EBRP gives creditors (state-owned banks and others) holding at least 30 percent of a public enterprise's debt the right to convert their claims into shares. In the case of SOEs, this conversion will automatically trigger a transformation into a joint-stock company [and the demise of employees' councils]. This provision constitutes nothing less than a breakthrough in the Polish Government's privatization policy since, for the first time, it makes privatization of an enterprise possible *without the legal consent of its workers.* (GOP, 1993, p. 30, emphasis added)[2]

The irony seemingly went unnoticed that in countries committed to eradicating their Communist past, undemocratic means were now used to achieve capitalist ends.

The World Bank's conditions with respect to SOE restructuring have made it the transition's most influential agent over the fate of such endeavors. Designating state-owned banks as the visible restructuring agent was a step forward for the Bank insofar as it signaled the Bank's recognition that something more than the invisible hand was needed to revive the huge SOE sector. Nevertheless, we would argue that the same Bank miscalculation that had grounded restructuring before 1993 persisted, namely, the idée fixe that the malaise of the SOE sector was due to the wrong "incentive structure" (an absence of private property), and that the situation would improve by privatizing and "getting the prices right." Bank belief ran along the following lines: "In a significant number of SOEs, the debt overhang and ongoing losses reflect not so much managerial incompetence or any inherent lack of viability as simply the fact that *under the current incentive structure there is no good reason not to incur losses and run up debt*" (GOP, 1993, p. 27, emphasis added). In other words, the Bank imagined that state-owned enterprises persisted in being unprofitable willfully and deliberately, as a consequence of not being privately owned. Moreover: "Some current loss-makers may have a viable future as going concerns *once their labor contracts and capital structure* are adjusted to new realities and the *new set of relative prices*" (GOP, 1993, p. 27, emphasis added). Yet as our case studies suggest, and as the ever more insistent demands of large foreign investors for protection against imports and for other government incentives further indicate, the problems of state-owned enterprises cannot be solved solely by reducing real wages, raising real interest rates, and adjusting other relative prices.

World Bank Conditions and Restrictions

The politics of the early transition period were generally marked by emotional enthusiasm for free market reforms, both by East European economists and their foreign advisers. Neoliberalism can by no means be attributed only to the latter. Nevertheless foreign banking institutions, in particular the World Bank, which arranged both the credit and the technical assistance so badly needed by Eastern Europe and mobilized not just its own financing but also co-financing from bilateral donors and lending agencies, have determined what neoliberalism means in practice. There are many variants of market economies, but the conditions the World Bank has attached to its structural adjustment loans to East European countries narrowly have limited their choices and tended to legitimate the ideas of the most ardent free marketeers.

"Rationalization" Defined as Cutting Subsidies

Bank practice regarding industrial development changed over the course of the 1980s, as was evident from the Bank's lending practices in Hungary. A Bank loan to Hungary in the early 1980s was intended to enhance the competitiveness of Hungarian industry through: technological upgrading of production facilities and rationalizing the product mix; focusing on high-value and skill-intensive industries; and promoting "background industries" for efficient import-substitution of specialized parts and components. This has proved to be the type of loan that Hungary and other post-socialist economies have needed from the Bank in the 1990s as well. According to the Bank: "This general approach was firmly based on the belief [of the Hungarian government] that the basic comparative advantage of Hungary was its technically competent managers, its highly skilled workers and its strength in applied research and development" (GOH, 1992). Moreover: "This approach to restructuring coincided with the Bank's thinking, and resulted in increased exports to convertible currency markets, introduction of more up-to-date technology in many production processes, and the development of a few 'background' [parts and components] industries . . . The project substantially realized its objectives" (GOH, 1992).

The problem, however, was that while this loan project "substantially realized its objectives," the whole Hungarian economy stagnated in the 1980s and partially collapsed in the early 1990s. Seizing an opportunity, Bank policymakers altered course. World Bank policy changed direction in Hungary the way it changed direction around the world, from one of fostering industrial development to one of subjecting existing industries to market rules of behavior ("structural adjustment"). Thus even before 1990 the Bank began insisting as a condition for further lending to Hungary that it reform its financial system, introduce trade liberalization and antimonopoly legislation, and slash subsidies to unprofitable public enterprises and consumers (for housing, fuel, and transportation). According to the Bank, "the main macroeconomic conditionality contained in the Industrial Sector Adjustment Loan [which was an adjunct to an IMF Standby Arrangement in 1988] was the Government's commitment to a three year program of subsidy reduction" (GOH, 1992).

Subsidies did, in fact, fall rapidly. Enterprise subsidies (industry only) in Hungary were estimated to have fallen from 5.4 percent of GDP in 1989 to 2.4 percent in 1991 (ILO, 1992). In Poland available data suggest that such subsidies fell to less than 2 percent of *budget expenditures* by 1991 (OECD, 1992a). In the same year in Czechoslovakia they fell to 2 percent of GDP and 4.3 percent of budget expenditures (OECD, 1991a, table 9).

However one views Bretton Woods institutions' conditions on loans to sovereign buyers in principle, it may not have been altogether unreasonable in practice for the World Bank to insist as a condition for lending to Eastern Europe that subsidies to chronically unprofitable state-owned enterprises (in, as it turned out, a relatively limited number of sectors, typically iron and steel, coal, and certain other heavy industries, depending on the country) be reduced.[3] But it is quite another matter for the Bank to insist that sovereign governments take no part in restructuring *promising* state-owned enterprises through industrial policy and the provision of supports to these enterprises with strict conditions determined by the governments themselves (as in East Asia), rather than the Bretton Woods institutions (see the discussion in OECD, 1992a). The Bank, however, insisted on both.

The Bank's approach is evident from a loan it made to Hungary in the late 1980s. In an audit report on the loan, the Bank stated:

> The experience with the restructuring of the steel and coal mining sectors indicates that enforcing financial discipline by cutting back subsidies is an essential step to the rationalization of obsolete facilities . . . Rationalization alone of obsolete facilities, however, will not lead to improved efficiency. This will require new investments in plant and equipment in the remaining facilities as well as reduction of overmanning and improved management practices. *Such physical restructuring is best done by private owners.* (GOH, 1992, emphasis added)[4]

An insistence that only private owners (if any) undertake restructuring is evident from the way in which the Bank whittled down the powers of the organization established by the Polish Parliament to undertake restructuring, the Industrial Development Agency (IDA), headed by the deputy minister of industry. The IDA was intended to provide both technical and financial assistance to promising state-owned enterprises. By parliamentary decree, the financial component of the IDA was to come from absorption of the Industrial Restructuring Fund, which had previously been the restructuring arm of the Ministry of Industry (the World Bank's bête noire). The Bank's contribution was to ensure that the operations of the IDA be limited to technical assistance, and that the financing of restructuring be privatized. According to a Bank appraisal:

> IDA's existing financial portfolio will be transferred to financial institutions. Loans to enterprises will be sold or transferred to financial entities capable of managing credit risks, such as the Polish Development Bank. IDA's equity investments in enterprises will be transferred to equity holding entities, such as independent companies, private funds, privatization funds or private equity holding companies. It was confirmed during negotiations [with the World Bank] that transfer of IDA's financial portfolio will be completed by June 30, 1992. (GOP, 1991)

It turned out that even the technical component of IDA's mandate was constrained by the Bank. IDA was limited to hiring consultants (with

Bank support) to undertake 150 or so industry and enterprise studies to further the goal of privatization.

The reason behind the Bank's insistence on no government-led restructuring was straightforward and to be expected on the basis of its experience with developing countries in financial distress. Whatever the Bank's underlying ideological hostility toward state-owned enterprises, especially those with active employees' councils (see, for example, Hinds, 1991), it did not want post-socialist governments to get involved in restructuring because this threatened to unbalance their budgets. Fiscal stringency, in turn, was elevated above all other goals as being necessary to prevent inflation and to facilitate Eastern Europe's repayment of its international loans, a preoccupation of international lenders strengthened by the Latin American debt crisis. In 1991 foreign debt stood at $48.4 billion in Poland, $22.7 billion in Hungary, and $9.4 billion in Czechoslovakia (Frydman, Rapaczyński, and Earle, 1993). Writing about Hungary, the Bank observed:

> Emphasis should be given to financial, organization, management and legal aspects of restructuring rather than physical restructuring which requires large resource outlays . . . and which will put great pressure on the resources of the State Property Agency [Hungary's privatization arm]. The Hungarian Government's expenditures are estimated at almost 60% of GDP, large by Western standards, and financed by high rates of taxation. (GOH, 1992)

Disempowering the Ministry of Industry

In capitalist enterprises, it is widely believed that a "champion" is needed if an embryonic technology or a new business plan is to succeed (Maidique, 1987). Similarly in the post-socialist transition, a cause was more likely to triumph if it had powerful backers. The Bretton Woods institutions were instrumental in aiding East European ministries of finance (to deal with the IMF) and ministries of privatization (to deal with the Bank). They lent least support to ministries of industry, which were tainted with responsibility for state enterprise before the transition, and whose equivalent in successful late-industrializing countries—say, the Ministry of International Trade and Industry in Japan (MITI) and the Industrial Development Bureau in Taiwan—were synonymous with industrial policy.

Among the most effective government bureaucracies in Eastern Europe after the transition have been the ministries of privatization (the Ministry of Ownership Change in Poland and the State Property Agency in Hungary). The Polish ministry benefited from World Bank assistance in its establishment as well as in the financing of a continuous inflow of foreign technical assistants. It was also exempt from ceilings on civil service pay scales, which enabled it to attract the most capable staff members. According to the Bank: "The International Finance Corporation [a member of the World Bank group] initiated a proposal, and helped secure European Community funding for financing the organization/establishment of the Privatization Agency, which was later expanded into the Ministry of Ownership Change" (GOP, 1991). But while the Bank was strengthening one ministry, it was politicking to weaken another. It stated:

> As Poland moves rapidly toward a market economy, and a large number of SOEs, previously controlled to a greater or lesser extent by the Ministry of Industry (MoI), are privatized, it is appropriate that the Government re-evaluate the role that MoI should play, focusing it toward supporting an enabling environment for the private sector. (GOP, 1991)

Similarly in Hungary:

> The Government is committed [to the World Bank] to reducing the role of the ministry (MIT—Ministry of Industry and Trade) in the economy rapidly, and the restructuring, revitalization and government of the bulk of industrial enterprises is to be left to market forces. (GOH, 1992)

The war against the ministries of industry was waged partly in the belief that they were infested with Communist Party officials of the ancien régime. In truth, however, in Hungary during the 1980s and even earlier almost all government agencies had ceased to be Party-dominated. In Poland as well, the *nomenklatura* were no longer to be found in key government positions (including state-owned enterprises) after the transition. The new director of the Lenin Shipyard, for example, was an engineer who had been with the company since his graduation from the university and had been a Solidarity activist for as long a time. The new director of a radio works (which, as mentioned earlier, quickly succumbed to East Asian competition) had been recruited by Solidarity from a research institute. In the view of most people (corroborated by a few pieces of indirect evidence) the *nomenklatura* had fled to the private sector, where they could make far more money. A survey in Gdansk showed that only 18 percent of private entrepreneurs used bank capital as an initial source of financing; most (73 percent) relied on personal savings, which the *nomenklatura* had been in the best position in the past to accumulate (Kreft, 1991). As early as 1987, 25 percent of people applying for licenses to run private enterprises in Gdansk were reported to be from the *nomenklatura* (Ost, 1990; see also Levitas and Strzałkowski, 1990).

The formation of ministries of privatization in the early stages of transition demonstrates that it is possible to mobilize competent and elitist state bureaucracies quickly. The defense of a do-nothing restructuring policy on the ground that competent state bureaucracies do not exist to formulate or administer one, therefore, is unsustainable, yet—as in the case of the ministries of industry—a self-fulfilling prophecy, given Bretton Woods conditions.

A Ban on Development Banking

A key institution of late industrialization is the *development bank*—that is, a public or quasi-public bank whose mandate is to mobilize largely foreign capital and fulfill development planning goals by extending long-term loans to targeted projects with high social rates of return at preferential interest rates. Such banks have operated in almost all successful late-industrializing countries, including China and South Korea. By contrast, the World Bank's conditions in post-socialist Eastern Europe have been intentionally designed to prevent the emergence of development banking.

In China, for instance, even after reforms announced in January 1994, a State Development Bank was entrusted with the task of financing development projects, and both commercial and specialized banks continued to handle government "policy loans" carrying below-market interest rates. In South Korea, the Korea Development Bank (KDB) was founded in 1954 to supply long-term credit for industrial rehabilitation. Later, "in accordance with the government's economic policies," it supported the development of export projects and heavy and chemical industries. From 1979 to the mid-1980s, in order to promote the structural adjustment of industry and strengthen the foundations for economic stability, the KDB fostered the development of energy conservation and parts and components industries and also supported industries suffering from cyclical depression, such as the shipping industry. After 1986 the KDB gave top priority to fostering high-tech sectors (BOK, 1990, p. 56). A major component of this effort involved paying credit guarantees to foreign lenders to help finance domestic industrial projects. Another function was to underwrite private corporate bonds and stocks (to encourage private financial intermediation) as well as government and public bonds.

By contrast, the Polish Development Bank (PDB), established by the Council of Ministers in 1990, found that its freedom to lend directly to industry was circumscribed by World Bank loan conditions. Eventually the PDB functioned as an apex bank, to funnel funds from abroad to private domestic banks, at market-determined interest rates, without credit guarantees attached, with private banks themselves deciding to whom to lend. According to the World Bank: "PDB will act principally as a wholesale bank, channelling the majority of its lending to the final borrowers through eligible Polish commercial banks." By way of a concession, the World Bank has allowed some direct lending:

> With the mandate of facilitating and promoting privatization, restructuring and development of the private sector, PDB will initially focus its operation on three "windows" providing financing, mostly through other intermediaries, for: (i) restructuring of private and state-owned enterprises, primarily those in the process of privatization; (ii) the development of new private small and medium enterprises; and (iii) minority equity investments in privatized or joint venture companies, *altogether limited to 15% of PDB's capital.*   (GOP, 1991, emphasis added)

World Bank policy in Poland has been directed at downplaying the importance of a public development bank and emphasizing the importance of private commercial banks: Korean government policy was the reverse. In Korea:

> From the institutional point of view, the domestic banks were facilitators and guarantors of external finance, but not intermediaries. The commercial banks did not try to develop skills in terms of lending. They basically issued guarantees on instruction from the government and took little responsibility for evaluating either the economic or financial feasibility of the project. Eventually, *when some of the projects proved unsound, the government . . . had to take extraordinary measures to relieve the banks of bad debts.*   (Cole and Park, 1983, p. 61, emphasis added)

The Korean case illustrates one pitfall of development banking: government liability for bad loans. In the absence of institutional safeguards, this can prove costly.

The problem with the approach advocated by the World Bank in Eastern Europe, however, has been that private commercial banks have been by and large unwilling to lend to public enterprises for physical restructuring. They have preferred to lend short-term to small-scale and mid-size enterprises, usually in the service sector, because such investments have quick pay-back periods. Amid the political uncertainties and inflation of the transition, quick pay-back periods are a rational business objective for private, profit-maximizing financial institutions. The preference for short-term loans on the part of private commercial banks has thus not been due to their inexperience, as the World Bank has imagined. Rather, these banks have been acting the way any profit-maximizing, capitalist agent should have behaved. Newly privatized banks in Poland have voluntarily continued servicing the loans to unprofitable state-owned enterprises that the government bequeathed to them at their founding as part of their paid-in capital, but only to avoid scaring off new customers with loan defaults, not to revitalize such enterprises.

The World Bank itself witnessed the strong resistance of private financial institutions in Eastern Europe to participating in restructuring, either by lending to state-owned enterprises or by accepting debt-for-equity swaps. A case in point was that of the Star Truck Company, whose problem immediately after the transition was financial. According to a study by the Boston Consulting Group, in charge of designing a business plan for Star (which employed some 12,000 people) in Poland, the company had to switch production from eleven-ton to seven-ton trucks to become profitable, and could do so at relatively low cost. Nevertheless, "The commercial banks were urged to come up with a financial restructuring package, and refused. The Industrial Development Agency [the Ministry of Industry's restructuring arm] was ready to take part in a financial consortium to rescue the company, but not alone, as it was far too expensive. *The whole episode illustrates the lack of willingness of the banks to take part in the restructuring process*" (World Bank, n.d., emphasis added).

The resistance of private financial institutions notwithstanding, the World Bank has been thus far unwilling to compromise. It has made no attempt to integrate the best elements of the private banking model along American lines and the traditional development banking model of late industrialization. Instead, it has effectively banned the latter: "Since during the transition period of the financial system [and often beyond], commercial banks may be slow to engage in new activities, such as medium- and long-term lending, it has been anticipated that there will also be a need for limited direct lending operations by the PDB" (GOP, 1991). Yet all the World Bank has been willing to concede on this point has been to allow the PDB to lend directly 15 percent of its total operations, and only for a period of three years.

Pseudo-Privatization and the Bias toward Bankruptcy

The trouble with depriving Eastern Europe of genuine development banks, or comparable institutions whose mission was long-term invest-ment, is that restructuring is thereby left to an indirect process, priva-tization. Privatization has been an indirect means toward restructur-ing because it has not been "genuine," meaning it has not taken the form of the purchase by a private buyer of a state-owned enterprise in exchange for money (but rather in exchange for debt, as in Poland, or a voucher, as in the Czech Republic). With this pseudo mode of priva-tization, there is a greater risk than otherwise of massive bankruptcy. With nothing paid for an asset, there is less to be lost in disposing of it. Moreover, with pseudo-privatization, there is greater risk than otherwise that the new private owner will have little knowledge of the acquired firm in question and even fewer ideas on how to restruc-ture it.

All this was evident in the Bank's 1993 Enterprise and Financial Sector Adjustment Loan to Poland (GOP, 1993). State-owned banks were chosen as the direct restructuring agent in this loan project, be-cause they allegedly held the largest share of debt of financially insol-vent state-owned enterprises (although it is almost certain, as in the case of Uniontex, that the government held a bigger debt share). Nine state-owned banks were supposed to "restructure" roughly two thou-sand state-owned enterprises. Even if we ignore the dangers of "finan-cial monopoly capitalism" inherent in this scheme (or the develop-mental merits of a close association between banks and industrial enterprises, as in Germany), the nine state-owned banks, in existence only since the start of the transition period, had few restructuring skills and little "hands-on" knowledge of most of these companies. (Their major clients in the past, accounting for the bulk of their nonperforming loans, were the biggest SOEs, which were slated to be restructured under a different procedure because of the political impossibility of bankrupting them.)

To avoid "an excessive bias toward liquidation" (GOP, 1993), the loan to Poland from the Bank encouraged state-owned banks to use Chapter Eleven–type "conciliation procedures," whereby minority creditors could be forced into a debt-restructuring agreement with an enterprise "willing to restructure," that is, willing to accept a debt-for-equity swap that transferred a share of its equity to its creditors (and thereby terminated its employees' council governance). Why state-owned banks would be interested in such swaps in 1993 when they were uninterested in them earlier is unclear, although it was probably to their advantage to clean up their financial statements and rid themselves of their nonperforming loans on paper by "buying" these loans from themselves.

Assuming that state-owned banks swapped debt for equity, they presumably had an incentive to make their newly acquired property productive. But how? The Bank had in mind the following: "Typically, the restructuring plans will involve closing loss-making production units, carving out non-essential activities, divesting non-productive or underutilized assets and shedding excess labor" (GOP, 1993, p. 30). That these steps constituted a sure recipe for declining output and rising unemployment did not seem to be an issue. Moreover, how this restructuring approach was supposed to relieve the bottlenecks of state-owned enterprises that related to poor product quality, obsolete technology, and impaired pieces of capital equipment was altogether unclear.

To avoid a bias toward liquidation and bankruptcy, it would have been better to allow the best of the two thousand state-owned enterprises to self-select themselves for financial support through a competitive process and actually undertake "restructuring," in the form of relieving their most pressing bottlenecks. This was the approach that had been proposed by the OECD (1992a), and while not foolproof in terms of achieving efficiency, it at least had the merit of being grounded in a realistic assessment of the actual problems of state-owned enterprises in the early transition.

East Asia and the Bretton Woods Institutions

Successful East Asian late industrializers also had to contend with the World Bank, or an equivalent foreign organization—the American Occupation Force in the case of Japan and USAID in the case of South Korea (before the Bank became active in Korea in the mid-1960s). Both countries' experience have important lessons for Eastern Europe. First, many policies foisted on Japan and South Korea by international organizations were less neoliberal than those foisted on Eastern Europe by international organizations in the 1990s. Second, Japan and South Korea tended either to ignore or circumvent many of the policies that were neoliberal in spirit.

In Japan's case, American occupying forces championed a more equal income distribution through land reform; in Eastern Europe, by contrast, the Bank has regarded the region's highly equal income distribution as a socialist artifact that would have to disappear with capitalist development. The occupying forces in Japan also championed democratization, trade union organization, and employee ownership of former *zaibatsu,* whereas in post-socialist Eastern Europe the Bank has regarded workers' organizations such as employees' councils with hostility, as blockages to change (for Japan, see Miyajima, forthcoming). Both the occupying force in Japan and the Bank in post-socialist Eastern Europe pressed for demonopolization. Concentration ratios did fall in postwar Japan (between 1950 and 1972) and the big business groups, or *zaibatsu,* were decapitated (although they later regrouped as *keiretsu*). Nevertheless, declining industry concentration ratios had almost nothing to do with antimonopoly legislation (which was greatly relaxed starting in 1949) and a great deal to do with rapid growth itself in the context of industrial policies that sometimes encouraged but sometimes discouraged competition (Amsden and Singh, 1994). Finally, when Japan was forced to abandon its Keynesian policies and adopt the monetarist, anti-inflationary Dodge Plan in 1960, "which would have pushed many firms over the brink into bankruptcy," "the Ministry of Finance and the Bank of Japan got in touch with the General Head-Quarters Economic Scientific Section, which was not on the best of terms with Dodge, and put into effect a Tight Money Neutralizing Measure (Kane Zumari Kanwa Hosaku) that would channel the fiscal surplus back into private hands" (Nakamura, 1981, p. 39).

In South Korea, the Bank was highly respected by American-trained Korean economists. The government was pro-Bank to the extent that the Bank lent it political legitimacy. According to Kim Mahn-Je, the first president of the American-sponsored Korea Development Institute: "The Korean government appreciated the recognition from the Bank partly because of its internationally favorable impact, but it was even more important for domestic purpose[s]. *It provided a powerful and persuasive justification to the Korean public for the existence of a dictatorial government* devoted to economic development" (M. Kim, 1992, p. 59, emphasis added). Moreover, in the 1970s, before the Reagan-Bush era, the Bank supported Korea's drive into heavy industry, a move the Bank later harshly criticized:

> Both Korean policy makers and Bank economists agreed on the desirability of heavy and chemical industrialization through highly selective government intervention and typical import substitution under tariff protection. The Korean government–World Bank relations in the heavy and chemical industry drive in the 1970s did not take the form of the neoclassical market economists from the Bank checking the interventionist Korean officials. Bank economists in general were not dogmatic and knew how to harmonize textbook principles with real world constraints. (M. Kim, 1992, pp. 40–41)

Korean officials, wearied by USAID administrators' aid conditions, had energetically lined up alternative credit agencies other than those of the United States and the World Bank. Thus when the Bank withheld approval of certain Korean projects (the Pohang Iron and Steel Company for one, and Hyundai Heavy Industries' shipyard for another), the Koreans could raise investment finance elsewhere.

Kim Mahn-Je concludes about South Korea's experience with the pre-1980s World Bank: "I believe that Bank economists, in concert with Korean technocrats and economists mostly working at government research institutions [such as his own], played the role of checking government actions from going to extremes" (1992, p. 47). In post-socialist Eastern Europe, unfortunately, no such forces have emerged to check the Bank's extremes.

That no serious attempts were made to restructure promising state-owned enterprises in the early stages of transition was in part a consequence of World Bank conditions, which were premised on the belief that whatever restructuring was required should be the responsibility of the private sector acting in response to market forces. With privatization proceeding at a snail's pace, "development banks" of the region not being allowed to undertake development banking, and "nouveau-riche" commercial banks unwilling to lend medium or long term, the public sector in Eastern Europe has been "deserted" (Nuti and Portes, 1993).

Ironically, the immediate effect of desertion and do-nothingness has heightened the worst fears of the international bankers. With no attempt at restructuring, even the best state-owned enterprises have suffered acute financial distress and have been unable to pay their taxes. This, along with rising unemployment and related social expenditures, has been largely responsible for the huge budget deficits that emerged soon after the transition began (Frydman, Rapaczyński, and Earle, 1993). In Hungary:

At the end of 1991 Hungary had a budget deficit of about 4.5 percent of GDP, after a minor deficit in 1990. The main reason for the unexpectedly large deficit in 1991 was that the tax revenues from industry were below target. (Ibid., p. 101)

In Poland:

Despite attempts to adhere to a strict fiscal policy, the state budget ended 1991 with a huge deficit due to the poor performance of most enterprises. Failure to meet its 1991 fiscal targets cost Poland the support of the IMF. (Ibid., p. 155)

A vicious circle, therefore, was activated before the international lenders could help East European governments introduce new taxes (value added and income). The failure to initiate restructuring has incapacitated the state-owned enterprises and worsened the fiscal deficit. The medicine of still more restrictive macroeconomic policies to reduce the deficit has injured the state-owned enterprises further, making the sale of public assets much more difficult.

We have seen that the restructuring of state-owned enterprises, even promising, inherently viable ones, involves a long, drawn-out process necessitating government coordination and support for diverse reasons: amid political instability, private owners are not likely to take a long-term, profit-maximizing view, especially if they have no experience in managing the property they have been given by the state. With pseudo-privatization, under which nothing is paid in exchange for receiving a public asset, there is less to be lost in disposing of it and a greater tendency to dispose of it rather than restructure it.

The sooner it is recognized that subsidies of some sort are necessary to restructure, the sooner government coordination and support can be made above-board, systematic, and sensible, thereby avoiding the need to deal on an ad hoc basis with demands for government favors by private investors (foreign and local). The sooner it is accepted that a "mixed economy" will exist in Eastern Europe for the foreseeable future, the greater the chances of creating productive interactions between state- and privately owned enterprises. World Bank conditions, however, and the Bank's preoccupation with pseudo-privatization, have tended to pull in the opposite direction.

6

Enterprise
and the State

Post-socialist economic performance is driven by interactions between the state and the private sectors. In this chapter we focus on structuralist and mainstream ideas about how state- and privately owned enterprises may evolve. Economic analysis offers insights into sectoral prospects, but ultimately is out of its depth in dealing with profound institutional change. The firm-level studies presented in Chapters 3–5 and the sociopolitical considerations set out in Chapters 7–8 complement economic theory in seeking to explain how the policy climate and SOE/POE linkages determine development patterns in the medium to long run.

We begin with a brief review of theories of public enterprise, and then summarize the results of a simple model (presented in the appendix to this chapter) illustrating how state and private firms jointly influence each other's output, profitability, and growth. The model asks whether continued SOE operations stimulate or retard POE activity and capital formation or, in other words, whether SOEs "crowd" POEs in or out. Mainstream analysis points toward crowding-out, a conclusion that calls for shutting down state-owned enterprises with all deliberate speed. There are reasons to be cautious, however, about a presumption of universal crowding-out. Difficulties with privatization since the beginning of the transition suggest that state-owned enterprises will continue to be major players (especially in industrial sectors) for a long time to come.

Other characteristics of SOEs and POEs are also explored. The extent to which privatization—the transfer of titles to companies' liabilities from the state to elements in the private sector—may be desirable and what forms of ownership are likely to emerge are central questions. With regard to scope, we advance evidence about the continuing importance of semi-public and public enterprises in semi-industrialized countries. With regard to ownership, an important distinction is drawn between insider control of firms along lines characteristic of Germany, Japan, and most developing countries, and outsider control via financial intermediaries or direct household ownership of shares as in the United Kingdom and the United States. Orthodox reformers assume that an Anglo-American ownership structure is the goal, but there are reasons to think that the inside ownership alternative is more appropriate for the middle-income levels to which post-socialist economies can reasonably aspire.

Different modes of privatization are also discussed: rental arrangements and "flow" versus "stock" transfers of enterprise liabilities. Flow transfers can be analyzed in terms of changes in claims on existing financial instruments or in terms of shifts in the macroeconomic flows of funds. Stock transfers involve the creation of novel claims such as the privatization vouchers proposed in the Czech Republic. Risks are implicit in both kinds of operations.

Under any form of privatization, new economic actors will have to operate in unfamiliar financial and other market structures. Drawing on previous lines of analysis and on the experience of developing countries, we examine other financial issues, the quest for market (especially foreign trade) liberalization, and the agrarian question. We conclude that the state will have to be an active participant in the production and financial spheres of the economy. In particular, it should create innovative agencies such as development banks to support reconstruction of the production base.

All these observations suggest that novel enterprise structures will have to be embedded in post-socialist societies if they are to survive at all. Economic doctrine says very little about how this operation can be carried out. In line with Polanyi's (1944) double movement thesis discussed in Chapter 2, successful embedding is not likely to happen without the active involvement of the state as the only actor at hand with sufficient institutional power to offset the destructive by-products of the market. As economic sociologists and historians have long emphasized, output growth and equitable income distribution emerge not just from policy but from the social fabric. The natures of their societies will finally determine whether or not post-socialist economies make successful transits to their own forms of market capitalism. Chapters 7 and 8 set out the preconditions in detail.

Theories of Enterprise

Defining a "firm" and describing how it intersects with the rest of the economy are not easy tasks, as decades of debate among both neoclassical and institutional economists attest. Recent neoclassical models follow Ronald Coase (1937) as refined by Olivier Williamson (1985) in emphasizing tradeoffs between the difficulties of arranging transactions in the market against the inefficiencies of undertaking them within the firm, with different forms of enterprise emerging via the minimization of transactions costs. In a related literature initiated by Michael Jensen and William Meckling (1976), how firms function depends on the limits on information available to and the types of transactions between their potential owners ("principals") and managers or workers ("agents"). SOE/POE interactions are often modeled in these terms.

For practical purposes, any functioning enterprise has to be defined with a long vector of characteristics, including the behavior of markets for its inputs and products; the nature and quality of its productive assets (physical capital stocks, access to technologies, claims on sources of raw materials, and so on); the structure and quality of its management; and its outstanding financial and nonfinancial liabilities (equity, debt, implicit obligations to "stakeholders" such as managers, workers, and the communities in which it operates) and the characteristics of the holders of these obligations.

The distinction between state-owned and privately owned enterprises rests on who controls (the larger part of) their financial liabilities[1]—the state or the private sector. In Eastern Europe under socialism, of course, almost all enterprises in the industrial sector were in the hands of organs of the state. With exceptions such as three-quarters of the farmland in Poland, the government controlled most productive capacity in the service and agricultural sectors as well.

In the mainstream view, differences in ownership of SOEs and POEs lead them to *behave* differently. Public firms are consistently accused of being less efficient than their counterparts in the private sector, for a variety of reasons. An initial attack on planning and by implication on state-owned enterprises was launched from Vienna in the 1920s by Ludwig von Mises (1935), reflecting the anti-socialist tradition of Austrian economics. Mises argued that "as if" socialist planners, mimicking enterprise owners, would merely "play" a market game, because they would not be economically disciplined if they made mistakes. Moreover, a complete set of market exchanges is required to generate prices that will underwrite the efficient allocation of resources. If planners interfere with even a few fundamental price linkages (in particular the profitability calculus underlying investment decisions), their bungling can badly upset production.[2]

Complete "market freedom" was inflated into a prior condition for "political freedom" by Friedrich von Hayek (1944), another member of the Austrian school. His *Road to Serfdom* was paved with public interventions in the private market; he argued that once bureaucrats began to usurp citizens' rights to act in a completely unregulated economy, they would soon move against other forms of liberty as well. One key rationale for global shock reform programs follows directly from Mises and Hayek. Unless *all* the preconditions for laissez-faire are created at once, the road to a market economy can never open up. Unfortunately for this theory, however, experience in Eastern Europe suggests that global shocks put the roadblocks more firmly into place (see Chapter 2).[3]

In the wake of this "calculation debate" about whether or not central planning could be economically effective, mainstream analysts produced a string of models indicating that state-owned enterprises are doomed to operate inefficiently in comparison with their enterprise ideal types—firms controlled either by one (or a few) individual owner(s) or by the "public" through ownership of joint-stock companies in perfect capital markets. Jan Winiecki (1991b) recites the litany of these privately owned enterprises' abstract merits.

1. Hands-on owner-managers of small firms are in the best position and have the strongest incentives to control their operations, closely followed by corporate management well and truly disciplined by the stock market.
2. Such managers are also not subject to temptations to overuse a common property resource or to have short time horizons, weaknesses to which labor-managed firms are allegedly prone.
3. The good entrepreneurs that laissez-faire puts in charge of firms (assuming there are no barriers to the entry of new competitors) will have appropriate attitudes toward risk.

4. Market systems ensure both political rights and economic possibilities to innovate, assuming that venture capitalists are on the scene.

5. Because they dance in part to nonmarket tunes, politicians or bureaucrats in charge of SOEs will automatically be less efficient than capitalist management. They may seek to use the enterprises that they influence for their own ends, or even dip into the till.

It is convenient to analyze market failures (1)–(4) together with the political difficulty (5) under the rubric of principal/agent models. Managers of state-owned enterprises typically report to politicians, who in turn report to "the public." In a market system, this two-tier delegation of authority is replaced by an ownership link between principals and agents (or shareholders and managers), which is supposed to pressure the latter to run enterprises in an efficient fashion.[4]

Under socialism, János Kornai (1981) pointed to the "soft" budget constraint as a specific manifestation of the state-owned enterprises' problem. The now vanished principal/agent structure of socialist enterprises had planners with imperfect information trying to control managers who had their own black market sales proceeds uppermost in mind. Both sides benefited from high material throughput lubricated by the soft budget constraint (Yavlinsky and Braguinsky, 1994). Because they really didn't have the public's interest in mind and wanted to build up their own comfort, the principals from the *nomenklatura/* party apparatus encouraged this inefficiency to persist.

We will return in later sections to ask to what extent the foregoing arguments about the potential inefficiency of state-owned enterprises make practical sense. The answer will not be clear-cut. In terms of Albert Hirschman's (1970) famous distinction, a principal's threat to "exit" by selling out shares of an inefficient POE may not be more effective than a politician's or bureaucrat's "voice" in threatening SOE managers with dire retribution unless they improve. As Max Weber made clear, much depends on how owners and bureaucrats, managers and workers fit into the ruling socioeconomic system.

Interactions between State-Owned and Private Firms

In traditional economists' fashion, we can begin by asking how the two forms of enterprise influence each other's demands and supplies over time. Not many observers have been concerned with the ways in which state- and privately owned enterprises fit into economic growth. Among structuralists, for example, Nicholas Kaldor (1957) and Luigi Pasinetti (1962) concentrated on distributional strife between workers and capitalists owning liabilities (bonds) of the *same* productive firms. They did not ask how outputs and profit levels of different kinds of producers get determined. Amitava Dutt and Bill Gibson (1993) do raise the question, but under socialist as opposed to post-socialist institutional circumstances.

On the neoclassical side, Philippe Aghion and Olivier Blanchard (1993) take up the potential sustainability of post-socialist growth, emphasizing two deficiencies of post-socialist SOEs. First, these firms are alleged to pay excessively high wages and/or to have relatively high unit labor costs.[5] Second, they may well run losses because of their soft budget constraints and require subsidization from the fiscal deficit or state-controlled banks (recall that enforced bank loans to loss-making state enterprises are considered "quasi-fiscal" deficits in the jargon).

Under such circumstances, common sense as well as the simple model set out in this chapter's appendix suggest that the activity of state-owned enterprises should be cut back. Shutting down high-wage plants will put their departing employees into the low-wage general labor pool, from which they can be hired by efficient private sector entrepreneurs. Subsidies to the SOEs will also be reduced, leading to lower interest rates, less inflationary money creation, and perhaps growing demand for the products of the new POEs. Through at least these two channels, state enterprises crowd private sector operations out.

This scenario seems superficially plausible, but is problematic on closer inspection. First, SOEs on the whole do pay their taxes—as Chapters 4 and 5 make clear, only a small set of post-socialist heavy industries are subsidy-guzzling dinosaurs. Moreover, we have seen that increasing fiscal deficits in post-socialist economies in 1991–92 were in large measure due to reduced receipts from previously profitable state-owned enterprises as they *began* to run losses in stagnant macroeconomic environments.

Second, the supply side cheap labor story can easily be offset by demand factors, in part because supply responses to lower wages are likely to be negligible for reasons elaborated in other chapters. On the demand side, many privately owned enterprises sell intermediate goods to state enterprises—higher output for the latter means more revenues for the former. In addition, consumer expenditures from SOE-generated incomes may at the margin flow strongly toward private firms, especially in the previously undersupplied service sectors in which they thrive.

Under these revised assumptions, SOE operations crowd in private sector activity in the short run. If investment demand responds to current output levels (a plausible first approximation in most corners of the world), overall growth would also be sustained by the state sector. Since crowding-in effects *do* appear to be important at the current range of sectoral output levels (see the evidence in Chapters 3 and 4), keeping SOEs healthy appears to be a useful strategy to pursue. This goal in turn involves continuing roles for a government ministry of industry and development bank of the traditional kind, especially under present post-socialist circumstances in which SOEs account for the bulk of economic activity overall.[6] The practical implications of this observation have already been spelled out in Chapter 5.

Public and Private Enterprise Sectors

Official estimates of the private sector share of GDP in Eastern Europe and Russia indicate the importance of state enterprises under post-socialism (see Table 6.1).[7] It is clear that progress in privatization has

Table 6.1 Official estimates of the private sector share of GDP (including agriculture) (in percent)

	1990	1991	1992
Bulgaria		5	10
CSFR	5	9	
Czech Republic			20
Slovak Republic			20–21
Hungary (1)	10	27	35
Hungary (2)	14	16	25
Poland	31	42	45–50
Romania			26
Russia			7

Source: UNECE (1993). The two estimates for Hungary are based on (1) tax returns and (2) labor force data, respectively.

been slow, for many reasons. Initially, establishing various levels of government in the democratic successor states to socialism as the *de jure* owners of land, productive capital, and the housing stock was a nontrivial legal task. Estimating the asset values of the SOEs was difficult, as was their "corporatization"—the creation of Western-style organizational and financial structures.[8]

As these steps were completed, most large firms have ended up in the hands of "privatization agencies" of diverse forms. The agencies' main tasks are to continue operating the companies that they inherited and ultimately to turn them over to the private sector, another difficult maneuver. Small firms in many cases were sold off fairly quickly, but there have been complex and lengthy negotiations regarding the restitution of assets confiscated by previous regimes, the transfer of title to housing units, and the reorganization of agriculture.

It is also worth emphasizing that privatization has been especially slow in manufacturing. Table 6.1 includes data for all sectors, and thus measures "easy" privatization (or even statistical reclassification) in agriculture and the service sector. In most post-socialist economies, the private sector accounts for 20 percent or less of industrial activity, as compared with 50 percent or more in branches such as retail trade.

The shares of GDP accounted for by the national private sectors in Table 6.1 are bound to rise as difficulties are gradually overcome. It is important to recognize, however, that a goal of 100 percent private sector operation of the economy does not make sense. Despite a recent wave of privatization of public companies, no country at post-socialist income levels has gone so far as to turn its entire economy over to private operators. .

Indeed, if the numbers in Table 6.1 set upper bounds on SOE shares of production, data through the 1980s show that in semi-industrialized economies corresponding lower bounds on SOE shares in GDP and gross fixed capital formation fell in the ranges of 10–15 percent and 20–40 percent, respectively (Chang and Singh, 1993). Public enterprises included the most efficient steel plant in the world, located in South Korea (Amsden, 1989); a bevy of state firms in Taiwan used at different times to spearhead sectoral big pushes (Wade, 1990); and well-known productive companies in almost all developing nations.

SOE shares of output were cut back drastically after the late 1980s in a few countries, notably in Latin America, under the strong ideological influence of the Washington consensus. This rush to privatize may well reflect what Hirschman (1982) calls a "public-private cycle," a reaction to the inevitable disappointment with whatever means happen to be in place for addressing the socioeconomic problems of the day. The Thatcher government made privatization the vogue in the United Kingdom early in the 1980s; as lagging indicators of global political trends, developing economies took roughly a decade to join the pack.

There is no reason to expect the cycle to remain in an extreme privatization phase. Public companies were originally set up under capitalism to remedy perceived deficiencies of the unencumbered market that private enterprise has historically been unable to resolve. State-controlled firms have proved able to seize economies of scale or stake out leading sectors, to generate countercyclical investments along with stable savings flows,[9] and to assist in meeting goals of achieving social equity through pricing policy and employment creation. All these factors have to be weighed in any serious decision about privatization, even when starting with low private enterprise shares as have the countries in Table 6.1.

Next we consider the details of ownership structures per se. Table 6.2 provides a bird's eye view of the patterns that exist. First, "outside" or "arm's length" ownership of firms by households who transact shares in a stock market (either directly or by way of financial intermediaries such as pension plans and mutual funds) is a somewhat special case, largely restricted to the United Kingdom, the United States, and other economies that have inherited the British financial system. For its defenders, the stock market provides an ideal vehicle for enterprise own-

Table 6.2 Different ownership structures

Types of ownership	Types of enterprises	
	SOEs	POEs
Arm's length (outsider)	Success cases in many countries	United States United Kingdom
Hands-on (insider)	White elephants (?)	
Bank-centered		Germany Japan
Groups		South Korea Taiwan Many LDCs

ers to solve the principal/agent problem by exerting their "exit" option (see, for example, Jensen, 1986). Because firms are always open to hostile takeovers, the argument goes, their managers will act in efficient fashion to avoid losing their jobs.

The one-trillion-dollar corporate merger and acquisition wave in the United States in the 1980s constitutes an important test of this proposition. Did the efficiency of the American economy rise as a consequence of the ownership exit options exerted during these financial maneuvers? The results will take years to be assessed, but early estimates place social *losses* in the range of hundreds of billions of dollars due to lower wages, increased unemployment, business failures, huge debt burdens, and stagnant investment and research and development spending (Crotty and Goldstein, 1993). Managers became obsessed with their firms' short-term survival as opposed to sustained output growth, and many enterprises' stakeholders were severely hit. The takeover premiums that Wall Streeters gained during the merger and acquisition decade came not from squeezing out poor managers but from the paper increases in asset valuations and rising debt that accompany any speculative boom.[10] As will be seen, similar frenzies are a clear and present danger under post-socialism.

Second, even if massive financial failures do not occur, asset prices under post-socialism will convey scant information about firms' performance because they have had no opportunity to establish a track record in a market setting. Such an environment facilitates chicanery; as a counterpoise firms' principals hold down their incentive payments to managers, who as a result will not actively search for ways to raise efficiency (Tirole, 1991).

Under outside ownership, this difficulty can be exacerbated by a "free rider" problem pointed out long ago by Adolph Berle and Gardiner Means (1932) and amplified into a fundamental critique of capitalism by John Kenneth Galbraith (1967). Rather than aggressively disciplining the management whose salaries they pay, individual owners may be lax in their supervision. There is not much incentive for a minor shareholder to intervene in corporate affairs, so that managers à la Galbraith can go their own way, for example, operating inefficiently within wide limits. As many commentators have pointed out, "insider" or "hands-on" finance can help keep the agents in charge of firms on their toes.[11]

In continental European, Japanese, and Taiwanese practice, for example, firms partially control each other through cross-shareholdings. Each enterprise's large stake in several others reduces temptations for free riding. An individual firm will typically have close relationships with external sources of finance such as a specific bank or (in Germany, for middle-scale firms) state or local governments. Such large investors will often have representatives on the enterprise's board of directors. With insider knowledge and their own institutional income flows in mind, bankers or government officials can impose discipline on managers while at the same time providing credit (often by rolling over short-term loans) at moderate cost.[12]

In the Anglo-American model, firms first pay for investment by borrowing from banks (or, more recently, by entering the money market) and then refinance short-term debt from internal savings and by issuing long-term liabilities in the capital market. One implication is that the final cost of funds tends to be higher in the United States, since German and Japanese shareholder banks can internalize information flows and exploit scale economies in credit provision. A broad, liberalized capital market along Anglo-American lines may provide allocative efficiency by equalizing returns to different sorts of holdings, but it can also be productively *in*efficient, creating high costs of finance and shortening economic horizons.

One major risk with hands-on ownership is insider speculation. In Chile in the mid-1970s, for example, firms that had previously been nationalized under the Allende regime were rapidly privatized, with financial "groups" linked to the government being the major buyers. These conglomerates began borrowing from banks under their control to bid up their own shares' prices as the stock market boomed. Total financial holdings ballooned in comparison to real output and capital stock, in a characteristic signal of financial fragility of the sort that Hyman Minsky (1986) describes.

After the inevitable crash, a quarter of the assets of the banking system were nonperforming and the two biggest banks (each central to a conglomerate) lost more than five times their capital. Refinancing the conglomerates' bad debt required the creation of stocks of liabilities amounting to one third of GDP—externally (from the government to foreigners) and within Chile (from the central bank to households, and from the government to the central bank). Associated payment obligations will cost taxpayers several percent of GDP per year well into the next century.

This experience clearly implies that as private wealth builds up under a post-socialist transition, a combination of strict regulation and productive investment outlets will be needed to prevent its financially unsophisticated owners from replicating Chile's adventure. Particularly risky will be rapid wealth transfers such as those resulting from voucher privatization schemes of the sort perhaps getting under way (after many false starts) in the Czech Republic in 1993. Claims and counterclaims supported by "confidence" and Ponzi schemes (shrewd operators borrowing ever more from naive lenders on the one hand to pay off their expanding interest payment obligations on the other) can easily balloon under such circumstances.

A third observation from Table 6.2 is that insider control of companies is not isolated to continental Europe and Japan. As Nathaniel Leff (1979) pointed out some time ago, company "groups" or conglomerate enterprises are ubiquitous in the developing world. The South Korean *chaebols* are prominent examples, nourished by "rents" created by state industrial policy interventions to become production powerhouses.[13] Ha-Joon Chang (1993) argues that the conglomerate structure can create transaction efficiencies, holding down proliferation of both free-riders and rent-seekers because the state and the groups deal among themselves as large entities. They can "bundle" issues, permitting a bargaining solution to be devised because there is room for side payments on many related questions.

Theoretical explanations aside, the worldwide presence of company groups suggests that they will appear under post-socialism as well. Privatization schemes such as those discussed in the next section should be designed with this eventuality in mind. Conglomerates' benefits in terms of reducing transaction burdens and costs in terms of creating monopoly power (with a corresponding need for regulation or creation of internal or external competition) are likely to be important policy concerns.

Fourth, the "white elephants" in Table 6.2 are meant to suggest that ownership structures affect SOEs' performance as well. Arm's length public ownership combined with other incentives may push state-owned enterprises toward efficient operation, but there are no sure guarantees; along with good performers, public sector subsidy sinks and patronage havens are notorious far and wide. For the enterprises that will remain under state control for extended periods in post-socialist economies, one can think of several policies to encourage their productivity.

Objectives can be clarified, especially with regard to provision of social services. As Chapter 2 made clear, safety nets will be sorely needed during the transition, but to what extent should they remain the responsibility of firms? Presumably reduced provision of benefits to stakeholders should fit into enterprise planning along with building up retained earnings and undertaking badly needed capital formation.

Incentives also have to be modified in line with rethinking SOE goals. The day of the soft budget constraint may have ended, at least for enterprises that cannot claim significant political favors. But that does not mean that public (or nominally private) company managers do not have to be pushed to perform. Experience in East Asia and elsewhere demonstrates that an ongoing role of the state in encouraging, reorganizing, and at times eliminating firms can play an integral role in economic success.

The task of creating incentives, however, should not be allowed to overwhelm the government, assuming that the bureaucracy's tendencies toward aggrandizement of its writ can be contained. Creation of (or directed evolution of the current privatization entities toward) small, elite agencies to monitor state-owned enterprises may contribute to this end.

Finally, competition can play a role. Within a country, state-owned enterprises can be forced to compete with other public or private firms in markets where economies of scale and "natural monopolies" are not dominant. Participation in export markets can be a stimulating test. It should be recalled, however, that Japanese and Korean planners consistently steered clear of "excessive competition," especially in industries with big sunk costs that tend to engage in short-term price wars and extreme investment cycles over time (Chang, 1993). A role for licensing and regulatory policy thus opens up.

The moral of the foregoing observations is that there is no single road to capitalism, let alone to the size of the public sector or to the patterns of firm ownership. The Anglo-American institutional model dominates both received theory and the advice that Bretton Woods institutions and associated advisers are imparting to post-socialist and other economies in transition. Economies with relatively large shares of GDP and investment in the hands of state-owned enterprises and with insider organization of corporate control, however, have performed better economically in several dimensions than Britain or the United States since World War II.

Modes of Privatization

None of the transition countries has chosen a coherent, easily traceable path toward privatization. As already noted, control of large state-owned enterprises has been consolidated in the hands of privatization agencies, which now have to run the firms while at the same time trying to sell them off (or else pass them along to still other agencies set up to do the same thing). Small enterprises, especially in the service sector, are in the process of being sold to the public at large or to previous stakeholders such as managers and/or employees through auction or buy-out schemes.[14] In many cases, immobile assets such as housing were simply transferred to occupants for nominal charges, in a form of social restitution.

The major privatization issues center around farms and large public enterprises. How can titles and/or rights to exploit these assets be transferred? Only three methods (each with many variants) are at hand.

Rental arrangements are possible, including leases and extensions such as franchises and management contracts.

Equity of firms can gradually be sold off, through buy-outs, auctions, share flotation, and so on. These methods involve *flows* of funds, in the sense that buyers pay for their purchases from current incomes or else by running down their existing financial assets or running up liabilities. Privatization in industrialized and developing nations has uniformly been done in flow fashion.

New financial assets can be created by fiat for households, which they can then trade in directly or indirectly for the liabilities of the companies held by privatization agencies. This approach boils down to transferring a *stock* of wealth from the state to the private sector. There have not been many examples under Western capitalism. One was the wholesale distribution of Western land in the United States in the nineteenth century, when 160 acres went to each eligible farm family and millions of acres to railroad companies, universities, and other institutions. Two thirds of the hopeful farmers failed to stay on their new homesteads for the five years required to obtain clear title; swindlers and speculators reaped the gains.

In post-socialist agriculture, few people are homesteading their way into private farming (UNECE, 1993). Rental, rather than other forms of transfer, appears to be the rule. The reason is risk. Market prospects are weak, and banks are unable to provide credit. Most Western farms are subsidized, but post-socialist governments are unwilling to take up this standard practice (at least until worries about either self-sufficiency or gyrating food prices begin to vex policymakers' minds). Peasants are wisely adopting a wait-and-see attitude about land transfers and opting for contract arrangments, cultivation without clear title, or maintaining ties with state farms and cooperatives whose potential fates are anything but clear. This stasis is not promising for the future. The difficulties it creates for reviving agriculture are recounted in the following section.

Flow transfers may ultimately prove important in industry, but they pose problems of mobilizing finance. If we assume for the moment that only citizens or national firms acquire public enterprises,[15] then José Fanelli, Robert Frenkel, and Guillermo Rosenwurcel (1990) observe that they can pay for their new ownership in just four ways: (1) an increase in private saving; (2) a fall in private investment; (3) a decrease in the private sector's new acquisition of financial claims besides those issued by privatizing firms; and (4) an increase in the private sector's flow demand for credit.

Alternative (1) could be helpful for output growth if accompanied by a jump in investment. The public sector would probably have to be the motor, taking into account crowding-in effects of public on private capital formation. In other words, governments selling off state-owned enterprises should reinvest the proceeds instead of cutting the current fiscal deficit. This observation becomes doubly relevant if the private sector reduces its own capital formation to take over public firms.

Alternative (3) is more likely than (4), especially in post-socialist economies with primitive financial markets. But then the government will find it difficult to place its own liabilities, which will provoke it to emit money or bear higher interest burdens or both. There will be strong pressures to use the proceeds of privatization just to cover the public sector borrowing requirement with no spill-over to capital formation.

Finally, to the extent that public firms can be sold to foreigners, is their direct foreign investment "additional" to what would have arrived in any case? What about remittance obligations in the future? It *is* true that transnational corporations that are engaged in more than simple "sourcing" (local assembly or production of intermediate inputs) do not readily leave a country once they have entered and built up sunk capital, and that they can serve as vehicles for technology acquisition. But even in this area, East Asian experience suggests that in the long run an economy may be better off if it strives for technological competence on the part of its own firms (Amsden, 1989; Chang, 1993).

These financial flow concerns will be macroeconomically important if practical difficulties turn privatization into a long, drawn-out process. Flow transfers could amount to several percent of GDP for many years, given the levels of POE activity documented in Table 6.1. Flow transfers also include processes such as "transformation" (in Hungary), via which companies are wound up and their assets sold at scrap value. The effect of these operations on public investment and on potential private sector output growth cannot be promising, especially in the absence of a coherent industrial policy. As Chapter 5 underlines, industrial planning is not likely to thrive under the Bretton Woods institutions' present ideological predilections.

At the level of rhetoric, at least, post-socialist governments were committed to stock transfers as of 1993. Potential claims on the productive assets of the large firms held by privatization agencies were to be issued gratis to the public, typically as "vouchers." These pieces of paper could then be converted into equity in newly privatized enterprises directly, or else into shares of mutual funds. In other words, an Anglo-American type of financial system was supposed to be created at one stroke.

Free-rider and principal/agent conundrums immediately raise their heads. In contrast to their transactions under flow privatization, people swapping vouchers for shares would not be operating with portfolios built up over time. Unfamiliar assets and liabilities would be involved, so that their market decisions could be erratic or even frivolous. To avoid such risks of "pseudo-privatization," Eastern European reformers are creating a layer of financial intermediaries—"holdings"—between households and the firms that they will ostensibly own.[16] These entities are supposed to be large and powerful enough not to free ride. Either by takeover threats or by voicing the power of their big blocks of shares, they may force the management of newly privatized SOEs to maximize owners' returns. The theory sounds good, but one should be seriously concerned about how well the holdings will function in practice.

They could, for example, behave like the pension funds, mutual funds, and life insurance companies, which own 70 percent of outstanding equity in the United Kingdom. These entities exert scant leverage on the companies whose shares they own, and are essentially a veil for widespread free riding (Corbett and Mayer, 1991). On the whole, American financial intermediaries are no more aggressive. During both the financially quiescent 1970s and the turbulent 1980s, their takeover threats failed to impose efficient management on many corporations.

Or holding companies might take an activist role, restructuring firms and trying to stimulate entrepreneurship and technology acquisition directly. How these activities would be coordinated with national industrial policy is not clear. Are there to be *chaebols* that interact with national planners along cooperative lines, or conglomerates with tendencies toward excessive competition, or cozy cartels? The regulatory problems that these possibilities raise cannot be addressed simply by creating the holdings.[17]

In addition destabilizing speculation is always a risk in stagnant economies with many financially inexperienced actors. If they see little room for gain by pursuing production, insiders may seek to raise their own incomes by playing financial games. Small cases of speculation and fraud (involving only thousands of people losing their wealth) had broken out in several post-socialist countries by 1992–93. Perhaps the largest was the "Caritas" Ponzi scheme in Romania in 1993, which may ultimately generate billion-dollar losses in an economy with at most a $40 billion GDP. In laxly regulated financial markets hynotized by the laissez-faire ideology, can a truly "big one" à la Chile be far behind?

Finally, if the holdings do become more than a veil and the regulatory and instability problems that they create are adequately addressed, then they will almost certainly evolve in the direction of becoming the conglomerate groups that flourish in middle-income capitalist environments. Economically, such a "normal" course is perhaps to be welcomed, because relatively well defined enterprise groups can provide a means for embedding progressive capitalism into the socioeconomic system.

Socially and politically, however, group formation could raise problems. In many countries, conglomerates are based on close control of productive companies by small, homogeneous sets of people, united by kinship or confession. In all post-socialist nations, as ancient communal animosities suppressed under socialism for forty years are reappearing (or flaring into wars in the Trans-Caucasus and the former Yugoslavia), the tendency toward formation of community-anchored economic power may become cause for unrest among the vast army of economic losers that the current pattern of transition seems certain to create.

Other Institutional Changes

There are obvious reasons why the post-socialist policy debate is obsessed with privatization, but many other institutional changes are urgent as well. Here we examine ways to help production on the part of both SOEs and POEs. We begin with financial issues beyond ownership and control, and then go on to market (especially foreign trade) liberalization and agricultural concerns.

The best analog for a well-functioning financial system is good plumbing—a set of conduits that take money from places where it is in surplus to other places where it is needed. In the experience of both developing and some post-socialist economies, specific pipes have repeatedly turned out to be essential, especially in the key area of mobilizing funds for new capital formation and research and development.

First, for the reasons pointed out in Chapter 5, private commercial banks are not necessarily the dominant investment finance institutions in much of the Third World (and in many industrialized economies as well). Nonbank intermediaries may be essential, whether "informal" in the sense of the South Korean nonbank finance for working capital or "public" in the form of directed credits from the treasury via a state-controlled banking system (South Korea) or development banks (Brazil). Credit provision by the state—either directly or through development banks—has functioned successfully all over the developing world. Most developing country governments have positive net saving in the sense that their current revenues exceed current expenditures; as observed in Chapter 2, finance in post-socialist nations is likely to remain unbalanced until their governments become net savers as well.[18] State development banks are natural vehicles for tapping such flows and directing them toward investment in both the private and the public sectors. Post-socialist recovery is not likely as long as World Bank bans on development banking remain in place.

Second, definition of the financial dimensions of the "government" is often not clear-cut. At the very least, one has to distinguish the actions of national and local authorities. One understated aspect of European industrial policy (in Germany, Italy, Denmark, and Spain, for example) has been the fact that it is implemented by local governments which take ownership stakes in or otherwise provide finance and other forms of support for a middle stratum of industrial enterprises. Both narrowly economic and more socially oriented goals have been furthered by these actions.[19]

Transition economy examples include the town and village enterprises that have flourished in China since economic reform got under way there in 1978. As Ajit Singh (1993) points out, town and village enterprises do face hard budget constraints, because local governments depend on them for a large share of their revenues. At the same time, they receive help in a variety of ways—bureaucratic support, assistance in obtaining bank credit and material inputs, and so on. As with the "Third Italy" of small and medium-sized firms that thrives under the benevolent hand of local power, a form of "municipal socialism" is involved. There is no reason why it cannot carry over to decentralizing post-socialist governments in Eastern Europe and (especially) Russia.

Finally, as observed in Chapter 2, the socialist planning system was particularly deficient in incorporating technical advances outside the military-industrial complex. In advanced capitalist economies, research and development activities are supported by big companies, the state, and (perhaps most important) venture capitalists who provide funds for new entrepreneurs. In middle-income economies, the economic bureaucracy has played a fundamental role in pushing firms toward the technical frontier. How these functions will be fulfilled under post-socialism is as yet unclear, but unless the small but vital financial pipes that direct money toward technological advance are put into place, sustained economic growth will not occur.

Liberalization of external trade is another major goal of orthodox reform. This policy thrust has been a touchstone of Bretton Woods institutions' recommendations for many years, as for example in the context of import-led growth discussed in Chapter 4. The emphasis of the Washington consensus on getting rid of obstacles to foreign trade is surprising, however, for several reasons: sustained output growth in many countries has taken place with distorted trade regimes; trade policy shifts were overwhelmed by macroeconomic forces in the determination of less-developed countries' growth rates during the 1980s; and most formal models show that eliminating distortions is likely to be of second-order significance anyway. It is interesting to explore the intellectual rationale for trade liberalization, and inquire whether the underlying economic model can be restated to make it relevant to post-socialist experience.

The mainstream position rests on textbook theorems about how interventions should be designed. If an economy is initially very distorted, with high and variable tariffs and a proliferation of import quotas, most economists agree that steps should be taken to simplify and perhaps cut back the interventions. There *is* professional consensus in this regard; the problem is that different authors' policy remedies diverge. David Evans (1991) suggests that the Bretton Woods institutions' pharmacopoeia can be described as follows.

The mainstream does recognize arguments for intervention, for example, nurturing infant industries, repelling foreign dumping (however defined), and imposing "optimal" export taxes. Extreme complexity, red tape, and inflexibility in setting quotas and tariffs vaguely aimed at correcting these problems, however, are part of the heritage of state planning.

When there is a market imperfection, the corrective policy should be applied as "closely" to it as possible. A subsidy for an infant industry makes more sense than a tariff, for example, because the latter will induce a by-product consumption distortion.

Under competition in the standard Heckscher-Ohlin model, an import quota has an "equivalent" tariff, which will let the same quantity of foreign goods come in. Because the government gets the tariff's proceeds while producers benefit from quota rents, the tariff is preferable.

If producers have market power, they can squeeze extra rents from a quota. If they go in for rent-seeking, (or "directly unproductive profit seeking," or DUP, activity) by devoting productive resources to lobby for more quotas, this form of protection looks even less desirable.

All these points lead to a standard sequence of recommended policies. First, there should be macroeconomic stabilization; thereafter, quotas should be "tariffized"; and then the tariff schedule should be simplified to two or three rates in the 10–50 percent range, sufficient to provide some protection and generate revenue.

As part of the exercise, there will probably have to be real exchange depreciation to hold the trade deficit constant as quota/tariff protection is cut back. For this reason, capital market liberalization, which may lead to appreciation, should be postponed.

It is impossible to refute these arguments on their own terms; as often occurs in neoclassical formulations, they superficially sound like limpid practical reason. Their deficiencies lie in incompatibilities between their underlying assumptions and the world as it really functions. One clear example is the implicit orthodox presumption that DUP activity is solely a response to state interventions, when in reality the private sector readily generates its own distortions and rents. For instance, national economic authorities have to deal with external agents with significant market power such as transnational corporations, local monopolies, and the divide-and-rule tactics of indigenous capitalists when confronting labor.

In addition, the model treats its "distortions" as small perturbations to an economy assumed to be at full employment with investment determined by available saving (perhaps mediated by a variable interest rate). When these hypotheses are relaxed in investment-driven growth models like the one underlying Figures 6.3 and 6.4 in the appendix to this chapter, protection to a given sector can easily lead to faster overall expansion if it shifts up investment functions and/or stimulates technical advance.

Finally, the mainstream approach does not incorporate the trade patterns characteristic of less-developed countries and likely to emerge under post-socialism—for example, a strong dependence on imported intermediate and capital goods. Programming the level and composition of such imports has been key to the success of developmentalist states. In South Korea, instruments such as quotas, directed credits, and targeting were used to promote import substitution, which led to export growth (Amsden, 1989). Brazil used protection and licensing to build an automobile sector, which flourished until the economy was destabilized by the debt crisis of the 1980s (Shapiro, 1991). In India, in line with the experiences of regional development policy already discussed, small-scale producers of bicycles and machine parts were helped by local authorities and cross-firm cooperation/competition in Ludiana and other cities in the Punjab—they now sell throughout India and are expanding abroad (Tewari, 1991).

Interlinked factors underlie these examples. Technology is imperfectly tradeable, because local producers and workers have to gain the expertise to operate physical capital goods that are not produced at home. There are economies of scale in both production and technology acquisition, and externalities among output levels, prices, and technical choice. Room is created for intervention, which can be rationalized in neoclassical terms especially if it creates two-way information flows among regulators and producers, which increase productive efficiency as they expand. Evans (1991) underlines the following implications.

Protection is justified, and may be programmed more effectively if it is based on quotas. Quota rents on strategic, technology-bearing imports can help subsidize export activity. Quotas on competitive imports (which in effect persist in Japan and South Korea to this day) turn the national market into a place for profitable learning. Costs can be held down if firms are exposed to foreign competition on the export side; real wage increases force the cost reductions to come from productivity advance.

Rent-seeking may characterize the process of allocating quotas, but they can be tied to export and output performance. Ideology and public pressure can help keep DUP within "reasonable" bounds.

Two-way information flows are essential, whether from the top down, as with Korean bureaucrats dealing with the vertically integrated, conglomerate *chaebols,* or among small producers and local authorities, as in the Punjab.

If a well-designed quota allocation system under this second line of policy action leads firms to use strategic inputs to acquire technology and expand nontraditional exports, it may well raise potential output faster than a Washington consensus trade reform, especially if investment responds. Moreover, it allows for more decentralized decision making than liberalization imposed from the top. Guessing tariff equivalents of quotas, phasing the liberalization to avoid bankrupting viable domestic producers by taking away effective protection, and getting the exchange rate "right" are not easy tasks. Policymakers never find themselves in a practical position to solve realistically dynamic computable general equilibrium models to reprogram the price system in a liberalization shock. Witness the exchange and interest rate gyrations in Eastern Europe and Russia since reforms began.

Of course, there have been failures with interventionist policies in developing countries as well. The bottom line is that there is no royal road to a productive, technically proficient market system. As Dani Rodrik (1992a) shrewdly observed, ". . . if truth-in-advertising were to apply to policy advice, each prescription for trade liberalization would be accompanied with a disclaimer: 'Warning! Trade liberalization cannot be shown to enhance technical efficiency; nor has it been empirically demonstrated to do so.'" If their external doctors give them a chance, post-socialist policymakers would do well to read the labels on the bottles of the medicines that shock therapy forced them to begin to take.[20]

In closing, a few words about the transition in agriculture. A first, essential, observation is that large-field collective agriculture combined with small plots operated by members of the collectives (the model in much of Eastern Europe and the Soviet Union) was *not* dramatically inefficient in comparison with the heavily subsidized farms of the West (Pryor, 1992).[21] Like much of the rest of the socialist system, the collectives also provided a framework for social support that will not be easy to replace. Under these circumstances, a rapid privatizing dash toward Lenin's (1964) "farmer" or (worse) "Junker" road to rural market capitalism may be a very poor choice. Production losses and societal disruption could be extreme (McIntyre, 1992). Moreover, only large, efficient agribusinesses will have a ghost of a chance of selling their products over the barriers created by the European Community's Common Agricultural Policy.

Just as in the rest of the economy, regulatory issues figure strongly in agriculture (Rao and Caballero, 1990). As in any commodity market with low demand and supply elasticities and long investment and production lags, the state will have to engage in stabilization and control. For example, creating and disseminating new agricultural technology is a public sector activity most places in the world, but supply enterprises can also be encouraged to act in these areas. Crowding-in effects of public investment—in irrigation projects, for example—on private farmers' own capital formation are likely to be strong.

Price incentives do matter in agriculture, but largely by affecting resource allocation among different crops and input packages. Overall land and labor productivity increases typically require capital formation, new technologies, and nonprice incentives such as access to valued consumer goods and improved rural quality of life. Private markets alone cannot be relied on to provide these stimuli. Even if rural capitalists gradually emerge from the existing collective/private plot model, they will need public help.

The Embedding Operation

The political risks discussed here are only an aspect of a more fundamental difficulty that the transition presents: how is capitalism to be embedded in societies in which for decades it has not been able to fit?

Mises, Hayek, and other deep minds have grappled with this question, without clear success. Nonetheless, one can learn from the attempts at synthesis made by Marx, Weber, Polanyi, and others. In his theory of the origins of capitalism, for example, Marx stressed the importance of the institutions supporting accumulation. They have not reappeared in Eastern Europe and Russia under allegedly "market friendly" reform programs.

The mature Weber (1968) pointed to a complex causal pattern underlying capitalism's original appearance: "All in all, the specific roots of Occidental culture must be sought in the tension and peculiar balance, on the one hand, between office charisma and monasticism, and on the other between the contractual character of the feudal state and the autonomous bureaucratic hierarchy." These factors were essential in setting up capitalism as a system of institutionalized strife among shifting but well-defined social groups (Collins, 1980). At a more practical level, all successful or semi-successful reform programs in semi-industrialized countries in recent decades—including those in Spain, Chile, Turkey, South Korea, and Taiwan—have involved complex causal patterns and contingent historical events.

Polanyi's great insight has already been noted, that the institutions supporting the market system have to arise from within society, which also defends itself against the worst excesses of capitalism—child labor laws were passed early in the nineteenth century, for example, and the collapse of real wages in Eastern Europe was arrested at 30–40 percent late in the twentieth. Double movements of creating and then regulating market institutions will have to occur systemwide if the postsocialist transition is to go through.

As society's superordinate actor, the state will have to play a central role in forcing both sides of the double movement. The experience of developing countries also shows that states can fail in several dimensions (P. Evans, 1992). They operate under fundamental uncertainty, and may or may not respond to the uneven advances of different sectors, disproportionalities, and balance of payments and inflationary pressures that will inevitably arise (Hirschman, 1958). They can try to do too much, thereby achieving little. They can become purely predatory, as in the countless petty dictatorships around the world (and in the successor states to Yugoslavia, perhaps, when war finally ends there). Nonetheless, as theoreticians of backwardness from Gerschenkron to Amsden have pointed out, when backward economies do catch up the process is mediated by the state, in particular by an autonomous bureaucracy accepted by (or embedded in) the society overall. In postsocialist as well as developing economies, policies proposed by the Bretton Woods institutions will have very little to do with putting these institutional prerequisites for modern capitalism into place.

A Model of SOE/POE Interactions

Figure 6.1 illustrates how private enterprises and state enterprises affect one another in the short run, when the latter pay relatively high wages and depend on subsidies from the state.[22]

In the northeast of the four-quadrant diagram, the curve labeled D_s shows that higher POE activity (X_p) stimulates output of state enterprises (X_s), by income generation, which adds to consumer demand, and by intermediate purchases—both are familiar channels. A steep D_s implies that these demand linkages are weak, that is, that POEs have

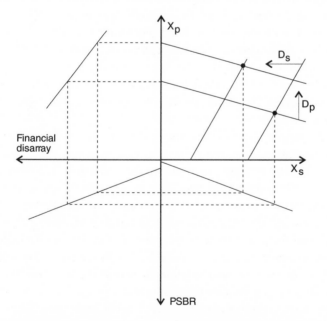

Figure 6.1 The orthodox view of state-owned enterprise/privately owned enterprise interactions in the short run. (PSBR = public sector borrowing requirement.)

marginal effects on the state sector, which still accounts for most of GDP (see the data in Table 6.1).

For reasons stemming from the supply side, the curve D_p for the effect of X_s on private sector activity slopes downward. The ruling hypotheses are that (1) a lower X_s creates unemployment by forcing SOEs to lay off their high wage labor and thereby reduces the wage level overall, so that (2) POEs are stimulated to raise their output X_p by lower labor costs.

POE activity will also be affected by the overall level of demand, determined in other quadrants of the diagram. In the southeast, the public sector borrowing requirement (PSBR) goes up with X_s: greater activity on the part of loss-making state enterprises forces their subsidy inflows to rise. In the southwest, this fiscal (or quasi-fiscal) problem is reflected in more "financial disarray," that is, inflation may speed up, interest rates rise, and contractionary policy be pursued due to the bigger PSBR. In the northwest quadrant, these responses to adversity cut demand for POE products and the intercept of the D_p locus slides down.[23]

Now we can ask what happens as SOEs are shut down by state actions such as decreasing subsidies, forced restructuring, and so on. The curve describing their activity level, D_s, shifts to the left by *force majeure*. Via a softer labor market and lower wages, POE output is crowded in directly along the downward-sloping curve D_p. At the same time, the intercept of D_p shifts upward due to a lower PSBR and reduced financial disarray. Both linkages imply that getting rid of public enterprises is a sensible policy to pursue.

The next step is to reverse the foregoing hypotheses, as discussed in Chapter 6. Figure 6.2 illustrates the implications. The D_p schedule slopes up instead of down, as a higher X_s raises X_p via stimulating increased sales (the standard assumption, at least in most models). In the southeast quadrant the PSBR declines due to higher tax revenues when X_s goes up. Cutting back on SOEs and shifting the D_s schedule to the left means that POE activity is crowded out, as the economy veers toward stagnation. In the world of Figure 6.2, shutting down SOEs on a large scale is not good medicine for the private sector, even if the state firms are inefficient in comparative terms.

Unsurprisingly, these cautions carry over to the medium and long term. The key questions are how capital formation and technological change respond to changes in short-run activity levels. Concentrating on investment, Figure 6.3 shows how shutting down SOEs may influ-

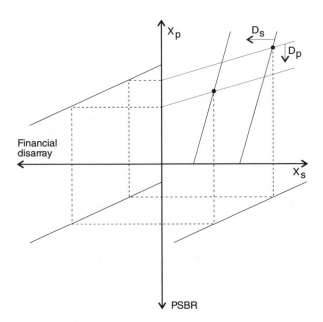

Figure 6.2   A more realistic view of SOE/POE interactions.

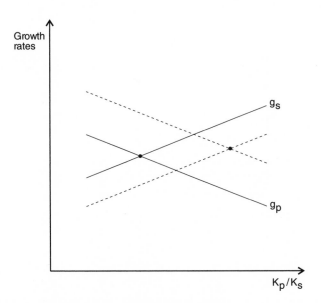

Figure 6.3   The orthodox view of SOE/POE growth.

ence resource allocation and the steady-state growth rate of capital stock under the orthodox hypothesis that higher state enterprise activity crowds out POEs.

Economists lack credible explanations for investment demand, especially under extremely uncertain conditions such as those prevailing under post-socialism. Two illustrative assumptions can be used to determine levels of capital formation in each sector, utilizing the ratio of sectoral capital stocks, K_p/K_s, as plotted on the horizontal axis in Figure 6.3.

First, when the ratio shifts toward sector i, its rate of profit r_i falls, that is, r_p (r_s) is a decreasing (increasing) function of K_p/K_s. In other words, a sector's profit rate (the ratio of its profit income to its capital stock) decreases as its relative capital stock increases, a thoroughly standard assumption. The second hypothesis is that each sector's capital stock growth rate g_i (the ratio of its net investment to capital stock in place) is stimulated by a higher profit rate r_i. Together with the first assumption, this means that g_s (g_p) rises (falls) with K_p/K_s, as shown. If SOE investment is insensitive to profitability, the curve for g_s would be roughly horizontal; profit-conscious POEs might have a strongly negatively sloped schedule.

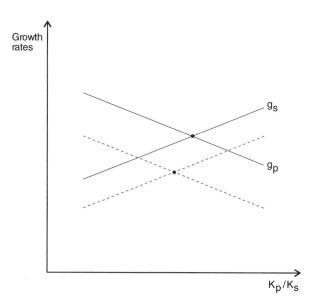

Figure 6.4 A more realistic view of SOE/POE growth.

When SOEs are shut down and POE ouput and profitability are crowded in, the curves shift to the dashed positions. SOE profit rates fall as they are curtailed and they invest less, moving down g_s. POEs respond to higher short-term activity levels by investing more. A new long-run or steady-state growth rate (with $g_s = g_p$) is determined by the point at which the two dashed schedules intersect. As Figure 6.3 is drawn, capital shifts toward the private sector (K_p/K_s rises) and the long-term capital stock or potential output growth rate speeds up.

As one might suspect, this growth rate result can reverse when state enterprises crowd in private sector activity, as illustrated in Figure 6.4, where both the g_s and g_p loci shift downward when SOEs are shut down. Output contraction in both sectors in the short run frustrates investment demand, leading to slow growth over time.

The moral of these scenarios is that it makes sense to look at how state-owned and private firms relate to each other in the economy at large. SOEs may well stimulate POEs by one channel and hold them back by another (various combinations of crowding out and in can be put together in the model just presented). These differential influences can go one way at low levels of activity and the other way at high levels; that is, the curves in Figures 6.1 and 6.2 could change slopes.

7

Challenges Facing
the State

Previous chapters have argued—theoretically and comparatively—
that the state must take an active role in the re-industrialization of
Eastern Europe. Yet even if one agrees that the market mechanism is
not enough, the question justifiably arises of whether the state can deliver. This question refers both to state capacity and to the various pressures to which the state is subject.

Before we address the problem of state capacity in the next chapter,
it is necessary to put the question of industrial policies in the broader
context of the challenges now faced by the post-socialist states and to
examine the extent to which these challenges are understood by the
intellectual and political elites of Eastern Europe. We argue that the
transition to capitalism—which, on the surface, might appear to be a
process of reducing the state's role—in fact calls for substantial state
efforts to make this very transition possible. We also argue that there
is only a dim perception of these challenges not only within the Bretton
Woods institutions but also among the elites of the East European societies themselves.

New Tasks for the State

It is not controversial to say that in any economic system the state has a
role to play. Even among the broadest circles of economists, neoliberals
included (with, perhaps, the exception of extreme libertarians), very
few would argue for the radical elimination of the state. Property rights
have to be defined and secured, and there always is a need to develop
and implement macroeconomic and social policies. Markets that must

be regulated include foreign trade, monopolies, labor, and drugs and hazardous materials as well as strategic commodities such as energy sources. The need to invest in infrastructure, research and development, and education is also universally recognized.

In post-socialist countries, however, there are additional reasons for the state to play a considerable role. Reasons include these nations' lack of adequate market institutions, their need to catch up with the world's technological frontiers, and their need to exploit their considerable human resources and semi-industrial capabilities. Industrial policies, which are the focus here, have to be seen as only one task within the wider context of the state's lengthy agenda.

In advanced countries, the institutional infrastructure of market and capitalism—together with the necessary attitudes and cultural framework—developed to a certain degree "organically," over the course of a long historical process. Friedrich von Hayek (1945) himself, one of the leading figures of economic liberalism, stressed the need for the historical, organic development of market institutions. In Eastern Europe, even before pseudo-socialism, capitalism never fully developed and markets were deficient (Chirot, 1989). Pseudo-socialism then destroyed most of the existing market institutions. In the post-socialist era, the process of market creation must be speeded up with the state as its main agent. But markets can hardly be constructed overnight.

In pseudo-socialist countries, moreover, there were only very limited possibilities for genuine voluntary associations (nonprofit nongovernmental organizations) which, in the West, fill the gap between the state and the private sector. While supporting the private sector, these associations meet needs that the market cannot satisfy and often cushion people from at least some of the market's adverse effects. Chambers of commerce, mutual insurance, education organizations, professional societies, cooperatives, churches, charities, and clubs—all these institutions, so vital for modern society, had almost no place under pseudo-socialism. Although similar associations now need to be developed, the state, which performed many of their functions, cannot simply shed its social responsibilities.

New welfare arrangements have to be created. Pseudo-socialism was a peculiar sort of corporatist society (Chirot, 1980; Ost, 1989), and welfare was provided in part through the work place and in part through specialized, comprehensive bureaucratic arrangements, financed from the central budget. Both those sets of institutions are now deteriorating. At the same time, expectations concerning the level of provision are quite high. A new, more efficient, and more flexible system has to be built for taking care of the unemployed and the disabled. This task cannot be postponed, not only for humanitarian reasons, but also because such a postponement might be politically explosive and destabilizing to the process of reform itself.

Another set of tasks for the state is related to its international economic position. Many East European countries, Poland, Hungary, and the Czech Republic in particular, aspire to membership in the European Community (EC). Even leaving aside the issue of the high level of regulation of West European economies, the process of gradually adjusting East European institutions and economies to the requirements of the European Community demands strong state leadership. After the breakdown of COMECON, state leadership is also needed for reconstructing trade and facilitating cooperation within the region. A weak state will not be a good agent for the tough negotiations required.

There are also several types of debts, some explicit, some implicit, that have to be repaid, including foreign debt and ecological debt (to clean up the environment, neglected for decades). Heavy investment is also needed in the infrastructure, which was largely disregarded under late pseudo-socialism. It is difficult to imagine how any of this can be accomplished without state involvement.

It also bears repeating that a huge sector of state-owned enterprises still exists, and the continuing process of privatization requires state involvement. State leadership is also needed to manage those state-owned enterprises that are either difficult or undesirable to privatize. Understandably, under the conditions of the transition, private capitalists have tended to take a very short-term profit-maximizing perspective. The state's longer-term investment horizon will be crucial for the re-industrialization of mid-tech industries and sustained economic development.

Even if, for purely ideological reasons, some form of liberal, free market economy is the ultimate aim, it cannot be produced instantly. For pragmatic reasons, the process must be gradual. In countries with strong traditions of market and capitalism, such as France or Germany, the process of liberalization after World War II took decades. It is an open question whether a free market economy can be achieved much faster in post-socialist countries.

The tasks the states face are formidable in themselves, and are often in competition with one another. The difficulty in addressing them stems not only from their inherent difficulties but also from the intellectual and political climate, which is hostile to the concept of the state acting as an autonomous agent of social and economic change.

The Collapse of Pseudo-Socialism and Neoliberal Ideology

When pseudo-socialism collapsed in Eastern Europe, anti-statist feelings predominated among the emerging political elites. Such sentiments were hardly surprising, since for years totalitarian bureaucracies had interfered with peoples' lives in every possible way, from the mass killings under Stalinism to the petty chicanery under the relatively lax regimes of Hungary or Poland of the 1970s. The state, while omnipresent, was also inefficient in solving the little problems of everyday life. Its officials were visibly corrupt, especially during the later phases of pseudo-socialism.

Communist ideology was never widely accepted in many East European countries. In Poland, it was contained by Catholicism and nationalism. In Hungary and Czechoslovakia, which had strong cultural bourgeois prewar traditions, the Soviet interventions of 1956 and 1968 destroyed whatever sympathies might have developed toward Soviet social models. Romania, though under the Ceauşescu regime unquestionably the most authoritarian of the East European nations, developed its own strongly nationalistic tradition (Verdery, 1991). On the level of intellectual discourse, communist ideology was contained by local prewar intellectual traditions and by the influence of Western thought. On the left, communism as a social project was always perceived as less desirable than a democratic version of socialism. The crushing of Dubček's reforms in Czechoslovakia in 1968 and the anti-intellectual and anti-Semitic campaign of the same year in Poland ended any wider sympathies to Marxism as well as any illusions about the reformability of "real socialism."

Attitudes toward state power have also been affected by the history of each country. Nearly everywhere in Eastern Europe communism was instituted by a foreign power, and the country's traditional relations with Russia tainted its attitudes toward the imposed state. (Bulgaria, with its Orthodox religion and sympathetic feelings for Russia owing to the latter's help in shedding the Turkish yoke, might be an exception.) The Poles never forgot that they had been forcibly incorporated into the Russian empire at the end of the eighteenth century, or that they had fought against Russian domination in two uprisings in the nineteenth century as well as a war in 1920. Poland lost half of its state territory to the Soviet Union in 1939, while nearly two million Polish citizens were deported and tens of thousands murdered. The Hungarians, Czechs, and Slovaks, whose modern culture developed under the Western influence of the Habsburg Empire, not only had communism imposed on them by the Soviet Union, but were invaded in 1956 and 1968. All over the region, the perception of the state as an alien force considerably weakened its authority.

The last fifteen to twenty years of communism, moreover, were accompanied by the anti-statist, neoliberal ideologies of the highly developed West European countries. During the 1950s and 1960s, the ideological climate of the West was substantially different than in more recent years. Then the goals of full employment, growth, and development were basic components of the prevailing ideology (Van der Vee, 1986, pp. 32ff.). Even if the aim was to construct free market economies, states were active in the postwar reconstruction of Western Europe (and Japan). Post-Keynesian theories lay at the roots of anticyclical intervention. In Europe, social democrats were active in designing the welfare state, while in the United States, Democrats worked toward the realization of the "Great Society." In many Third World countries, planning and even direct state involvement in production were considered a means of combating poverty. The same Bretton Woods institutions, particularly the World Bank, that now advocate a free market approach were then much more in favor of development planning. Even Soviet-style economies, while treated with political suspicion, were regarded as possibly feasible systems that might be attractive to less-developed countries. Indeed, much of the Western economic aid effort in Third World countries was an effort to provide an alternative, non-Communist method for state involvement in development. Intellectually, this approach was rationalized by a whole new discipline of development economics.

During the 1970s there was a profound change, and different views, advocating minimal state intervention, triumphed. The reasons for this shift included stagflation in the highly developed countries (of which excessive public spending was considered an important cause), the failure of many development projects in Third World countries, and the growing debt crisis. In the late 1970s and then the 1980s, there was a growing realization that the experiment with centrally planned economies had failed. Considerable segments of voters in the West, the middle classes in particular, grew dissatisfied with the ever-expanding state, which in part explains the phenomenal popularity of Ronald Reagan and Margaret Thatcher. At the same time, the exceptional communication talents of both these leaders gave an additional boost to anti-statist sentiment. In Western Europe, the social democratic parties unequivocally withdrew their earlier support of partial nationalization. The welfare state structure also came under criticism and was to some extent dismantled.

But despite the shift in popular sentiments, there were only marginal practical changes in the economic institutions and policies of the highly developed countries. Compared with the overall structure of their economies, there were small changes in the scales of taxation, some budget cuts here and there, and this or that institution was reduced. Even the highly acclaimed British privatization affected only a limited number of enterprises over a rather long span of time.

Anti-statist sentiments, however, acquired a strong theoretical basis owing to the fast growth of traditional branches of neoclassical economics—microeconomics, and even more so macroeconomics, the basis of the monetarist approach. They also grew due to the neoliberal "new political economy," which claims that state involvement distorts price signals and also inevitably produces rent-seeking activities (Krueger, 1974; Buchanan, Tollison, and Tullock, 1980). A younger generation of economists in the West and elsewhere grew up within this new paradigm. The majority of Nobel Prizes in economics have gone to proponents of unregulated markets, close to the Chicago school. Because the prevailing mood is that one economic approach is suitable for interpreting any set of circumstances and is, moreover, a good guide for interpreting human behavior in general (Becker, 1976), development economics has been proclaimed in decline even by some of its creators (Hirschman, 1981).

As is usually the case, dissenters to the new orthodoxy have appeared. They call for "bringing the state back in" (Evans, Rueschemeyer, and Skocpol, 1985), but they are largely gathered within the disciplines of sociology and political economy, and have only recently appeared within formalized structuralist macroeconomics (Taylor, 1991). It is difficult to disregard the East Asian experience, but proponents of neoclassical orthodoxy have tried to incorporate it within their paradigm and show that the state's role has been either irrelevant or harmful (World Bank, 1993; Amsden, 1994b).

These intellectual and political developments have had a profound effect on intellectuals, analysts, and policymakers in Eastern Europe, especially in the most open countries, Poland and Hungary. There are, obviously, great differences among the East European nations. In Poland, and even in Hungary, many intellectuals were able to be openly rebellious; but in Bulgaria, for example, "economic and social science was very conformist: most of the country's scholars and institutions were closely connected with the government and remained loyal to the 'party line'" (Nikova, 1994). In the more open countries, outside influences had effects much deeper than many Westerners realize. The elites of these countries were in search of categories that could help them to come to terms with their everyday experience—namely, the visible material, social, and moral decay of their societies. The liberal idea that the more state is engaged in the economy, the less efficient the economic system is, seemed to fit their experience perfectly. It also fit well with the popular belief that people care more about things they own.

While acknowledging that there are substantial differences among these nations due to both their intellectual traditions and their degree of openness to the West, we can still note general changes in the perspective of East European economists. Primitive, dogmatic, official Soviet Marxism, an obligatory staple of every East European student of the social sciences during the early fifties, began to soften in 1956, giving rise to ideas of "market socialism." This term, however, was not in use, and the discourse was initially within the Marxist categories of "the law of value" rather than in the marginalist terms that Oskar Lange used when he launched the idea in the 1930s. (The full version of his classic text was not even available in Polish until the late 1970s.) Party reformers in Poland, in Hungary, and to a degree in Czechoslovakia, trying to decentralize and rationalize command economies, worked within this paradigm. Although they realized the inefficiencies of the existing system, both academic economists and party reformers stopped short of questioning the political constraints and the problem of ownership. The dynamics of both this ongoing debate and the actual systemic changes are described by the Polish economists Włodzimierz Brus and Kazimierz Łaski (1989). Both were engaged in pressing for reforms, and both were forced to emigrate after 1968.

In Poland, mainly due to the work of Michał Kalecki and Ignacy Sachs, growth and development economics became an important subject, especially in regard to less-developed countries. Kalecki, Oskar Lange, and Czesław Bobrowski (the father of the Polish pragmatic, pre-Stalinist reconstruction planning of 1946–1948), with many others, often served as United Nations advisers in developing countries. Their methodology was applied to analyze the growth possibilities of socialist economies and to devise methods of long-term planning.

Intellectual life, particularly in Poland and Czechoslovakia, was dealt a serious blow in 1968 by the Soviet invasion of Czechoslovakia and by the anti-Semitic and anti-intellectual purges in Poland. In the next decade, except for the lip service paid by official ideologues, very little Marxism was left in Hungary and Poland. The developmental ideas of Kalecki (who died in 1969) and Sachs and Bobrowski (who left the country) were largely abandoned. Since Poland and Hungary (in contrast to Czechoslovakia after 1968) were relatively open countries, however, their intellectuals were receptive to Western thought. Under late pseudo-socialism, there were many ways for Western ideas to disseminate. Poles and Hungarians (and Czechs to a much lesser degree) traveled and studied in the West, read the books and journals that were available, and consumed samizdat publications (Skilling, 1989).

The career of Leszek Balcerowicz provides an example of Western influence. Balcerowicz, who introduced Poland's stabilization plans in 1990, had been a Communist Party member but left the party when martial law was declared in December 1981. He had earlier worked for a party research institute. He received part of his training at Johns Hopkins University, however, and he was the author of the most radical, pro-market proposal for economic reform in 1980–81. During the 1980s he chaired a seminar on comparative economic systems, and some of his students later became his close collaborators in 1990.

During the 1970s, the more independent thinkers (sociologists were at the forefront) engaged in a critical analysis of the economic system. Although very little of their work was published, the idea that the Soviet-style economy was inefficient and dysfunctional gradually became universally held. At the same time a parallel view also developed that market reforms could have only a limited effect within the existing political framework.

One of the important discoveries during this period was that the informal industrial and regional lobbies were very strong and able to manipulate the central planners. The lobbies had a monopoly of information as well as political strength that they used to their own advantage, mostly pressing for investment funds and for wages. According to this interpretation, the central planning authorities were, despite their apparent political power, weak in relation to the enterprises and regions, and were often unable even to obtain a correct picture of the ongoing economic processes. The central authorities could not decide on the course of economic strategy and were unable to demand compliance from the enterprises. The behavior of the firms was characterized by extremely powerful "investment hunger"; they were motivated by both economic and noneconomic reasons and were not restrained, unlike under capitalism, by fears of failure (Kornai, 1980, pp. 189ff.). Although these findings were not formulated in terms of rent-seeking, the parallels are obvious. This behavior is still remembered in the 1990s and may partially explain the discomfort East European economists feel when dealing with large industrial organizations. Such firms or groups of firms are often automatically perceived as inefficient giants, hungry for subsidies and ready to resort to manipulation and political blackmail.

More generally, Kornai's (1980) volume on the economics of shortage (which was in fact a synthetic model of the functioning of a Soviet-type economy at a late stage) and his widely read article (1986) on the limits of economic reform provided testimony for the newly emerging paradigm shared by the more independent-minded East European analysts. David Stark and Victor Nee (1989, p. 10) comment: "The significance of Kornai's theoretical breakthrough is that he showed how the same mechanisms that produced rapid economic growth in planned economies give rise, in the long run, to an economy of chronic shortage, hindering further economic growth."

In this analysis the market system, as the opposite of real socialism, has naturally tended to be idealized. Highly abstract theoretical models of markets, however, have been better understood than the real, everyday management practices of Western business enterprises. In addition, mainstream neoclassical micro- and macroeconomics has had more of an appeal than, for example, post-Keynesianism or macrostructuralism. The East Asian experience has not been studied in a detailed way, in part for prosaic reasons such as distance and in part because the Eastern bloc had no diplomatic relations with South Korea and Taiwan until the end of pseudo-socialism. Adam Lipowski and Jan Kulig published the first Polish work on the South Korean economy only in 1992. Generally, as far as the Asian model has been known or, rather, imagined, its characteristic authoritarianism, social conformity, lack of individualism, and, last but not least, labor discipline have been perceived as unattractive and so remote from the culture of East European societies as to make it irrelevant.

Members of the younger generation of post-socialist economists, often educated in the West, have been fascinated by the mathematical elegance of neoclassical economics. Despite the lack of textbooks, these ideas were transmitted into the classrooms of better universities, where the students read samizdat editions of Hayek and Friedman essays. Although there was constant talk about reforms, the idea of introducing capitalism was perceived as politically unthinkable until the late 1980s. The domino-like collapse of communism brought an abrupt turnabout and a triumph for economic liberalism.

In the case of Poland, one can rightly ask how neoliberal attitudes have been accommodated within the presence of a strong trade union movement, especially given the active role of employees' councils in Polish state enterprises since 1981. This question cannot be answered without taking into account strictly political factors. Solidarity in 1980–81 was not so much a trade union as a political, and almost revolutionary, national movement against communism. As such, it received the wide support of many intellectuals, who under different circumstances might have been much less sympathetic toward union power—as, indeed, they are today. Many intellectuals were deeply involved with Solidarity as advisers and even activists in 1980–81, and during the clandestine part of its history (it was relegalized in 1989). Most of them, however, left it after 1990. They had either become engaged in the newly emerging political parties or left simply because they objected to the redistributive politics of the union after 1989. The union, abandoned by talented leaders, often turned to cheap populism, and the workers' attitudes in general began to be perceived as unfortunate residuals of the epoch of "real socialism." Because strong unions are usually found in large enterprises, the whole structure (the large enterprise and its unionized labor force) tended to be viewed as a leftover from earlier times. Although many liberal economists simply spoke of the unavoidable costs of transition, more sensitive observers regretted that the workers, who had rebelled against communism, then became victims of the change to a market economy.

During the 1980s, employees' councils were accepted by many people as an independent force against the system (similar to unions). At the same time their management functions were treated, under the circumstances, as a politically feasible approximation of private property, as they made enterprises more independent from the government. Referring to his experiences in designing blueprints for radical market reform in the early 1980s, Balcerowicz (1992, p. 12) explains the favorable position he and his associates developed at that time in regard to the employees' councils: "To have an independent enterprise, it is necessary to sever its links to the planning center. In such a way, we arrived at an idea of employee councils."

After 1989 radical neoliberal ideas had, perhaps paradoxically, wide popular support. As Jerzy Szacki (1993) has pointed out, however, it is necessary to distinguish between political and economic liberalism. Liberal parties have become active in many post-socialist countries, and are usually represented by relatively young, well-educated, and Western-oriented politicians. This orientation has also been very visible in the media, especially in the press, which, at least in Poland, has had a very liberal, pro-market bent. Solidarity is probably the only trade union in the world that, for a short period of time at least, supported radical market reform. It is not difficult to explain this apparent contradiction. In the popular mind, capitalism was, at least initially, positively associated with a consumer society, and there was a universal feeling that the previous system had been a total failure.

The widespread popular support for neoliberal ideas started to crumble after the effects of "shock therapy" took hold. (The small Polish liberal party, which even had a prime minister for several months, lost out completely in the 1993 elections.) Neoliberal opinions, however, are still predominant among academics, journalists, and politicians. Because there is a huge demand for skilled white-collar personnel in business, media, and government, many members of these highly educated groups gain from the new situation. Their attitudes are also reinforced by the fact that academic exchange with the United States is much easier than, say, with Japan, that the new economic textbooks available for translation are American, and, last but not least, that the Bretton Woods institutions are an important employer for local consultants.

It would be a gross oversimplification, of course, to claim that neoliberal views constitute the only prevalent ideology in Eastern Europe. There are voices among the older generation of economists that have been raised in favor of state interventionism and industrial policies, but the credibility of such positions is weakened by their authors' association with the previous regime. Indeed, the recent split within the Polish Economic Association is along these generational, political, and theoretical lines. Moreover, and probably more important, these views are weak in an intellectual sense. They are not powerful enough to challenge the neoliberal orthodoxy on its own ground, with full appreciation and understanding of the force and refinement of neoclassical arguments.

Proponents of a social democratic way of thinking, who stress a greater role for the state and argue for a more gradual transition, are also evident. The views they hold are sometimes labeled "a Third Way," to denote their differences from both communism and capitalism. This name is confusing, however, because it was used earlier with different, and often ideologically loaded, meanings. Stafania Szlek Miller (1992) provides a comprehensive review of the various ways the concept of the third way has been used. In Poland, Karol Modzelewski provides a very good example of the social democratic critique of crash market reform. He is an important figure not only as a prominent intellectual (and medieval historian) but also because of his impeccable political credentials. A Communist until the early 1960s, he then spent several years in prison for publishing a neo-Marxist pamphlet criticizing Soviet-type bureaucratic socialism. He was a spokesperson for the Solidarity trade union and inventor of its name. After martial law was declared, he was once again imprisoned. In the early 1990s he became an honorary chairman of the new social democratic party, the Labor Union. He is against "pseudo-privatization," and has argued (1993) for mixed state-private ownership as an intermediate step in the process of transferring ownership of state-owned enterprises. He believes in taking employees' councils as partners in systemic change, and disagrees with taxes such as the *popiwek* (excess wage tax). He also argues, although in an unspecified way, for interventionism and industrial policies, using protective tariffs, preferential credits, and subsidies or state investments. His views, however, represent only a minority of those of Polish intellectuals.

There is no question about the significance of the attitudes of intellectuals. The types of categories they try to forge and the content of their discourse are important because, through the media, they reach a wide public. Earlier they affected popular opinion through samizdat publications, and since 1989 they have been heard through the press and the electronic media. They form the core of the post-socialist political class, and many have become members of cabinets all over Eastern Europe.

When fulfilling the neoliberal vision was attempted in the economic sphere at the very beginning of the post-socialist period, it was often conceptualized as a return to something "normal" and "proven." There were implicit assumptions that the simple removal of the market's institutional barriers would cause its organic, spontaneous development. Apart from the popularity of Western thought, there were many objective reasons for such attitudes in Poland, Hungary, and Czechoslovakia. Czechoslovakia, despite the freeze of the Husak period, had always had a strong tradition of bourgeois culture. There were also strong pro-market tendencies within the Polish and Hungarian economies. Polish agriculture was not collectivized, while in Hungary there had been a de facto reemergence of family farming within the statist framework, with strong embourgeoisement tendencies (Donath, 1980; Szelenyi, 1988). A small craft and trade sector operated, and there was always a black market, which, during the 1970s and especially the 1980s, developed into a full-fledged "shadow economy" (Bednarski, 1992). The shadow economy had many advantages. Its existence alleviated chronic shortages, and encouraged the rise of entrepreneurs, a class of capable people, ready to seize opportunities. The shadow economy flourished on the borders of the legal economy, and involved, to a considerable degree, many members of the ruling *nomenklatura*. At the end of the 1980s, with the relaxation of rules for private business, many of these shadow enterprises emerged into legality. The fast rise of small business misled some analysts, who confused the rise of the market economy with the rise of full-fledged capitalism, capable of producing long-term growth.

The Contingency of Capitalism

The fathers of "shock therapy," when claiming a return to "normality," misunderstood the historical experience of the West. In a historical sense, capitalism is anything but "normal." On the contrary, it is accidental. It spontaneously developed only once—in late medieval Europe, in northern Italy. It later spread north of the Alps and to North America. Capitalism then produced the industrial revolution at the turn of the nineteenth century.

Both classical economists and Marxist economists have tended to believe (on totally different grounds) that there was something "natural" (liberals) or "inevitable" (Marxists) in the development of market and capitalism. Today this view is no longer commonly held by historians, who now generally agree that the birth of capitalism in Europe was the outcome of a rather unusual set of ecological, economic, social, and political circumstances—a result of, as E. L. Jones (1981) and others described it, a "European Miracle." Looking at economic history from a comparative perspective, they point out that other, more ancient and highly sophisticated civilizations, China for instance, did not spontaneously develop capitalism.

In the context of our interest in the development of market and capitalism in Eastern Europe, it is useful to differentiate between the two, since although they are deeply related, they are not the same. When we look at highly developed agrarian civilizations, we see that market exchange was the nearly universal, though not exclusive, mode of organizing economic life. Although the market was usually highly administered, it was, as Polanyi, Conrad Arensberg, and Harry Pearson (1957) have shown, accompanied by reciprocity and redistribution. Capitalism, however, is unique. Fernand Braudel (1981–1984) analyzed in detail the relation between the unplanned development of market exchanges on the family level and the rise of capitalism in Europe during medieval and modern times. The former, Braudel noted, were truly spontaneous, organic, and "normal." People need things that they are unable to produce themselves, so someone specializes in producing them. Capitalists, on the contrary, are not numerous, and they can flourish only under particular circumstances. Capitalists are not simply people engaged in market economy. They operate in markets that are distant in time and space. They have specific, rare skills, and they try to monopolize their activities. The market economy, in the Braudelian sense, needs a relatively simple set of institutions: a marketplace, a shop, an itinerant peddler, and quite simple money devices, which is not the case with capitalism. Here specific, complicated, and abstract institutions are required: accounting, letters of exchange, credit, stock exchange, specified property rights, banking arrangements, and so on. Europe took centuries to develop these institutions, and they are in a state of constant change. This is sometimes recognized even by those Westerners who would prefer a fast transition in Eastern Europe. Michael Camdessus, head of the IMF, once noted: "It took my country 2,000 years to develop capitalism" (*New York Times,* April 26, 1992). If we think in terms of a distinction between a market economy and capitalism, the quick rise of small business and entrepreneurship in Eastern Europe is clearly a manifestation of the former rather than the latter.

Even in capitalism's birthplace, Western Europe, its development cannot be separated from that of the state. Economic historians, even these with a neoclassical bent, have recognized that capitalism was by no means inevitable, and required a specific set of conditions. The neoclassical explanation is expressed in terms of theories of property rights and transaction costs (North and Thomas, 1973; North, 1981), and these are impossible to explain without introducing the state. The birth of capitalism, therefore, was "accidental," and was contingent on special conditions that emerged only in Europe. It was also aided by a specific European development: the rise of what historical sociologists call the "national state" (Poggi, 1978, 1990). Europe produced, for geographical reasons among others, not comprehensive empires (as was the case in Asia), but a system of mutually dependent and competing national states. War technologies, gunpowder, and standing armies made the survival of such states dependent on their capacity for raising revenues, usually in the form of taxes and/or public debt. Under the particular circumstances of the sixteenth and seventeenth centuries in Europe, it was more useful for the national states to protect property rights and to tax the emerging capitalist classes than to seize their wealth and to organize redistributive economies along Asian-imperial lines. This suited the rising bourgeoisie, and the public debt helped to develop capital markets.

The state became even more important during industrialization, especially in the less-developed or "peripheral" parts of the world, as was shown by Alexander Gerschenkron (1952). During nineteenth-century industrialization, the state protected infant industries almost everywhere, except in Britain, of course, whose leading position did not require such measures.

Germany, Japan, and Russia provide good examples of the state's role in economic development during the late nineteenth century. There is one important difference between Germany and the other two cases. While Germany's success was the result of introducing new products and technologies, Russia and Japan were mainly imitators. The role of the state, however, was crucial in all three cases. The Prussian state prepared the preconditions for modern growth: a customs union, agrarian reforms, and a legislative environment that was favorable to industrial progress. Prussia also organized a state industrial sector (mining, heavy industry, and textiles). The Meiji bureaucracy abolished the formal status system and the privileges of samurai and introduced agrarian reform, Western-type administration, an army based on conscription, national currency, taxation, banking laws, and compulsory education. In Russia, serfdom was abolished in 1861. After a phase of liberal economic policies, Russia, during the last decade of the nineteenth century, went through a phase of a very intensive industrialization in which the state initially played a dominant role (Von Laue, 1963; Crisp, 1976).

The state was involved in creating infrastructure, and was often directly involved in production as well. During the imperial era in Germany, the state built canals, railways, and ports. It also organized a postal system. Similarly, the Meiji state was also directly engaged in the economy. As the government was improving the infrastructure and working to create modern industries, public investment initially exceeded private investment. In Russia, the government, though already controlling a considerable sector of the economy, took over the construction and management of railways and organized the telegraph service. During the 1890s, it introduced a protective tariff policy. State armament factories were modernized, and the government took over certain private enterprises.

The governments of these then less-developed countries supported the concentration of production. Germany integrated concerns, diversified combinations, and unlike the United States, encouraged cartels (Kocka, 1978). The Japanese developed *zaibatsu,* powerful commercial combines. These established their own banks, some of which enjoyed state help in the form of government deposits (Yamamura, 1978, p. 240). In Russia, there was a very substantial concentration of production and cartelization, while business developed due to state contracts.

Financing was organized differently than in earlier developed countries. In Germany, the industry was financed and to a large extent controlled by banks. Banks combined investment and commercial activities, channeled shares into the stock market, provided long-term investment credits, and accepted risks and losses. Although the central bank was not a state institution, its president was nominated by the government, and shareholders had no say in its policy. The majority of savings banks, which controlled more capital than commercial banks, were municipally owned (Stolper, 1967, p. 43). German entrepreneurs and managers were part of a complicated structure, with blurred boundaries between the state and the private sector. In Japan, investment banks of the German type also started to play an important role after World War I (Yamamura, 1978, p. 241). The government was an important provider of capital, which it mobilized in part through taxation and in part through the subscription of foreign loans. The capital went mostly to the shipbuilding and armaments industries (Ohkawa and Rosovsky, 1978, p. 265; Broadbridge, 1989, pp. 1112, 1116). In Russia, the state was also instrumental in developing modern banking. Tax policies were favorable for the accumulation of capital and industrialization. The Russian government taxed the peasantry very heavily in order to obtain capital. The governments of Russia and Japan "used a combination of tax power of the state and the specialized talents of the bankers to shift resources from taxation to production" (Crisp, 1976, p. 155).

The state protected new industries. From the early 1870s on in Germany, national industries were protected from foreign competition (Schremmer, 1978, pp. 483ff.). In Japan, there was close cooperation between the state and the private sector (Broadbridge, 1989, p. 1114). In contrast to Russia, however, where the government kept industries under its control for a long time, the Japanese state privatized them once they reached maturity.

Late modernizers paid special attention to investments in human capital and in research. The Prussian state, and then the German Reich, placed great stress both on universal, public education and on the development of universities. Although the development of universities was undoubtedly related to attempts at forging a national culture, it also gave a boost to research and education in science. At the end of the century, these institutions "were providing the best technical and scientific training in the world" (Chandler, 1990, p. 425). Between the institutes of universities and the laboratories of private firms a whole sector arose, producing knowledge and innovations, especially in the chemical and electrical industries. Germany became a leader in the numbers of new patents granted, which rose from about 4,500 in 1878–79 to almost 13,000 in 1910–1913 (Łuczak, 1984, p. 9). Research became a form of long-term investment, and the heads of laboratories became involved in the strategic decisions of the enterprises (Kocka, 1978, p. 571). Germany's rapid development during the imperial era was based on original innovations.

Germany was also one of the first countries to develop a system of compulsory primary education. The German labor force was better schooled than that of the British, and its universities produced well-prepared bureaucrats, managers, and researchers. Entrepreneurs and managers traveled extensively abroad.

The Japanese, in contrast to the Germans, made an effort to adapt foreign technologies. Students were sent abroad to learn and practice, and foreign specialists were invited to Japan (Broadbridge, 1989, p. 1118). The system of secondary and higher education was expanded on both state and private initiative. These efforts were built upon strong cultural traditions that emphasized the importance of learning. From the beginning of the twentieth century, Japanese firms increasingly sought to hire university graduates. The stress on education changed the status-oriented society into a merit-oriented one. In Russia there was also considerable educational effort, although it did not spread to the lower classes of society.

The same state-led pattern of change was visible in some Eastern European and Latin American countries during the interwar period. They developed a set of protective policies, sometimes referred to as "economic nationalism," which at times targeted industry, at other times agriculture, and were often combined with a strong sector of publicly owned enterprises (Szlajfer, 1990). Poland, Brazil, and Turkey offer cases in point. In Poland, the port and town of Gdynia was created out of nothing to counterbalance the German-dominated Danzig. During the 1930s, the state invested heavily in the so-called Central Industrial Area. Criticism of these policies by liberal economists encouraged the state to develop sophisticated methods of management in order to safeguard the efficiency and profitability of these enterprises—and to escape criticism. The Polish government did not adhere to any special doctrines different from those of standard economics. State involvement in the economy was treated as a necessity dictated by the logic of the situation.

After World War II, the state played a considerable role in economic development in most of the newly industrializing countries. In Latin America, developmentalist ideologies were at the roots of a system sometimes called state capitalism. In many countries, import substitution strategies led to the establishment of a significant sector of state enterprises. Although these policies were criticized after Latin American countries found themselves in debt crisis with high inflation, they nevertheless contributed to a substantial economic and social modernization.

In East Asia, the policies undertaken took the form of a close cooperation between the government and private business rather than a concentration on building a state manufacturing sector. Because none of these countries had the competitive advantage of new products and processes, industrial policy played a much bigger role than had been the case for earlier latecomers. The state promoted both import substitution and export orientation. It helped to create the private sector and big, strong companies, but the private sector was subjected to state guidance or control. In Korea and Taiwan subsidies were given, but only in exchange for meeting performance standards (Amsden, 1989). The state helped private companies, but only in order to force them to develop and to compete in foreign markets. The successful process of mastering acquired technologies was possible owing to the strong emphasis placed on education.

Eastern Europe: Disintegration and Recomposition

This lengthy excursion into the patterns of the development of capitalism enables us to take a closer look at the economic situation of Eastern Europe. It also brings us back to the question of whether an "automatic" revival of capitalism is very likely. Paradoxically, the experience of the early 1990s is often used as an argument both for and against this thesis.

Shock therapy, which was applied in its most drastic form in Poland, is cited as a success. Not only there are no more lines, which were a constant nightmare, but people learned the rules of the consumer market in a surprisingly short time. The danger of hyperinflation was contained, although inflation is still 3–4 percent per month.

In the Polish case, the positive aspects most often mentioned are the revival of growth (although, as must always be kept in mind, the statistics of the transition are extremely unreliable) and the explosion of private entrepreneurship. The development of private business after 1989 has been, to a degree, the process of the shadow economy surfacing. New forms of activity have also developed. On the surface, the easiest to observe is trade, which quickly moved from street peddling to shop space, market halls, and even malls. The number of small-sized business establishments (registered not as companies, but as individually owned) rose from 800,000 in December 1989 to over a million and a half in mid-1992. The number of private companies reached 45,000, and more than half of the labor force was employed by the private sector. Since, however, most of the newly established firms are small- rather than medium-sized, since trade and services are preferred to manufacturing, since capital comes from family savings rather than from banks, since firms operate locally, and since the motivating force is a desire to find an independent source of income for the family rather than dreams of building a fortune, we are within the realm of a Braudelian "market economy" rather than capitalism. Moreover, the small- and medium-sized firms have a very high rate of mortality (Webster, 1993b).

Although successes do exist within the small private sector, the story of state-owned enterprises is much more complicated, as has been illustrated in earlier chapters. Privatization was supposed to be a magic cure. Despite pronouncements of commitment to privatization, however, the results are not impressive and are often restricted to what we call pseudo-privatization.

Recession and unemployment have evoked criticism of the stabilization measures. Undoubtedly many points are debatable: Should tariffs be reduced so much? What categories of prices should be de-controlled? (In Poland, for example, energy is still under state control.) Should internal convertibility be introduced? What exchange rate should be set? Given the conditions in Poland (though not in Hungary), however, some form of stabilization—that is, the drastic reduction of consumer subsidies, budget cuts, and control of the money supply—has been necessary, because the budget deficit had to be controlled.

The problem, therefore, is not the stabilization measures themselves but the lack of a long-term strategy for institutional change, for creating conditions conducive to the emergence of markets and development, and especially for restructuring some of the existing state-owned enterprises. In retrospect, "shock therapy" was not simply a set of economic measures; it was also, perhaps primarily, a way to circumvent the inertia of the old regime. It was a political-psychological "rite of passage" that demonstrated to the society that a new order was now in place. It was also a costly economic therapy, however, that was unsuited to the task of capitalist construction.

The Challenges

What post-socialist countries need is modernization and, most important, re-industrialization. International competitiveness is crucial. Countries of this region have already developed industrial sectors, which need to be restructured and adapted to the requirements of the world economy. This restructuring requires considerable investment.

These industries were considerably developed under pseudo-socialism, but according to the needs of a system that, though not autarchic in a literal sense, was evidently not geared to mass exports of manufacturing goods outside its borders. Moreover, after the crisis began in the late 1970s, the rate of investment decreased considerably and much of the equipment became outdated and technically worn out.

The modernization that is needed in post-socialist economies differs in at least two respects from the earlier cases touched on in this chapter. First, the early cases of modernization involved, roughly speaking, building industries from scratch. In the case of post-socialist countries, we deal rather with the necessity of restructuring already developed industries, as discussed in Chapters 3 and 4. Second, in the nineteenth and early twentieth century, domestic markets played a more important role. Under the present conditions, in order to be successful, countries must be deeply involved in the world economy. This last difference stems in part from the character of technological development and in part from the international demonstration effect.

Each subsequent generation of technology is more complicated, more dependent on other industries, and in particular, more dependent on specific research and development. It is increasingly impossible to capture all the repercussions of technical progress within one firm, one branch of industry, or one national economy. Galbraith's (1967) comparison of the tremendous difference between the design process of the first Ford automobile in 1903 and the Ford Mustang in 1962–1964 is a good illustration of this point. For countries that industrialized as late as the interwar period, it was often sufficient simply to copy existing designs and then to develop their own technologies for their production. Soviet technologies of the 1930s and 1940s are good examples of this approach. With almost any known Soviet consumer product, it is possible to find its Western (often its American or German) model. (The Soviets never mastered real mass production with a low rate of defects, however.) With the passage of time, this reverse engineering process became increasingly difficult and costly. In the 1970s, at least in the pseudo-socialist countries, it was already impossible simply to buy a piece of machinery and reverse engineer it. (South Korea, when it engaged in such reverse engineering during the 1960s, had a much wider access to foreign—especially American and Japanese—technologies, expertise, and advice.) In pseudo-socialist countries, it became necessary to purchase full technological processes (complete assembly lines) and often to hire foreign experts to make them work. In the 1980s, with many advanced products, it was necessary to buy specialized machines and to have a constant supply of spare components and specialized service. A well-known example is the machinery necessary to produce silent submarine propellers, which the Soviets managed to buy indirectly from Toshiba in defiance of a Western embargo. Although it is relatively easy to assemble a computer, only a handful of firms in the world produce processor chips. In order to manufacture any sort of more advanced product, therefore, a country must import. In order to import, it must have access to foreign currency. In other words, the country must export.

The second reason for international involvement is the international demonstration effect, especially in the sphere of consumption patterns. In earlier epochs, industrialization took place when societies were relatively culturally isolated. Demonstration effects, an attraction to the consumption of more advanced societies, affected mostly elites, people who traveled, read books, met foreigners, and lived in urban centers. In the last four to five decades, owing to the presence of modern, mass consumer products almost everywhere and to the electronic media, this attraction now affects all strata of society. Social stability often requires providing the masses of population with the promise of a higher standard of consumer goods than was the case fifty years ago. The importance of this "international demonstration effect" has been convincingly demonstrated by Janos (1986, pp. 84–95). Translated into economic terms, it means a powerful pressure for a rising standard of living for wide masses of the population as well as for access to fashionable consumer products. Since politicians are expected to deliver economic well-being, this pressure is amplified by the development of modern mass democracy.

Both technological developments and the demonstration effect exclude, practically speaking, the possibility of semi-autarchic development of the type pursued by some Latin American countries between the 1930s and the 1960s or, in an extreme sense, by the Soviet Union and other pseudo-socialist countries until the end of Stalinism. Post-socialist countries must follow the path of increasing involvement in the international economy and must therefore be able to produce goods that are competitive on international markets. This is one of the aims of their re-industrialization.

As we argue in this volume, re-industrialization is unlikely to occur solely through the automatic operation of market forces. Both the theoretical arguments and historical evidence demonstrate the necessity for the state to take a considerable role.

This does not mean that the state is the only key to success, or that it can guarantee such a success. That illusion is over. There is too much evidence of the inefficiency and rent-seeking tendencies of bureaucracy. The Asian successes, apart from the lucky coincidence of factors unconnected to state policies (Cumings, 1988; Vogel, 1991), were achieved through pushing companies to compete abroad. The successful method was not statism (understood as constructing a huge public manufacturing sector), but was made up of a close cooperation between state and business and of constructive administrative guidance. Intellectually and politically, the state should not be opposed to the market, but should be treated as complementary to it.

Historical evidence demonstrates the inseparability of capitalism and state. In successful late-comer countries, the state has created the externalities for private business, established a legal framework for the market, and acted as an agent for the accumulation of capital. It has also pursued active industrial policy, especially because these countries could compete neither on the basis of new products nor solely on the basis of low wages. Given the level of development of East European countries, it does not seem possible for them to be the exception to this rule.

8

Reconstructing the State

Post-socialist states face special challenges in the process of modernization and building capitalism. Whether the state is able to meet these challenges depends, first, upon how they are perceived by state elites, and then upon the elites' ability to exert leadership and develop the conditions that allow the state to remain an autonomous actor despite pressures from divergent social groups and interests. Meeting the challenges of modernization also depends, further, upon the state's technical capacity to formulate and implement specific policies. The first category of conditions belongs to the realm of ideas, which were analyzed in the previous chapter. We have seen that the elites of Eastern Europe, particularly in Central Europe, tend to perceive the proper course of action to be reliance on market forces pure and simple (contained, at most, by only the exigencies of social policy) and are hardly prepared to formulate ideas for active development policies.

Examining the next two categories requires a sociopolitical analysis of the relations between the state and social groups and an analysis of the technical capabilities of state operations. We begin with a brief analysis of the concept of a "developmental state," some form of which would be desirable for the countries under consideration, and then turn to an investigation of the East European case.

Most of the experience of a given society is local. It is bounded by language and by a depository of national traditions (whether they are real or invented is of secondary importance). The challenges facing a given society are usually articulated in terms of metaphors that come from the local culture. As noted in Chapter 1, people learn from their own history. They then use the models that their history provides to interpret the situations they face. In Poland, for example, Communists loyal to the Soviet Union were accused of colluding in another "Targowica"—referring to the site where in 1795 a group of Polish magnates agreed to the final dissolution of the then Polish state and submission to Russia, Prussia, and Austria. In another reference to tradition, what is currently the most important peasant party in Poland uses the same name as a prewar peasant party. Lech Wałęsa, when he proposed a new, "non-party" to compete in future elections, gave it the same acronym as a prewar, pro-Piłsudski organization.

Historical associations are very appropriate and, indeed, unavoidable when communicating with a specific population. At the same time, modernization in a late-comer country depends upon the adaptation of foreign concepts—be they political arrangements, administrative structures, or technological solutions. Precisely because these were initially developed for different social, cultural, and even ecological conditions, the adaptation process is often difficult and painstaking. The arrangements must be modified to fit a different setting. Their workings have to be explained within the context of local language, traditions, and metaphors. In a late-developing country, the pool of individuals who are sufficiently prepared to understand how this should be done is limited. They must play the roles of "interpreters" and explain the adapted arrangements to their fellow citizens, which is often not an easy task. This problem is often apparent in the introduction of "hard" technologies, and there are many cases of their rejection or of the difficulties they pose in adaptation. But the problems are even more pronounced in political and organizational arrangements, where it is much more difficult to find a language that is sufficiently free of foreign associations: neutral, technical, and void of emotions. Here the national tradition often becomes a straitjacket that is difficult to loosen. Foreigners, and locals accustomed to foreign ways, may be received with great mistrust. Analysis of the local political tradition is therefore as important as insights into social structures and political coalitions. All innovations must be filtered and mediated through these traditions.

The Problem of the Developmental State

Is there any specific model of a developmental state that is required for effective industrial policies? What are its salient characteristics? Can such a state be "constructed" by the effort of a political elite, or is it only the accidental product of particular historical circumstances? How does it relate to the question of political democracy?[1] These are important questions, much easier to pose than to answer.

The question of economic growth versus democracy is particularly elusive (Haggard, 1990; Przeworski, 1992). In Europe, capitalism preceded democracy, but the American experience was different. In most East Asian countries, strong interventionist policies were introduced by authoritarian governments, except in Japan, though its form of government, too, has sometimes been described as "soft authoritarianism" (Johnson, 1987, p. 137).

Theorists have mixed opinions about the relation between capitalism and democracy in general. The modernization theorists of the 1960s argued for the compatibility of democracy and capitalism, but there is also a strong tradition, from Joseph Schumpeter (1950) to Mancur Olson (1982), which claims that democracy is dysfunctional for capitalism, because it allows for the crystallization of specific interests, favors redistribution and rent-seeking, and hinders the efficient allocation of resources.

The experiences of the Third World and the newly industrialized countries brought a new wave of theorizing. Questions were posed about why so many programs failed (Africa), why successful countries went wildly off track (Brazil), and why other countries were so successful (East Asia). Some analysts, reflecting upon why state actions had failed in certain Third World nations, looked upon them in terms of "weak states, strong societies" (Migdal, 1988), arguing that social control tends to be dispersed. Others developed typologies, introducing concepts of "predatory states" (Zaire, for example) and "developmental states" (P. Evans, 1992).

The developmental state has antecedents in modern European history, several of which were referred to in the previous chapter. Early examples, such as Prussia under Frederick the Great and Russia under Peter I, are interesting, because they indicate that attempts at state-induced modernization took place when social classes were either relatively weak or incorporated into the ruling bureaucracy. In both cases the burgher class was relatively weak, and the ruler was able to fend off the nobility's possible resistance to modernization by incorporating that class into the governing structure. In contrast, the Russian government, during its push for industrialization at the end of the nineteenth century, turned the peasantry against those in command. The peasantry was then the main force in the 1905 revolution (Shanin, 1986). In the cases of the interwar statist policies of Kemalist Turkey and Poland, civil society also found itself in a weak position. In Poland, after the successful coup of Marshal Piłsudski in 1926, *dirigiste* policies were pursued during the 1930s.

The concept of the developmental state tends to be used loosely (P. Evans, 1992, p. 147). For Chalmers Johnson (1982, pp. 315–320), four characteristics are crucial: an elite bureaucracy, a political system in which "bureaucrats rule and politicians reign," a use of market-conforming methods of economic intervention (that is, preserving competition) of which administrative guidance is the most important, and a role for pilot organizations in designing industrial strategies. Government policies that provide incentives for enterprises are particularly important (Johnson, 1987, p. 141). An example is Amsden's concept of (1989, pp. 139ff.) "getting the prices wrong," although, especially in South Korea and Taiwan, the state went far beyond that.

A developmental state should ideally be able to, first, act with relative autonomy with respect to social groups and, second, have the intellectual, ideological, and technical capacity for designing and implementing development strategies. It is not easy to list the social and historical conditions under which such a state is likely to arise. With respect to East Asia (ignoring, for the moment, the high educational levels), the factors most commonly noted are relative cultural and social homogeneity, relative equality (hence the historical importance of land reform and the demise of old rural elites), strong and easily perceivable economic and political challenges, and a specific cultural tradition, elements of which can serve as building blocks for new social institutions. Thus Ezra Vogel (1991, p. 93) considers "the development of a meritocratically selected bureaucracy . . . one of the great contributions of East Asia to world civilization." He emphasizes that the bureaucrat had broader responsibilities and enjoyed more authority and respect than in the West. If so, Weber's (Gerth and Mills, 1947) description of the characteristics of bureaucracy (professional, apolitical, selected on merit through an examination system, operating on the basis of clear rules and written records, and so forth) may be not complete. In the Asian case, we must add the bureaucrat's sense of social responsibility, the counterpart of which is the high respect in which he is held in society.

Even without these cultural aspects, the quality of a bureaucracy remains crucial. The East Asian states provide many examples of state agencies dealing with development that have been institutionally designed to hold down their inefficiencies and reduce private sector rent-seeking. East Asia also provides examples of how bureaucrats are formed, recruited, and selected to ensure their high quality (Johnson, 1982; Amsden, 1989; Wade, 1990, pp. 195–227). Education is an extremely important factor in nurturing an elite bureaucracy.

The political sustainability of a developmental state requires social policies that ensure the equitable distribution of wealth produced by growth. Supporting inefficient industries, such as agriculture, may be the price paid for maintaining social peace. Investment in universally accessible education, apart from serving growth, equalizes the chances of participation in its results. The World Bank in its report (1993) lists "shared growth" as an important factor in East Asian success.

It has been argued that a certain degree of authoritarianism is necessary for a developmental state to function (Johnson, 1987, p. 143). Bruce Cumings (1988) calls South Korea and Taiwan "bureaucratic-authoritarian industrializing regimes," and demonstrates that in Korea "the accumulation of state power rose considerably at the precise time when the ROK [Republic of Korea] began a deepening industrialization program in steel, chemicals, ships, and automobiles." In Taiwan, where social groups were "weak," there was no need to strengthen state power, which, "once strong for retaking the mainland and guaranteeing KMT power, . . . is today strong for economic development" (1988, p. 235). An authoritarian state ensures stability and predictability, propagates ideologies of national unity and common goals, mobilizes society through a one-party system, forestalls the creation of mass alliances against its goals (labor unions, in particular), and represses opponents. It is able to discipline not only labor but also capital (Amsden, 1989, pp. 14–18). A one-party state, however, is likely to appear in the early to middle stages of development, rather than later (Wade, 1990, p. 229). Historical examples of state-led industrialization also demonstrate the importance of authoritarianism. In interwar Poland, without the authoritarian state structures built after the 1926 Piłsudski coup, it would not have been possible for the architect of economic policy, Finance Minister Eugeniusz Kwiatkowski, to take measures such as freezing hard currency accounts, limiting the amount of foreign exchange allowed citizens, and introducing extra-budgetary funds.

A comparison of successful East Asian cases with the countries of

Latin America that also engaged in ambitious, state-led development programs sheds some light on the question of which social conditions are necessary for a successful developmental state. In Latin America, old, patrimonial elites were not removed from the stage when new elites emerged with industrialization. Strategies of growth were targeted on parts of urban segments of society, with political cooptation serving an important role. Thus the state often became a hostage of powerful interest groups, unions and large (state) enterprises in particular, although in all the major postwar Latin American countries, growth was, nonetheless, rapid. Patterns of patronage and clientelism, characteristic of nineteenth- and early twentieth-century oligarchic politics, spread to more modern sectors of society. The fact that large groups were excluded from the process of modernization not only produced tensions but also undercut state authority. Latin American societies have rarely achieved a high degree of national cohesion. Their bureaucracies, even if highly competent in a technocratic sense (Brazil), never achieved Weberian characteristics to a degree comparable with East Asia, especially in regard to social respect and authority. On the contrary, they became deeply embedded in clientelistic relationships of various sorts (Schneider, 1991). These elites, though motivated by the same kind of developmental goals as in Asia,[2] were operating within a different set of social and institutional conditions—with different, less positive, results.

In Europe there are certain parallels with the East Asian experience of successful state involvement in development. Leaving aside the experience of Russia or Prussia in the nineteenth century, and looking at more recent times, we find an approximation of East Asia's pattern in Europe's war economy and postwar reconstruction. It is of particular interest that reconstruction succeeded under democracy. To determine how this occurred, we must look into the ways that social discipline was achieved. First, the challenges and the goals were clear, and around them social consensus was built. Second, the state's level of authority was high.

This authority has a very specific character in the West European case. It rests not only upon the state's legitimacy but also upon a functional cooperation between the formal state and civil society. Democracy and political liberalism, respect for individual freedoms, separation of powers, and the rule of law have been accompanied by a high degree of social discipline and by a deeply internalized respect for state institutions. Legal arrangements are as important for the functioning of this social order as informal habits and customs and historical traditions. The gradual inclusion of citizens in politics, and the development of social discipline can be understood as the internalization and legitimization of norms that otherwise would have to be enforced (Poggi, 1978, 1990). Some European states, of which France is the best example, were also successful in developing competent and honest bureaucracies (Suleiman, 1974). In the postwar (and earlier, in the post-Depression) years, moreover, West European societies were well disciplined. Only later did rising expectations, particularly those relating to welfare arrangements, cause the state to stretch its efforts beyond its capabilities.

Bearing in mind the importance of state authority and capacity, the role of social consensus and mobilization for clear national goals and the need for a good, meritocratic bureaucracy, we may now look at the particular state traditions and political configurations of East European countries.

State Traditions in Eastern Europe

The state traditions of Eastern Europe differ from those of the West. The burgher class and bourgeoisie were much weaker, and the modern state emerged in a specific way. "Although almost thirty different peoples called East Central Europe their homeland, geographers drawing the map of this area in the middle of the 19th century needed but three different colours to represent the three big empires which ruled it" (Berend and Ránki, 1977, p. 11). The region was dominated by the Russian, Habsburg, and Ottoman empires. (Part of present-day Poland was also dominated by Prussia, which over the course of the nineteenth century became part of the German Reich.) Poland, which had been a powerful state in the sixteenth century, gradually lost its strength and ultimately collapsed at the end of the eighteenth century. Its territory was divided among Prussia, Russia, and Austria. Except for Poland, the states of this region developed strong absolutist systems (Anderson, 1974). Executive powers and the bureaucracy were strong, and civil society was much less pronounced than in the West. Democratic traditions also developed to a lesser degree, resulting in a decreased identification of citizens with the state.

Poland was an exceptional case in Eastern Europe because it never had an absolutist state. From the sixteenth to the eighteenth centuries, its government was dominated by representative bodies of the nobility on both the local and the national level. Fearful of "absolutum dominium," the nobles even introduced a principle of "liberum veto," which allowed a single dissenting voice to block the introduction of any new law. Polish monarchy was elective, and subsequent monarchs, often foreign, granted more and more privileges to the gentry. By the end of the eighteenth century, Poland's taxation, standing army, and administrative apparatus was almost nonexistent in comparison with those of the three neighboring monarchies, Prussia, Russia, and Austria. The partition of Poland at the end of the eighteenth century was a result of this weakness of the state.

All over Europe, the nineteenth century is crucial for understanding later periods. It was an epoch of industrialization, social modernization, nationalism, and the emergence of mass society. In the leading countries of Western Europe, modern democracy and modern systems of government were built in the second half of the century. Eastern Europe too saw the formation of nations as we know them today. Most of these nations achieved full statehood only at the beginning of the twentieth century, however, as the empires dominating the region disintegrated. Prior to this, the elements of the modern state—government, civil service, tax authorities, army, judiciary, and the symbols of state power—had all functioned under the authority of the partitioning powers and were therefore perceived as alien. National uprisings occurred in many countries. For the Poles and others, patriotism was associated with resistance *against* the state.

A few new sovereign states emerged in the nineteenth century, when the Ottoman empire disintegrated. Romania was proclaimed an independent state in 1859, Bulgaria in 1878. Poland, Hungary, and Czechoslovakia became independent states only in 1918, as did the Baltic states. Ideologically, the situation was easier for the nations that had a long, pre-nineteenth-century tradition of statehood, such as Poland or even Hungary. Politically, most of the new states began as parliamentary democracies. Administrative and judicial experience, as well as the legal system, came primarily from the nineteenth-century imperial powers. The interwar years were used for building new institutions and traditions, mostly in the executive branch of the government rather than in the representative. During this period all the countries of the region except Czechoslovakia shifted from rather inefficient parliamentary systems into various forms of authoritarianism, sometimes with fascist overtones. Nonetheless, sophisticated party structures developed. During the authoritarian phase, many countries of the region responded to the Great Depression with policies of "economic nationalism" (Szlajfer, 1990), sometimes targeted to develop industry (Poland) and sometimes to strengthen agriculture (Bulgaria). In Poland, the growth of state-owned enterprises, or "statism" *(étatisme),* was of particular importance.

World War II ended these traditions with respect to both the countries that fought on the Allied side (Poland, Czechoslovakia) and those that joined the Axis (Bulgaria, Hungary, Romania). In Poland, the whole ethos of resisting the enemy greatly intensified. During the Nazi occupation, a sophisticated organized underground state developed, complete with armed forces, party structure, and even a judiciary. It was loyal to the Polish government in exile, based in London. After the Nazis were defeated by the Red Army in 1944–45, the remnants of these structures were thoroughly destroyed by the Communist security apparatus.

After the war, communism was established from above all over Eastern Europe, a process that "was greatly facilitated by the fact that, domestically, the Great Depression and World War II not only destroyed the old political systems, but also greatly weakened the old political classes throughout East Central Europe" (Rothschild, 1989, p. 122). Communism and its mutant, pseudo-socialism, profoundly changed East European societies, in part through industrialization and social modernization and in part through specific policies that aimed at the persecution and social elimination of the remaining former upper classes and elites. In the longer run, in the course of industrialization, urbanization, and social modernization, new social structures emerged and crystallized. Urban workers and new intelligentsia, mostly of peasant origin, and a new "middle class," composed of skilled blue-collar and educated white-collar workers, in part overlapping with the ruling *nomenklatura* but much larger, were the social bases of the new Communist state.

This state, like the whole pseudo-socialist system, went through phases of growth and then decay and decomposition. Its base was laid during the 1940s and completed during the Stalinist period. Its basic characteristics are well known and include the party's domination of the legislative, executive, and judicial branches of the government, administrative rule over the nationalized economy, and ideological control of the society. Certain features of this state are important for our analysis of state traditions in Eastern Europe. Although generalizations across countries do not always hold, a clear pattern emerges.

First, the state was built "from scratch," after a purposeful break with continuity and tradition (as far as it was practically possible) in every sense imaginable, including ideological legitimization, legal foundation, organizational tradition, and the feeling of identity among the ruling elites.

Second, although the pseudo-socialist state was bureaucratic, both the party and the state bureaucracy were far from the Weberian model. Rules and norms of operation were unclear and changed according to the political needs of the moment. The bureaucracy did not work within any constraints resembling a "Rechtstaat." Recruitment was according to political loyalty, not professional merit. (*Bierni, mierni ale wierni*—Passive, mediocre, but loyal—was a popular Polish rhyme characterizing the Communist bureaucrat.) Communist civil servants were different from their French and Japanese counterparts in every sense. They were accustomed to avoiding responsibility and were notoriously inefficient.

Third, in Poland, Hungary, and Czechoslovakia, the question of the legitimacy and acceptance of the Communist state, and the consequent respect accorded to it, has been very complicated. On the one hand, substantial segments of the new middle classes gained from modernization under communism (especially after the Stalinist phase), and their members had a personal stake in supporting it. In general, both modernization and a certain social equality were treated as positive achievements. On the other hand, there was a feeling that the system was installed by the Soviets (mistrusted for their own sake and as heirs of Russia, a traditional enemy) and that the country was not sovereign. The entire ideological justification for the system, especially its antireligious elements, ran against deeply ingrained national sentiments. Finally, the state was omnipresent and took responsibility for every sort of need. At the same time, it was hopelessly inefficient, and the officials, especially on the lower levels, were corrupt in petty ways. This inefficiency and petty corruption led to a disrespect for the state's institutions and representatives.

Fourth, although pseudo-socialist states began with command economies during the Stalinist period, the actual influence of the central planning authorities over the economy was relatively weak, especially during the later stages. Technically, the sheer size and complexity of the economy (thousands of enterprises and hundreds of thousands of types of goods and prices) made it unmanageable. Sociopolitically, the dynamics of the system led to the emergence of powerful informal interest groups, formed along branches of the economy and in the industrial regions. Through networks of political alliances, these groups were able to influence the decision-making process of planners and shift resources (investment funds, in particular) to their own use. Although the central authorities formally controlled resources, the lower levels had a monopoly of information, which they used to manipulate the center (Rychard, 1987; Żukowski, 1988). This process, present from the very beginning of the system, grew in importance after political terror was phased out.[3] (Stalin's purges, or Mao's Cultural Revolution, for that matter, can be interpreted as attempts to block the formation of interest groups independent of the central authorities.)

The political and economic history of the pseudo-socialist period is relevant to the present because it left vivid memories of a particular perversity of statism—the process of a powerful state becoming a victim of its own subjects. The heritage of an inefficient and easily corruptible bureaucracy susceptible to powerful local and industrial interests in part explains the subsequent total lack of trust in state intervention in the economy.

Fifth, pseudo-socialism was a sort of "welfare state," which took care of most of its citizens' needs (Chirot, 1980; Ost, 1989). Health and education were free, and housing (when available) was subsidized, as were basic foodstuffs. Pensions were automatically granted from the state budget. Enterprises provided not only work, but welfare. The state also served as an institution of social control and political affiliation. As a result, expectations and claims on the state increased.

Post-Socialist States

State organization in the post-socialist era is very peculiar, stemming from the character of the political transition of the regime. This transition was at the same time revolutionary and evolutionary (not to mention reactionary, as noted in Chapter 1). It was revolutionary in the ideological and symbolic sense. Every possible aspect of the pseudo-socialist regime was called in question: its legal basis, its culture, its economic efficiency, its political rules of operation, and even the morality of those who supported and served it. Ideologically, there was a desire on the part of East European countries to treat the forty years after World War II as an unfortunate and forgettable historical episode. After the socialist regimes' collapse, every possible ideological symbol, from the names of states to national emblems to the names of streets, was changed. Powerful voices have demanded de-communization, that is, to ban former party functionaires from holding official positions. Laws to that effect were passed only in Czechoslovakia. In Poland and in Hungary, most of the high-ranking officials of the former regime had left their posts anyway. The new political elite legitimized its rule by stressing the idea of a total break with the past.

At the same time, the change was evolutionary and peaceful. In post-Soviet Eastern Europe, apart from Romania, there were no shootings and no arrests. In Poland and Hungary, there was also no legal persecution of officials of the old regime. The institutional structure of government was handed over to newcomers, and—except for the political police—there were no mass shake-ups of staff. The legal continuity of states, though verbally attacked, was in fact respected. Their nature was changed only through step-by-step amendment of existing law.

By and large the administrative apparatus inherited from pseudo-socialist times was not up to the task of economic and political transformation. Its structure and organization had been tailored to the needs of a command economy (although it was accustomed to economic reforms) and its staff members' training and experience had occurred under nondemocratic systems. The new political elites were, at least initially, unable to introduce reforms in the civil service. Given their concentration on political problems and the everyday details of government, they were probably not even conscious of the scope of the necessary changes.

Once the transition to the new regime began, the administrative apparatus of the state started to show visible signs of disintegration. Analytically, at least three reasons for this disintegration can be found. The first was the disintegration of the pseudo-socialist system in general. It was a long process, which in Poland, Czechoslovakia, and Hungary, at least, had begun as early as the 1970s.[4] The political transition after 1989 and "shock therapies" obviously accelerated this dynamic. For our purposes, the disintegration of the management structure of state-owned enterprises and the disintegration of the institutions of the welfare state are of special importance.

The fiscal crisis is the second closely connected reason for the disintegration of the states' administrative apparatus. This crisis was caused by a grave recession and the decline of the state sector, which was the main source of state revenues. Depending on the country, neither the tax system nor the fiscal authorities were prepared (or able) to collect revenues from the quickly emerging private sector—let alone the gray economy. The low salaries in government administration caused the best staffers to leave, and there was no money for welfare and other statutory programs or sectors (army, health, industrial support). Although foreign lenders, especially the Bretton Woods institutions, were willing to lend to Eastern Europe to promote privatization, they were unwilling to lend to reconstruct the state.

Political reasons were the third cause of disintegration. Good and competent bureaucrats from the old system were not only dissatisfied with the low pay but also afraid of the new political climate. They were aware that as former members of the *nomenklatura* they would never be promoted under the new conditions. Consequently, many of them left. Many went to the private sector and foreign firms, which were happy to hire such well-prepared and well-connected employees.

As a result of all these processes, the entire government apparatus has been in great need of reorganization and restaffing. Some attempts in this direction are already visible. The salaries of some civil servants have been visibly increased (to the disappointment of other public employees such as teachers, university professors, and doctors and nurses). Schools of public administration have been opened. Proposals for laws on civil service reform have been put forth.

The question of creating an efficient bureaucracy is particularly difficult in the context of fiscal duress and the immaturity of political parties and parliamentary systems. The civil service should be not only competent but also at least partially autonomous relative to the political process. What we observe in some East European countries is quite the opposite, with parties treating ministries as turf to fight for. They try to "capture" ministries and then offer jobs to their supporters. After each change of cabinet, consequently, there are shake-ups and changes in most of the ministries. Whatever experience has been recently gained is thereby lost. Middle-level functionaires, furthermore, are trained to be loyal to powerful leaders rather than to the state in general.

Even assuming that the performance of the civil service will improve, industrial policies will face another, extremely powerful obstacle—the traditionally established claims on the resources of the state, reinforced by the democratic political game. It is these competing claims that make the state "weak." The first category of claims includes political pressure from troubled state enterprises asking to be bailed out. The stronger the trade union movement, the greater the pressure that is applied. The ability of state agencies to identify which cases truly deserve help is not only a technical problem (which can be helped by upgrading the quality of the agencies in question), but, more important, a political one. The second sort of claims involves the pressure to keep or increase welfare benefits, of which the most serious is the pension system. This system is mostly financed from state budgets, and in some countries, such as Poland and Hungary, it already consumes a sizable portion of state revenues. But as parliamentary elections demonstrate, pensioners are an important segment of voters. Even if we focus on "developmental" questions, we find strong competition between aims such as industrial policy and, for example, education and research and development.

Political Change

Is it possible to reconstruct the weak East European state? To answer this question, it is necessary to examine the social and political context within which the state must operate. The disintegration of pseudo-socialism and then "shock therapy" and the process of transition toward a market economy have brought about enormous changes in the structure of society and in the nature of the political actors and the process they are engaged in. This upheaval in turn has consequences for the prospects of the state and its autonomy.

Communist society, although somewhat stratified, was relatively egalitarian. Full employment and welfare provisions (free education and health care, subsidized food and housing) provided a sense of social security and a relative equality of chances. Decades of state-led development produced a specific middle class, defined mostly on the basis of education and links to the state. Although the middle class ultimately lost any illusions it might have had concerning the ideological foundations of the social order, it took its situation for granted. When it engaged in political protests, it did so against the malfunctioning of the welfare state rather than in the name of its abolition.

The collapse of pseudo-socialism and the beginning of the transition process changed this situation dramatically. Real incomes, at least within the official sphere of the economy, fell dramatically. Owing to the profound structural crisis of the post-command economy, welfare state provisions were already vanishing before the ultimate collapse. But the stabilization program brought about the final shock: prices of social services went up, while the fiscal squeeze on the state made it unable to pay for the services in full. Schools and hospitals as well as municipalities and police grew short of funds. The unplanned, spontaneous processes of privatization of public services that began have been particularly painful for the poor.

Other social changes have taken place as well. One of them, owing to the fast growth of trade and services, is the rise of a classical middle class, defined by its ownership of small property. Statistical indicators of this period are extremely shaky, but everyday observation reveals a considerable increase in conspicuous consumption by the new bourgeoisie. At the same time that the middle classes have been beneficiaries of the nascent capitalism, however, workers of many state-owned enterprises have often been its victims. Their incomes have stagnated, their welfare benefits have been lost, and they face the possibility of unemployment.

Pensioners are extremely important as political actors. In Poland, they number 8,500,000 (with a total labor force of about 17,500,000, out of which almost 2,500,000 are unemployed). In the face of stagnation or the decrease of real incomes, pensioners have pressed for redistribution. The problem is a serious one for macroeconomic stability. Because of the insufficiency of Polish state pension funds, for example, almost 19 percent of 1992 budget expenditures went to subsidize pensions (GUS, 1992, pp. 145, 215).

The unemployed themselves have become a new segment of society. Unemployment has skyrocketed throughout Eastern Europe, reaching double-digit levels almost everywhere. It particularly affects the less skilled, the young, and women. There are towns and regions in every East European country where lack of work has become a tragic reality amid the once-high hopes for the post-socialist era.

These social and political changes have been reflected in the redefinition of old political actors and in the emergence of new ones. New parties have developed, but the patterns of their formation differ from region to region. It is difficult to arrange them according to a simple "left-center-right" formula (Roskin, 1992). We argue that the main axis of political divisions have not been explicable in terms of left and right alone, as András Körösényi (1991, pp. 60ff.) shows convincingly for the emerging Hungarian party system. Former Communist parties have not vanished; rather, renamed as socialist or social-democratic, they reappear on the political stage. Their electoral successes are explicable in terms of their organizational practice and well-developed local networks, which the newly emerging parties lack. Labor unions have become important actors as well. Even leaving aside the special case of Solidarity in Poland, which in 1980–81 was a social movement rather than a union, in many countries of the region old, official labor organizations (OPZZ in Poland, CITUB in Bulgaria, MSZOSZ in Hungary) were revitalized during the last years of the old regime, while new organizations also (Solidarity; in Bulgaria, Podkrepa) arose. Although labor groups initially went along with pro-market changes, after a year or two they began to object to many of the market's effects, particularly compressed real wages, shrinking welfare arrangements, and the loss of job security. These groups have often resorted to militant actions such as street demonstrations, wildcat strikes, and roadblocks (Nelson, forthcoming).

The transformation has also affected the rural population, which, in some countries, remains a large segment of society (in Poland, one fifth of those employed work in agriculture). A relatively small strata of modern, commercial farmers have been hit by both a rise in input prices (interest rates, in particular) and a simultaneous decline in demand for their products, caused both by stagnating urban incomes and by the competition of cheap Western imports. In addition, most peasants have lost the opportunity to augment their incomes through part-time work in state industrial enterprises.

It is perhaps too early to speak of the reemergence of class conflicts—although they may appear soon. The processes of social exclusion have certainly started. Sizable social groups have had little chance of even entering the market, because they are handicapped in a cultural (educational) sense or constrained by local conditions such as inflexible housing systems. According to some researchers, East European society is dividing into two parts, each holding totally different attitudes regarding the region's changes, with the level of education as a strong correlate (for Poland, see Marody, 1993). These circumstances provide a breeding ground for populist discontent.

Social Structure and Politics in Poland

Are changes in the social structure reflected in some regular way in the nature of the new political structure? It is always difficult to relate the party system to the social structure, and it is even more difficult to do so under conditions of rapid change. Still, a few general observations can be made with respect to Poland.

The initial bipolar political structure produced by late communism—of "we" and "them," society and authorities, Solidarity and communists—deteriorated within a year from the moment pseudo-socialism collapsed. Solidarity split into many groups and parties, while former Communists and their satellites regrouped and redefined themselves in terms of democratic politics. To explain the ideological differences among these groups in traditional terms of "left" and "right" would be difficult, because they differ in terms of more than one criterion. There are at least four axes along which the parties might be arranged according to their ideological profile. The first concerns the degree of state intervention they seek. Some political groups advocate a fast march toward classical, relatively unregulated capitalism, of which the United States is the closest approximation. Others argue for more intervention, with the state acting as both a provider of welfare and a guide for the process of growth.

The second axis refers to the degree of cultural and political affiliation desired with the West. While some argue for a quick march toward Europe (NATO, EC), others are afraid of foreign competition, foreign capital, and foreign ideas and stress the value of national identity.

The third criterion of difference concerns the role of the church and religion in public life, a problem particularly important in a country that is predominantly Catholic and where the church played a leading role in building the elements of civil society under pseudo-socialism.

The final difference concerns attitudes toward the past. Is pseudo-socialism, in an ideological sense, a part of national history, or is it just an aberration, an episode brought about by foreign force, alien to the national spirit, that should be erased and forgotten? As already noted, the adherents of the latter position demand de-communization—a ban of some form that would forbid former Communists from participating in public life. Such a position alienates considerable numbers of former liberal and reformist Communists, of course, who are often highly skilled and well educated. A ban also goes against the idea of the rule of law, which usually does not permit punishment for deeds that were not criminal when they were committed.

The position of a political group on one of these axis does not necessarily correspond to its place on another one. There are nationalist parties that are pro-church and others that are indifferent to the church. There are parties that are interventionist in an economic sense, but open to the world in a cultural and political sense. The fact that there is more than one reason for ideological differences at times makes the reading of Polish politics difficult and confusing. The political actors themselves often behave in ways that seem inconsistent.

From our point of view, the most important pressures on a developmental state include the following: pressure from workers and managers of endangered state-owned enterprises; from pensioners; from farmers; and from regions particularly hard hit by the recession. Each of these groups pushes for redistribution of national income, using a combination of political pressure and ideological arguments. The debate, not surprisingly, is highly emotional.

In the area of industrial policy, therefore, the state itself, given both its weakness and the claims made on it, is in great danger of being captured by interest groups of inefficient industries, which cloak their redistributional demands in terms of industrial (or agricultural) policy needs. Such groups can easily gain the support of other disgruntled parties or organizations. It is very likely, moreover, that the officials responsible for particular regulations and subsidies may be corrupt. The problem is thus whether an institutional design and/or a course of policies exists that can minimize the state's vulnerability.

The elections of fall 1993 considerably changed the Polish political scene. The 1993 parliament became dominated by coalitions and parties usually referred to as "the Left." The most important members of the Alliance of the Democratic Left are the Social Democrats (former Communists) and the Peasant Party (also one of the parties of the pseudo-socialist period). In the West, these election results have been generally interpreted as signifying opposition to rapid market reforms. Although this conclusion simplifies the problem (issues other than market reform, such as church involvement, affected voting patterns), it is basically correct.

What are the prospects after such an election, when a coalition government, formed by Social Democrats and the Peasant Party, is in power? The Peasant Party is a special interests organization, likely to call for some form of protection of Polish agriculture: tariffs, subventions, and the like. Despite its historical lineage, socially it tends to be a Christian popular party. The Social Democrats have a strong electorate composed of the urban working classes, members of former Communist labor unions, and pensioners. These groups are likely to press for social transfers. Yet the Social Democrats have also received considerable support from the entrepreneurial class. This is not surprising, because many of the new businesspeople come from the ranks of former Communists and are interested in forging connections with the present power elites. The leadership of this party has a very pro-market ideological orientation and has declared its intention to continue the course of market reform. But these declarations lack specifics, so their interpretation—including whether these reforms might include some form of national industrial policy—remains an open question. The new government has also stated its intention to keep the budget deficit low and to work very hard at establishing good relations with Bretton Woods institutions.

Social Structures and Politics in Eastern Europe and the Former Soviet Union

We have examined the Polish case—the country that was the first to undergo political change and, in some respects, the most advanced in building capitalism. Can the same observations be generalized over the much larger area of Eastern Europe, including the post-Soviet states? This enormous and complicated subject can be only briefly touched on here.

These countries appear to have many features in common. All (save the Czechs) went through social changes under pseudo-socialism from peasant societies with small urban and industrial sectors into semi-developed industrial economies with large urban populations, with many of the characteristics that sociologists use to describe "mass society." All these nations developed a middle class of sorts. (In the more liberal Poland, Hungary, and even Czechoslovakia, however, the overlap of this middle class with the *nomenklatura* is less than elsewhere.) All developed a huge industrial and relatively educated working class, which became restless under the stagnation of the last two decades and which has shouldered the burden of the change to a market system. In addition, all developed (though with varying degrees of efficiency) comprehensive welfare arrangements (now collapsing), which not only made people dependent on the state in a material sense but also produced learned helplessness.

There are also differences—economic, historical, and cultural—among the former pseudo-socialist countries. At least six are important enough to produce distinct patterns of politics.

First, the religions practiced in Eastern Europe and the former Soviet Union range from Catholicism to Protestantism to Orthodox Christianity to Islam. In some countries (such as Poland and Lithuania), one religion predominates; in others, there are many denominations. Religion, suppressed under pseudo-socialism, has now reappeared, and feelings of affiliation overlap with other social changes.

Second, there are tremendous ethnic differences, both within and across borders. This issue may be the most explosive, as wars in the former Yugoslavia and in the post-Soviet states demonstrate. Stabilization measures that result in mass unemployment, the shrinking of the state, and the collapse of law and order may fuel further ethnic violence.[5] More generally nationalism, once again rising in Eastern Europe, may have very different effects. It can create a sense of social cohesion that helps in answering developmental challenges, but it can also produce perverse outcomes. Katherine Verdery (1991, p. 318) argues, speaking about the possible future of Romania, that a "socialist form of totalization" may be replaced "with a national one," which could lead to "chauvinism, intolerance, and a rhetoric of purification." There is a short road from the rhetoric of purification to ethnic cleansing.

Third, these nations have experienced varying degrees of Western cultural influence. Some countries received Christianity from Rome, others from Byzantium. Some were within the sphere of the Habsburg Empire, which was basically Western, for a long time; others were subject to Russia or the Ottomans. Some had at least a passing experience with democracy, while others had none. Legal traditions, the whole idea of the rule of law, intellectual traditions, and institutions differ according to the country's distance from the West.

Fourth, the time span of the pseudo-socialist experience differs from nation to nation. In Russia, and in most of the territories of the former Tsarist empire, pseudo-socialism lasted for well over three generations. In this region, no one can recall living under another system. In other parts of Eastern Europe, the duration of a Soviet-style regime was much shorter (especially when one remembers that elements of a multi-party system were present until 1949). In these countries people have memories of their former system that often serve as a frame of reference for present politics.

Fifth, within the newly forming capitalist middle classes *cum* bourgeoisie, differences exist in the degree to which these new strata are formed out of the ranks of former members of the *nomenklatura* or from the independently rising business class. Poland and Hungary differ substantially from, for example, Bulgaria in this respect (Nikova, 1994). The change of *apparatchiks* into capitalists is (apart from possible moral objections) generally positive. It allows for the translation—to use Bourdieu's terminology—of "political capital" into economic capital. It also acts as a safeguard against the possible political mobilization of former ruling elites against democratic change. The overall domination of business life by people who rely on informal connections, however, raises the danger of change in the direction of predatory regimes of the African kind—especially we recall that, under late communism, in some countries (the Asian Soviet republics, for example), close connections between the power elites and a Mafia-like crime sector already existed.

Finally, there is one important difference between Russia and the rest of Eastern Europe. Russia's military strength, imperial traditions, and strong nationalist ideologies make it very unlikely that it will remain content to be just one among many players. Any efforts by Russia to regain a position of world power will affect both its internal and its foreign policy.

In each country the mix of factors is different, as are the societal responses to market change. It would be unwise to build a too general predictive model for the whole region. If one looks across the vast areas of the former pseudo-socialist countries, the only safe prediction is that the states will take a different shape in the near future. Given the open or latent civil wars that are tearing apart or threatening various populations, even the existence of some of these states cannot be taken for granted. Which of the post-Soviet states will remain independent of Russia is also an open question.

Hungary, the Czech Republic, and Poland are most likely to develop patterns of politics that bear at least some resemblance to the democratic West. It will be much more difficult, though not impossible, for

Bulgaria and Romania.[6] In Russia, the development of a political structure somewhat like the West's seems unlikely, or at least appears so after the events of October 1993. If anarchy is to be avoided, some form of semi-authoritarian rule seems probable, with a significant role played by the military-industrial complex. In some of the Asian post-Soviet states, there is a high likelihood that regimes will emerge that resemble dysfunctional, predatory state models.

Toward Restructuring the State

The most persuasive argument for the rise of a developmental state in the more Western-oriented countries of Eastern Europe is functional. Such a state, given the compelling evidence of the first five years of the transition, is badly needed. A magic recipe or a medicine that can be easily administered with a high chance of success in creating a developmental state does not exist. There are, however, many prior examples, bits and pieces of which could be adapted by Eastern Europe with far greater success than it has gained through wholesale mimicking of nineteenth-century free market capitalism. The experiences of late-industrializing nations are worth studying, and politically, at least some of the factors behind their success are worth a try.

We have already referred to the experience of East Asia. With all the caveats about its timing and its particular coincidence of economic and geopolitical factors, this region still provides several lessons:

- Industrial policy must be conducted through close cooperation between government and private business, with the government retaining the upper hand in the sense that it does not fall victim to interest groups.
- An important agent of this policy is a highly competent bureaucracy, insulated from day-to-day political pressures and from the undue influence of business groups.
- Trade is critical for stimulating competitiveness, but economic "openness" must be carefully controlled—in terms of guarding against negative interference by the Bretton Woods institutions, admitting foreign investment selectively, and generally emphasizing the building of domestic technological capabilities.

As noted earlier, East Asia and Eastern Europe share in common two very important ingredients for rapid economic development—high levels of education and equal income distribution. Whether or not they also share much in common politically remains to be seen. If economic conditions continue to deteriorate and social unrest worsens, politics in Eastern Europe may become more authoritarian (even if, in some countries, "democracy" technically survives).

There are many reasons why the authoritarian solution is neither desirable nor likely to succeed in the more Westernized countries of Eastern Europe, however. These nations shed pseudo-socialism in the name of democracy. They are now relatively well-educated, urban mass societies, and pro-democracy feelings are strong. Stable authoritarian regimes usually arise in countries during earlier stages of transformation from agrarian society. Countries such as Poland, Hungary, and the Czech Republic are close to democratic Western Europe, and to realize the wish of substantial parts of these societies to be admitted to the European Community depends upon preserving democratic systems. And perhaps most important, it is not likely that any social "founding myth" other than democracy (be it the idea of religious or ethnic identity or a historical mission) can hold these societies together as communities with a shared sense of historical experience, future fate, and mutual responsibility.

These factors do not preclude the possibility of authoritarian change. On the contrary, it is likely during times of serious social and/or political crisis. Fragile new democracies are easy to destroy. The point is that authoritarianism is not very likely to be efficient or successful. Short of democracy, these societies risk anarchy.[7]

In terms of economic matters, although democratic arrangements slow down the decision-making process and often make the introduction of necessary solutions impossible, they do provide a much higher legitimacy for the decision taken—provided there is, of course, a consensus regarding respect for law. Historically, however, democracy seems more easily compatible with advanced capitalist society than with earlier stages of growth, because it supports the redistribution of incomes from accumulation to consumption. The challenge facing Eastern Europe—pro-growth policies under democratic conditions—is new. Actual solutions will be found through practice. But what institutional and sociopolitical conditions are conducive to making growth and democracy work?

The institutional conditions are more straightforward, and the first concerns constitutional arrangements for ensuring government stability. Presidential systems carry the considerable risk of putting too much power in the hands of one individual. Swings in public mood may also lead to the election of the "wrong" candidate. Consequently, cabinet rule should be strengthened. The constructive "vote of no confidence" used in Germay appears to be one way of avoiding too easy a dissolution of the cabinet.

Another institutional safeguard is to construct a good bureaucracy. Here not only the East Asian experience but also that of France, for example, is illustrative. The basic ideas are fairly simple. The bureaucracy should be relatively well paid, entry should be on a competitive basis, the prestige kept high, and the lines of promotion based on performance and merit. Bureaucrats should be prevented from entering business or politics while in service. Retirement should be relatively early to provide the chance to join the private sector. Japan (MITI especially) provides the best-known example of this sort of bureaucracy, but quite a few East Asian countries succeeded in reforming their civil services along these lines relatively quickly (World Bank, 1993). The agencies in particular need of reform are the ministries of industry and developmental banks.

The matters mentioned so far, however, are of a technical nature. Another, much more profound problem exists that involves the social consensus in regard to the state, its authority, legitimacy, and power. To look at it from another angle, the problem is one of social discipline. Historically, social discipline and national consensus have been achieved in various ways. In East Asian countries, they were guaranteed not only by authoritarian political regimes and Confucian ideals but by the reaction to losing a war and the need for reconstruction. In addition, it is probably easier to maintain social discipline in an authoritarian way in an agrarian society than in an urban one.

To achieve this discipline in a democracy, there must be a widespread sense of belonging to the national community. The processes of social exclusion that accompany the building of a market economy pose the worst kind of danger (except, perhaps, for ethnic conflict) to democratic stability and social discipline. Members of the society must have the feeling that they share in the benefits of growth, if there is growth, and that the burdens of recession are distributed in a fair way (which does not mean an equal way). For example, despite the fact that developing East Asian countries were not democratic, they were egalitarian. East Asians (Singaporeans and South Koreans, in particular) made a conscious effort to achieve "shared growth"—that is, growth whose effects would be felt by as wide a segment of society as possible (World Bank, 1993). One method used to achieve this is education, which considerably improves the chances that an individual can participate in modernization. Another is the protection of certain inefficient industries (agriculture, in particular) in order to minimize unemployment. In Japan, highly efficient industries still subsidize substantial numbers of people employed in other parts of the economy.

Another example worth mentioning, much closer to Eastern Europe, is that of Western Europe during the late 1940s, the 1950s, and the early 1960s. Here too deliberate industrial policies were pursued, and the reconstruction of whole branches of the economy (especially agriculture) was achieved through a conscious effort on the part of the state. There was redistribution, but there was also a social discipline that, until the late sixties, safeguarded these countries against the dangers of overspending and inflation. One of the factors responsible for this discipline may have been the experience of World War II. Once this discipline started to dissolve, these countries entered an epoch of stagflation, which dragged on through the 1970s.

Although neither of these regional experiences can be repeated in Eastern Europe under the present conditions, they demonstrate the need for social policies that lead, first of all, to building the authority of the state as a common good and common value and, second, to industrial policies that are pro-growth measures (Bresser Pereira, Maravall, and Przeworski, 1993). An economist must be aware, however, that no policy is cost free. Both social policy and building state authority come at a price. It is not true, however, as some claim, that one must have a Swedish economy in order to have a Swedish welfare state. Sweden started to build social protections when it was poor.[8] Neglecting social policies brings the risk of exclusion, populism, anarchy, democratic instability, a weakened state, and ungovernability.

Finally, what East European societies require to develop economically are not only good institutions and social discipline. They are also in great need of new ideas. Their intellectual and political elites must realize that future growth requires more than simply putting market mechanisms in place. Perhaps time is needed for these ideas to develop—time to observe the actual process of transition, to digest the experience, and then to create new visions. Time, however, is running out.

9

Economy, Society, and the State

Despite all its problems, the post-socialist transition can still succeed. The essential precondition is that orthodox economics yields to common sense. In Eastern Europe in the mid-1990s, common sense dictates four courses of action: encouraging macroeconomic expansion; creating conditions under which viable state enterprises can self-select themselves into growth; giving these state-owned enterprises (as they turn into privately owned enterprises) adequate institutional support to generate saving, aid investment, and further technical advance; and empowering a government bureaucracy that can harmonize political democracy with the degree of economic governance that modern capitalism requires.

Some of the conditions from which recovery must commence are indeed disastrous. During the first stages of transition, the market's successes were infrequent at all economic levels: overall, in the different production sectors, and for enterprises. We have observed each country's depressing numbers regarding output and inflation, described avoidable enterprise collapses and financial misadventures, and pointed out privatization's halting course. Even more disheartening is the extent to which the decay throughout the production structure continues.

There has been a political reaction to these economic failures, and the implications for the future are not entirely bright. In Poland, a center-left coalition supplanted the reform government (which itself had begun to back away from shock therapy eighteen months earlier) in the fall of 1993, but it had no coherent alternative program. In Russia in December, nationalists, former Communists, and independent reformers dominated the vote in the lower house and the orthodox reform party became a weak minority. Somewhat earlier the Czechoslovak federation had fallen apart, and right-wing governments consolidated power in Hungary and Romania, growing increasingly nationalist in orientation as the economic situation grew steadily worse. Although too facile, the commonly drawn political parallels between the early 1930s and the early 1990s in Mitteleuropa were not entirely off the mark. Elsewhere, the ongoing armed conflicts in the former Yugoslavia and the Trans-Caucasus made the 1930s look almost like a pleasant interlude.

After all these conflagrations, will the phoenix rise from the ashes? It can, as various lines of argument suggest. Despite the many problems, other initial conditions in East European nations are good. Most important among these are the equal income distributions and the high education levels of post-socialist nations. Unless present tendencies toward increasing inequality continue and social tensions rise sharply, there are not likely to be strong pressures for fiscally destabilizing redistributive programs (although reconstituting the welfare state will be difficult enough). A high level of education is certainly a necessary, though far from sufficient, condition for productivity and income growth.

To realize these advantages, prudently aggressive macroeconomic policy will be helpful, despite the risks it entails. Analysts concerned with stability often call for more austerity than sustained re-industrialization can endure. In the postwar period, semi-industrialized countries that achieved steady output growth—including South Korea since the 1950s, China since the late 1970s, and Brazil between 1945 and 1980—did so under consciously expansionary macroeconomic regimes. When conflicts arose between, say, enhanced subsidies or cheaper credit for industrial development and macroeconomic restraint, the latter was often sacrificed.

This is not to say that one should not be wary of severe macro imbalances. After all, there was a wrenching stabilization in Brazil in the mid-1960s, and its thirty-five years of rapid growth were cut short by the debt crisis. But maintaining industrial growth seems to require robust expansion of domestic and export demand. There is nothing worse for the private sector's investment plans and learning process than a few cycles of repeated stop-and-go production. Well-designed public investment projects, by contrast, usually stimulate private capital formation.

To evade recurrent stabilizations, both the balance of payments and inflation have to be kept under tolerable control. Continued export growth and access to foreign borrowing are essential to external balance. Restrictions on capital movements—to the extent that they are geoeconomically feasible—can help keep the overall balance of payments in line and also permit internal cheap credit policies.

Fiscal balance[1] and real wages growing no more rapidly than labor productivity are essential for holding price increases in check. Certain institutional symbols—an "independent" central bank, for example—may help the anti-inflation fight. Under moderate inflations of 1 or 2 percent per month, however, price and wage regulation of the sort that the South Koreans have applied since the early 1970s may be more to the point. Combined with austerity, foreign exchange support (perhaps anchoring a new currency to the deutschemark or dollar), and luck, rigorous wage and price controls may be essential for stopping double-digit monthly inflations in the republics of the former Yugoslavia and Soviet Union.

Crucial macroeconomic details can aid the industrial restructuring task. Cheap, directed credit has already been mentioned; it should accompany closed international capital markets and a state role (if not control) in banking. Public development banks are the preferred model in most corners of the world, as suggested in Chapter 5.

Externally, a weak exchange rate is certainly an adjunct to export growth, but may be difficult to maintain in places like Russia, which have ample raw material endowments. Exports from such sources can obviate the need for a high local price for hard currency, making directed incentives for other export lines that much more essential. An undervalued currency also goes hand in hand with a low real wage. Given the dramatic wage-cutting during the early transition period, the political feasibility as well as the likelihood of favorable economic responses to further income reductions is unlikely.

In a buoyant macro environment, companies themselves can surmount the problems of the past—with the cooperation of the state. The now vanished principal/agent structure of socialist enterprises put planners with imperfect information in charge of managers who had their own black market sales proceeds uppermost in mind. Both sides benefited from high material throughout, lubricated by the soft budget constraint. Outside easily privatized sectors like retail trade, the former principals have been replaced by public agencies that now own the bulk of large firms and must help make them tick. Managers must learn capitalist mentalities, with their ongoing technical, investment, and marketing education being more essential than "hard" budget constraints to industrial recovery and growth.

The key initial task is restructuring. Management and technology problems of the sorts discussed in Chapters 3–5 have to be resolved, to allow potentially healthy enterprises to get under way. Certainly, state-owned enterprises will have to continue shedding the welfare responsibilities that they assumed under socialism. This transformation may cause fiscal difficulties, as already noted, but will be essential if any sort of Western-style corporatist social order is to appear.[2]

As firms (whether SOEs or POEs) reconstitute themselves, they will need institutional help. Finance for expansion has to be available, along with a favorable investment climate. Experience around the world shows that for nations not at the technological frontier, jointly mediated state and private sector procedures for "picking winners" *are* feasible and indeed necessary for growth.

The old Japanese criteria of supporting industries that sell products with high income elasticities of demand and in which rapid productivity growth is likely apply just as well to post-socialist Europe as they did for MITI in 1950–1970, for Korean planners in 1960–1980, and for Chileans in 1970–1990.[3] So does the Korean practice of tying incentives to enterprise performance, especially in exporting, while using tariffs and quotas to ensure cash flow from sales in the protected domestic market. Through indicative planning, self-destructive price competition and wide investment swings in sectors with scale economies can be avoided.

Such a planning operation will be needed because the price system is not the only bearer of economic information. Transmitting the messages it elides[4] is far easier among a reduced number of actors, and this simple fact points functional economic systems in the direction of large and/or collaborating enterprises, labor federations, and a bureaucracy that can guide producers to operate coherently with directed supports. All parties can ease the transmission of newly acquired technologies to the factory floor.

The free market models that have been applied to Eastern Europe do not recognize that successful semi-industrialized economies share these features; in due course, the world view of the Washington consensus is bound to be replaced. There are also specific interventionist actions—cooperation between private firms and regional authorities all over Western Europe and in Punjab, the town and village enterprises in China, even American innovations like the Tennessee Valley Author-ity—which may find emerging analogs under post-socialism.

With corporatist capitalism as a general target, the last operational question is how to constitute an economically functional bureaucracy to control restructuring, privatization, and then regulation and guid-ance of efficient enterprises (whether privately, publicly, or otherwise owned[5]). As Chapter 8 makes clear, the human capital base and politi-cal traditions for an effective bureaucracy in Eastern Europe exist. It will take a political act of will, however, spurred by recognition of neces-sity and legitimacy, to bring it into being. Well-paid, competent priva-tization ministries have been set up in several countries, in line with reformers' ideological predilections. The political process itself will de-termine how long it takes for effective indicative planning offices to emerge.

Reinventing planning, in fact, is the other side of effective priva-tization's coin. What will not work is pseudo-privatization, or the imple-mentation of an idealized Anglo-American system in which owners/principals use voice and threats of exit to impose economic efficiency on the managers/agents who run their firms. Such a capital market is a textbook fiction. In practice, Eastern Europeans are likely to follow their Western cousins by moving toward cartels, conglomerates, and insider-based mechanisms for financial control. Embedded public/pri-vate collaboration in managing change go together with this sort of ownership structure.

How can such economic development be made consistent with demo-cratic politics? Sustained output growth (with enterprise ownership swinging gradually toward the private sector) will have to be guided by politicians and bureaucrats sharing the long view and holding con-siderable power over management and labor. Can all these parties coex-ist with changing elected leaderships, and can they monitor both recon-structing the means of production and reweaving the social safety net?

Societal answers to these interlocking riddles will have to be found before sustained output and employment growth can provide legiti-macy for democratic politics and ratify the replacement of socialism by a humane system in Eastern Europe and the former Soviet Union. The verve and ambition that have been demonstrated in the first years by the peoples undertaking post-socialist transitions suggest that all the riddles will one day be solved.

Notes

References

Index

NOTES

1. From Pseudo-Socialism to Pseudo-Capitalism

1. The bias in our country coverage is toward Poland, Russia, and Hungary. When we refer to "Eastern Europe" we include Russia but not the former East Germany, which, owing to its political integration with the former West Germany, is sui generis in many respects. When we refer to Central Eastern Europe, we mean Poland, Hungary, the Czech Republic, and Slovakia. We emphasize Poland because of its role as a trailblazer in being the first country to undergo "shock therapy" and to create state-owned banks for the purposes of financial reform.

2. For a controversial World Bank publication on Poland, see Pinto, Belka, and Krajewski (1992).

3. For example, according to Lawrence Summers, vice president and chief economist of the World Bank in 1991, "Much of what is said about the propensity of economists to disagree is vastly exaggerated. I suspect that the discussion here [the World Bank Annual Conference on Development Economics, 1991] on the problems of socialist transition will not belie my impression that there has been a striking consensus in the advice that mainstream economists have given on the transition in Eastern Europe" (Summers, 1992, p. 7). See also OECD, 1991c.

2. Transition Macroeconomics

1. See, for example, successive issues of the U.N. Economic Commission for Europe's *Economic Survey.*

2. The consensus is codified in Williamson (1990) and the World Bank's *World Development Report* (World Bank–OED, 1991). Fanelli, Frenkel, and Taylor (1993) give a critical assessment. The consensus's central political dogma— starkly put—is that state intervention in markets leads toward economic

inefficiency and dictatorship. Such arguments were pioneered by the Austrian economists Ludwig von Mises and Friedrich von Hayek, who are often invoked by post-socialist reformers. See Chapters 6 and 7 for more discussion.

3. Zhukov and Vorobyov (1991) and Taylor (1991) present the framework underlying the analysis here. They emphasize the likelihood of severe price inflations and output contractions following post-socialist global shocks. Inability to control prices after the collapse of planning led to similar outcomes even in nations such as Ukraine, which did not fully accept the orthodox liberalization package but was inevitably drawn into Russia's policy-induced economic collapse.

4. Zhukov and Vorobyov (1991) observe that according to input-output tables for the USSR, intermediate input costs made up over half of gross output (intermediates plus value added) on average across the economy, even with low energy prices. A typical share in a semi-industrialized market economy would be about one third. In applied analysis, interindustry complications in cost structures are often ignored on the assumption that final goods prices can be reduced to direct and indirect labor costs (plus a markup) through the input-output table; in other words, overall cost and price changes are basically driven by wages. This treatment does not fit post-socialism, because prices of energy, raw materials, and other intermediates have risen sharply with respect to labor costs (Vorobyov, 1993).

5. The "efficient" American capital market failed for many years to discipline antiquated management at GM, IBM, and Kodak, until outside directors reluctantly stepped in. On the other side of the Pacific Ocean, Japanese and Korean conglomerates flourish despite their closed ownership and management structures, in which decision making is largely unaffected by movements in equity and bond prices. These contrasts are explored in the following chapters.

6. In the post-1945 Western literature, forced saving is usually associated with the work of Nicholas Kaldor (1956), but it was also the dominant adjustment mechanism in mainstream theory between the world wars and traces at least two centuries further back in economic thought (Taylor, 1991). Formal models are usually set up in terms of redistribution between workers and capitalists, but under socialism the latter's high savings rate was assumed by the state. With the advent of post-socialism, nouveau riche, "Mafia," and speculative classes are moving into the high savers' role. Also note that in socialist times, consumption fell when goods were simply not available; lower spending was involuntary under explicit rationing. This sort of noninflationary abstinence was labeled forced saving, in contrast to the definition here. It helps explain the relatively high household savings rates observed prior to the transition. As noted later in this chapter saving-investment balance may be difficult to achieve under post-socialism as savings rates drop off in response to the new availability of imported goods in the market.

7. Forced saving may have especially weak effects on demand in post-socialist systems where the boundary between enterprise wage and surplus funds is vague. The base for the inflation tax may rapidly erode as people flee from local currencies with minimal credibility. These considerations suggest that inflations and income and wealth redistributions large even by developing-country standards are needed to curb excess aggregate demand during rapid transitions away from administered allocation systems. The data reported below support these conjectures.

8. Over the past decade or two, Indian industrial planners have made a virtue of necessity by developing effective multi-tiered pricing systems for their nationalized industrial firms and even in agriculture (Alagh, 1991). China, with its rapid growth rates over the past decade, also relies on multi-track pricing (Singh, 1993). Intermediate inputs such as steel and energy are subsidized, generating paper losses on the part of the relevant state-owned enterprises but an important stimulus to export growth. Markets for land, labor, and financial capital do not exist in China, and in effect these inputs are made available by various levels of government to enterprises at differentiated and often subsidized costs.

9. A caveat about data is in order. Numbers describing economies during the post-socialist transition are approximations at best, and they differ widely among sources. The data in this chapter were assembled from published and unpublished information appropriate to the issue at hand, but in no way should they be taken as definitive.

10. Bruno (1993) reports the following approximate ratios of M_2 to GDP in 1990: Hungary, 0.4; Poland, 0.9; CSFR, 0.7; Bulgaria, 1.3; Romania, 0.6. A typical value in a market economy could range from 0.2 to 0.5 or more.

11. When monetary emission via loans from the banking system to the state ("printing money") becomes more than 5 percent or so of GDP, it can be destabilizing. By differentiating the famous equation of exchange $MV = PX$ (where M is money supply, V is "velocity," P is the price level, and X is real output), one can show that 5 percent emission $[(dM/dt)/PX = 0.05]$ is consistent with 12.5 percent annual steady inflation at zero output growth when $M/PX = 0.4$ (or $V = 2.5$). In the short run, however, inflation can jump up. The permissive factor is an increase in V as people try to hold less money when price increases speed up—from greater emission, adverse movements in costs, or rising social conflicts over the distribution of total output. Monetarists usually finger the fiscal deficit as the culprit behind emission, but in the Yugoslav case the "quasi-fiscal deficit" created by the central bank's financing of the subsidy schemes was at fault.

12. The traditional definition of hyperinflation is price increases at a rate exceeding 50 percent per month, for six months running. A more telling symptom is a jump in velocity, as the flight from holding money turns into a stampede.

13. Note 11 illustrates the calculations.

14. Price increases in proportion to exchange rate devaluations are sometimes called a "dentist effect," in honor of the price-making activity of all local practitioners with some degree of market power. Dentists and their colleagues are active worldwide, especially in post-socialist and similar countries where economic information is scarce, turning the exchange rate into the key pricing signal.

15. Along with other reformers, Sachs (1993b) argues that living standards in 1991 in Poland were higher than in 1989; hence real wages could not possibly have fallen as far as is shown in Table 2.3. His assertion is controversial. Data based on both price and wage deflation (UNECE, 1993) and consumer expenditure surveys (Sachs) are imperfect means for capturing real spending changes during the transition from the planning system. Linked declines in wages and consumption *do* fit into the coherent macroeconomic model sketched earlier in this chapter, adding to their mutual credibility.

16. According to estimates compiled by the UNECE (1993), net fixed capital formation fell by over 50 percent in Bulgaria (1989–90); almost 100 percent in the CSFR (1989–1991); 20 percent in Hungary (1989–1992); 40 percent in Poland (1989–1991); and 75 percent in Romania (1989–1990).

17. Current price GDP in 1990 was 626 billion rubles (World Bank, 1992), while the average money supply over the year was about 863 billion (Table 2.5). The resulting overhang was comparable to Poland's and Bulgaria's as reported in note 10.

18. In appropriate circumstances, price controls can tip the policy balance against inflation, as in the successful Israeli and Mexican stabilizations of the late 1980s. They are likely to fail, however—as they did in the "heterodox shock" Argentine and Brazilian anti-inflation packages of the same period—unless they are combined with a degree of austerity and access to foreign exchange (Taylor, 1991).

19. In practical situations, even eliminating distortions can be an inappropriate program. For example, Amsden (1989) argues that South Korean planners during 1955–1965 pushed exports to raise aggregate demand close to potential supply by setting prices (rightly) "wrong." They subsidized capital in a "basket case" country in which even subsistence wages were not low enough to give comparative advantage in critical export lines.

3. The Black Box of State-Owned Enterprises

Epigraph: See Pinto, Belka, and Krajewski (1992), pp. 1, 29.

1. Amsden undertook studies of more than 15 Polish and five Hungarian enterprises in various industries in 1991, 1992, and 1993, initially in conjunction with the preparation of OECD (1992a), as noted in the *Preface*. Where possible, the two case studies presented in this chapter use supplementary firm-level and industry-level data and information collected by other consultants.

2. The contrast with postwar Japan is striking, as discussed in Chapter 5. American occupying forces in Japan were New Dealers, rather than free marketeers, and instead of trying to dismantle Japan's Ministry of International Trade and Industry they tried to use it for their own purposes and worked with it (Nakamura, 1981).

3. How to define a "promising" enterprise, other than by using current profitability data, and how to select among promising enterprises for government support, are serious questions that are considered in OECD (1992a).

4. A study of employees' councils in fifty enterprises in Poland in 1991 by Dąbrowski, Fedorowicz, and Levitas (1991) found that "despite their wide competencies (the hiring and firing of directors, etc.), employees' councils are often weak or controlled by management. In this sense, they neither block nor facilitate reform." Moreover, some employees' councils were a positive factor in restructuring: "There are firms in which the councils are the carriers of change, forcing management to pursue more dynamic adjustment strategies, and moderating work force claims so that they do not exceed the financial capacities of the firm. The dynamic employees' councils represent a widening of managerial skills for the future." Finally, the study suggests that employees' councils do not necessarily either oppose privatization or want a pure employee-owned enterprise: "Employees' councils do not opt uniformly or generally for majority ownership schemes. Often employees' council activists are inclined to support mixed ownership schemes, in which the sale of stock to the work force is one element in speeding reform of the property system." None of this supports the view that employees' councils were an impediment to enterprise restructuring.

5. The management of almost all the firms we studied were interested in some foreign equity participation (but of their own choice). In the fairly representative case of Avia, a Polish machine tool company that had been restructured in the 1980s and that was profitable at the time of the transition, the management (in conjunction with its employees' council) preferred the following ownership structure: 35 percent of equity shares to employees (typically the Polish government insisted on a maximum of 20 percent); 30 percent to remain with the Treasury; 15 percent to go to a foreign partner for gears; 15 percent to go to a foreign partner for machine tools; 5 percent to go to a bank; and 5 percent to go to a foreign trading organization.

6. The degree to which SOEs could retain the profits from restructuring themselves in the form of selling their land or parts of their enterprises versus the degree to which such profits reverted to the State Property Agency (in the case of Hungary) was unclear in the early stages of the transition.

7. Pinto, Belka, and Krajewski (1993) find that "hard budgets and import competition—essential ingredients of Poland's reform package—can exert adjustment pressures even when changes in ownership and governance lag behind" (p. 214). But it remains unclear how adjustment is supposed to be accomplished after "pressures" on firms register.

4. Overloading the Market Mechanism

1. As noted in Chapter 2, wages determine the rate of growth of output and employment, but then changes in output exert a further effect on employment and wages, which is what we consider here.

2. The comparison is not ideal because concentration ratios for the United States are calculated at the four-digit industry level whereas they are calculated for Poland at the three-digit industry level, and the more finely disaggregated the industry (as in the United States), generally the higher the concentration ratio (data availability determined the choice of the benchmark). Thus the data in Table 4.4 *underestimate* Polish industrial concentration in relative terms. An off-setting factor, however, may be country size (being a smaller economy, Poland could be expected to have higher industrial concentration than the United States).

3. Industry information is from UNIDO (1991, 1992) unless otherwise stated. The UNIDO data probably do not include Russian entries.

4. Some of the details on import and export liberalization may be found in Hanel (1992); OECD (1991a, b; 1992a, b); Frydman, Rapaczyński, and Earle, 1993; and Rodrik (1992). As in many other aspects of transition policy, Hungarian exceptionalism manifested itself in less import liberalization and more export promotion than in Poland or Czechoslovakia (ILO, 1992).

5. According to a survey of seventy-five large state-owned Polish enterprises undertaken in 1991, sixty-five firms changed suppliers after the transition. Of the sixty-five (= 100 percent), 35 percent changed from one domestic supplier to another domestic supplier and an additional 26 percent changed from one foreign supplier to another foreign supplier. Only 15 percent changed from a foreign to a domestic supplier, while 23 percent changed from a domestic to a foreign supplier, due to lower prices, higher quality, and greater reliability of services (Pinto, Belka, and Krajewski, 1992).

5. Pseudo-Privatization and the World Bank

Epigraph: UNIDO (1992), p. 238.

1. At the time the World Bank made its Enterprise and Financial Sector Adjustment Loan to Poland, the Polish government was already in the process of planning the restructuring of some heavy industries. The Bank got on board this restructuring exercise as well, tying it to privatization: "The Bank is currently helping the Government draw up restructuring plans in the steel and chemical subsectors, and it plans to support the Government in implementing these restructurings *and linking them with enterprise privatization*" (GOP, 1993, p. 29, emphasis added).

2. As noted in the case of Uniontex (see Table 3.5), the largest share of enterprise debt was often held in the form of tax arrears by the central government or another government agency—the Social Security administration,

National Health service, and research and development institutes. The Bank ruled out converting *public* debt into public equity, however. How, exactly, the government's share of SOE debt was to be disposed of was unclear.

3. In Poland, most loss-making enterprises before the transition were concentrated in two industries, food processing and coal mining (see Schaffer, 1990).

4. As the Bank came to realize, its initial definition of "rationalization" (the withdrawal of subsidies and the bankruptcy of unprofitable enterprises) made sense only if (a) past subsidies were allocated to unprofitable enterprises, *and* (b) after the withdrawal of subsidies, only profitable enterprises remained. Owing to the dislocations of the transition, many enterprises remained that were not profitable but that were inherently viable, as discussed in Chapter 3.

6. Enterprise and the State

1. In economies like those of the United Kingdom and the United States, "financial liabilities" in the text should be replaced by "equity." Elsewhere in the world, nominal bondholders such as patriarchs of family conglomerates or lenders such as banks can have an audible voice in company affairs. The discussion in this chapter emphasizes how the Anglo-American form of finance is not likely to emerge under post-socialism.

2. In arguing that socialism is bound to be inefficient, von Mises ignored a long line of conservative scholars from Pareto and Barone on through Schumpeter who asserted that a planning system *could* replace (or certainly supplement) the market—it just had to get the marginal conditions right. We must credit von Mises with a degree of common sense that his colleagues lacked. Even if incorrect incentives for planners were not a problem, computational and informational gaps alone would soon overwhelm any potential super-Gosplan, as the failure of its real world incarnations under the Leninist system amply confirmed.

3. Shapiro and Taylor (1990) point out that market friendly economists who followed von Hayek kept up his *Road to Serfdom* theorizing about how perfect laissez-faire fits with vanishing states, benevolent dictatorships, and other impossible political configurations. His successors forget Hayek's (1949) almost Burkean insistence that if capitalist institutions arise, they do so in historical, organic fashion. He argued that their complexity defies human understanding, so that planners' (or reformers'?) attempts to improve on their inherited market systems are bound to fail. The successful developmentalist states in East Asia and elsewhere are obvious counterexamples.

4. Chang and Singh (1993) provide a good review of the SOE/POE literature, noting that (as often in economics) theory dominates the discussion because

the evidence is weak. There are not many empirical studies directly comparing the efficiencies of the two forms of enterprise, and on the whole they are inconclusive. The World Bank (World Bank 1991 and elsewhere) frequently argues that SOEs are suspect because their investment exceeds their saving, but the observation is irrelevant at best. Apart from odd cases like South Africa (where output and investment have been stagnant since the mid-1980s and there have been strong incentives for corporate capital flight), the enterprise sector in capitalist economies always invests more than it saves. Transferring savings flows net of own investments to cover this gap from the fiscal side of government, households, or the rest of the world is what the financial system is—or should be—all about.

5. The two concepts are not the same—see Chapter 4 for more detail. Under post-socialism, the second accusation holds more water than the first.

6. Aghion and Blanchard (1993) draw different conclusions from a model incorporating labor market crowding-out (plus other standard mainstream paraphernalia such as Say's Law as modified to incorporate a dole to the unemployed, determination of POEs' investment by their available saving, and generalized perfect foresight about wage and employment changes—all a bit alien to observable post-socialism). They conclude that "the equilibrium speed of transition is likely to be too slow, justifying measures by the government to accelerate the transition. These measures may include restraints on wages in the state sector, and top-down privatization and restructuring, imposed on firms rather than chosen by them." To be fair, Aghion and Blanchard also recognize that "going too fast may lead to too high unemployment and derail the transition" along the lines of the growth stagnation illustrated in Figure 6.4 in the appendix to this chapter.

7. Participants in the roundtable discussion edited by Slay (1993) report small upward movements in private sector shares of GDP in 1993.

8. Successive annual numbers of the UNECE *Economic Survey of Europe* provide useful detail on these and other matters. Another recent review is Slay (1993).

9. For example, Carneiro and Werneck (1993) emphasize how public enterprises in Brazil both undertook strategic investments and generated substantial savings flows until their prices were held down in the 1970s for anti-inflationary ends and to turn the firms into net borrowers so that they could serve as vehicles for capital inflows prior to the debt crisis. Recovering their previous positions will be difficult for these companies, regardless of whether they are publicly or privately owned.

10. Hyman Minsky's (1986) theory of speculative finance helps explain the merger and acquisition episode and the insider maneuvers in Chile discussed below. In a typical scenario, a financial intermediary (for example, a bank or a brokerage firm) might offer liabilities (insured deposits or junk bonds) to acquire speculative assets (shares of companies undergoing merger and acquisition action). As long as the prices of the speculative

assets go up (feeding back into expectations of future capital gains), both sides of the intermediary's balance sheet expand, along with the ratio of its debt to real asset holdings (essentially the real capital stocks of the companies concerned). When the speculative asset prices stabilize or start to decline, the intermediary's liabilities become bad debt. Cleaning it up may be essential for saving the financial system, with the taxpayers typically picking up the cost. During the course of the speculative excursion, the principals of the intermediary are often guilty of fraud and theft, plundering the public's willingness to hold dubious claims supported by unfounded hopes for limitless gains. Moral hazards created by overly generous deposit insurance schemes, the Anglo-American notion that corporations "belong" just to shareholders, as opposed to stakeholders, and lack of prudential regulation all prime the financial market for such self-delusions.

11. This point has been raised in several contexts. Corbett and Mayer (1991) and Akyuz (1993) present useful surveys for post-socialist and developing-country circumstances respectively.

12. Germany's bank-based financial system is solidly built into the socioeconomic structure, having emerged in the nineteenth century as a response to the challenges posed by "economic backwardness," as Alexander Gerschenkron's (1952) celebrated essay pointed out.

13. For example, an import quota allows its holder to earn "rents" by buying importables cheaply abroad and selling them dearly within the country. A large literature criticizing industrial strategy asserts that directed policy interventions such as quotas tempt firms to engage in nonproductive "rent-seeking" activities, such as bribing bureaucrats, instead of efficiently manufacturing goods (Krueger, 1974).

14. Definitions and details vary enormously across countries, but the UNECE (1993) reports that through 1992 well over half of "small" production units had been privatized in the Czech and Slovak republics and the ex-GDR *Länder*. The share in Russia was about one third. Public receipts from these sales have been tiny shares of GDP.

15. In fact this hypothesis is not far off the mark. Apart from Eastern Germany, post-socialist economies have not proved attractive to foreign investors. Hungary's share of foreign control of capital is the highest in the region—at about 3 percent (UNECE, 1993).

16. In 1992–93, holdings were being established by the state in Poland and Romania, while "investment privatization funds" organized by entrepreneurs arose spontaneously in the CSFR. Russian schemes went in all the Eastern European directions, but with more opportunity for inside ownership.

17. Nor can they be circumvented by stating *ex ante* that the holdings will have to sell themselves out to create a decentralized capital market after five or ten years, as Blanchard and Layard (1991) propose. *Ex post,* if sufficiently powerful holding units emerge, they will find ways to reconstitute them-

selves as did German and Japanese conglomerates after World War II—or the law can simply be changed. If powerful units don't emerge, then the whole exercise will be pointless.

18. For supporting evidence, see Taylor (1993). In a representative sample of eighteen developing countries in the late 1980s, only four had negative public sector savings as defined in the text. All had suffered severe macroeconomic shocks—either armed conflict (Nicaragua and Zimbabwe) or large external imbalances (Uganda and Zambia). Positive public savings rates ranged from 1 percent (Argentina) to 11 percent (South Korea) of GDP.

19. For example, Udis (1987) points out that West German local governments used full or partial ownership of firms as an instrument to increase employment in depressed regions, prevent private monopolies from forming, provide low-income housing, encourage innovation, and strive for self-sufficiency in key sectors. These are the classic aims of state-owned enterprises worldwide.

20. To be fair, it bears note that World Bank (1993) researchers are beginning to recognize the central role of East Asian state interventions in the market in support of growth. Whether this realization will influence the policy practice of Bretton Woods institutions remains to be seen.

21. A macro-level political obsession with food self-sufficiency led many marginal lands to be put under the plow under socialism; one implication was that measured production inefficiency was high. Comparative efficiency studies of East and West have also been biased by underestimation of outputs and overestimation of inputs in vertically integrated socialist agricultural sectors as contrasted to unintegrated Western farms.

22. For simplicity, the analysis here is presented in terms of diagrams. Taylor (1991) provides the algebra underlying models like the one that follows.

23. Implicit assumptions are that tax and subsidy flows associated with POEs are minor, and that demand for SOE output is relatively autonomous, in part because many of them produce intermediate goods and deal with one another. Recall from Chapter 2 how SOEs in Russia in 1992 kept their output flowing by advancing credits among themselves as attempts at contractionary credit policy fell apart.

8. Reconstructing the State

1. Not to confuse democratic institutions per se with the social and cultural conditions under which they function, we understand democracy here in a narrow sense: free elections, responsibility of the government to parliament, free media, respect for civil rights.

2. Sikkink (1991) gives an extremely interesting account of these ideas.

3. Stefan Jędrychowski, the head of the planning agency during the 1960s, remembers that his branch departments acted as de facto representatives of interests of specific branches, while he and the coordination department

had no way of checking the data and the claims presented (Kalecki, 1970, p. 470).

4. Analysis of this process is beyond the scope of this book. But it should be noted that this process of disintegration had various aspects: economic (diminishing, and then negative, rates of growth; rising output/input ratios, unmanageable hierarchical organizational structures; a growing parallel economy or "gray sector"); political (loss of effective central control); ideological (loss of legitimacy); and even moral (double standards in public and private life).

5. Observation of the Yugoslavia specialist Susan Woodward during a November 1993 Overseas Development Council meeting.

6. Nikova (1994) offers a review of Bulgarian circumstances.

7. The idea of democracy as the only founding myth possible I borrow from Marcelo Cavarozzi.

8. I thank Ignacy Sachs for this observation.

9. Economy, Society, and the State

1. It helps to have positive government saving (current revenues in excess of current expenditures including interest payments), and the difference between public investment and government saving (essentially the public sector borrowing requirement) should be no more than a few percent of GDP.

2. We use "corporatist" to refer to a system in which there is significant extra-parliamentary intermediation of organized interests and extra-market determination of prices and incomes, typically based on bargaining among organizations structured at least in part from the top down. Modern corporatism descends from European "guild socialism" of the interwar period. After 1945, it was perhaps first referred to (critically) by von Hayek (1960). Among social democrats, it did not lack subsequent defenders.

3. Despite its free-market rhetoric, the Chilean government under Pinochet did in fact pursue "industrial" policy by supporting exports of processed raw materials (fruits, forestry products, fisheries, and the traditional copper) which had strong market prospects and in which rapid technical upgrading was feasible. Policies were both targeted (public investment, enterprise restructuring, technical assistance, cheap credit) and generalized (cheap labor, worsening an already unequal income distribution that may still prove to be the Achilles heel of the Chilean miracle).

4. For example, technical information, signals among competing/cooperating enterprises in a given sector, and what Keynes called "the tone and feel" of the market.

5. Although they in no way dominate Western capitalism, some employee-owned companies have a successful track record in both the United States and Western Europe. This form of enterprise may fit naturally into the post-socialist environment.

REFERENCES

Aghion, Philippe, and Olivier Jean Blanchard. 1993. "On the Speed of Transition in Eastern Europe." Department of Economics, Massachusetts Institute of Technology, Cambridge, Mass. Mimeo.

Akyuz, Yilmaz. 1993. "Financial Liberalization: The Key Issues." United
Nations Conference on Trade and Development, Geneva.

Alagh, Yoginder K. 1991. *Indian Development Planning and Policy.* New
Delhi: Vikas.

Amsden, Alice H. 1989. *Asia's Next Giant: South Korea and Late Industrialization.* New York and Oxford: Oxford University Press.

―――― 1992. "A Theory of Government Intervention in Late Industrializa-
tion." In Louis Putterman and Dietrich Reuschemeyer, eds., *State and
Market in Development: Synergy or Rivalry.* Boulder and London: Lynne
Reinner Publishers.

―――― 1993a. "Big Business and Urban Congestion in Taiwan: The Origins
of Small Enterprise and Regionally Decentralized Industries (Respectively)." *World Development* 19, 9: 1121–1135.

―――― 1993b. "Trade and Performance in South Korea." In M. R. Agosin and
D. Tussie, eds., *Trade Policy for Development in a Globalizing World.*
London: Macmillan.

―――― 1994a. "Can Eastern Europe Compete by Getting the Prices Right?:
Comparisons with East Asia." In Andrés Solimano, Osvaldo Sunkel, and
Mario Blejer, eds., *Rebuilding Capitalism: Alternative Roads after Social-
ism and Dirigisme.* Ann Arbor: University of Michigan Press.

Amsden, Alice H. 1994b. "Why Isn't the Whole World Experimenting With
the East Asian Model to Develop?: A Comment on the World Bank East
Asian Miracle Report." *World Development* 22, 4: 615–670.

―――― 1995. "Big Business-Focused Industrialization in South Korea." In
A. Chandler, Jr., F. Amatore, and T. Hikino, eds., *Global Enterprise: Big
Business and the Wealth of Nations.* Cambridge: Cambridge University
Press. Forthcoming.

Amsden, Alice H., and Takashi Hikino. 1994. "Project Execution Capability, Organizational Know-How, and Conglomerate Corporate Growth in Late Industrialization." *Industrial and Corporate Change* (March).

Amsden, Alice H., and Rolph Van der Hoeven. 1993. "Manufacturing Output and Wages in the 1980s: Labor's Loss towards the Century's End." International Labour Organization, Geneva.

Amsden, Alice H., and Ajit Singh. 1994. "The Optimal Degree of Competition and Dynamic Efficiency in Japan and North Korea." *European Economic Review* 38: 941–951.

Anderson, Perry. 1974. *Lineages of the Absolutist State*. London: Verso.

Åslund, Anders. 1994. "Lessons of the First Four Years of Systemic Change in Eastern Europe." *Journal of Comparative Economics* 18 (August).

Awanohara, Susumu. 1992. "Question of Faith: Japan Challenges World Bank Orthodoxy." *Far Eastern Economic Review* (March 12): 49.

Bain and Company. 1991. *Polish CTD-Industry*. Ministry of Industry and Trade, Warsaw.

Balassa, Bela, and associates. 1982. *Development Strategies in Semi-Industrial Countries*. Baltimore: Johns Hopkins for the World Bank.

Balcerowicz, Leszek. 1992. *800 dni: Szok kontrolowany* [800 Days: A Controlled Shock]. Warsaw: Polska Oficyna Wydawnicza BGW.

——— 1993. "Lessons and Consequences of the Left's Victory in Poland." *Transition* 4, 8 (October–November).

Bank of Korea (BOK). 1989. *Economic Statistics Yearbook*. Seoul.

——— 1990. *Financial Systems in Korea*. Seoul: Bank of Korea. December.

BCG. *See* Boston Consulting Group.

Becker, Gary S. 1976. *Economic Approach to Human Behavior*. Chicago: University of Chicago Press.

Bednarski, Marek. 1992. *Drugi obieg gospodarczy: Przesłanki, mechanizmy i skutki w Polsce lat osiemdziesiątych* [Second Economy in Poland: Basis, Mechanisms, and Effects in Poland in the 1980s]. Warsaw: Warsaw University Press.

Berend, Iván T., and György Ránki. 1974. *Economic Development in East-Central Europe in the 19th and 20th Centuries*. New York: Columbia University Press.

——— 1977. *East Central Europe in the 19th and 20th Centuries*. Budapest: Akademia Kiado.

Berle, Adolph A., Jr., and Gardiner C. Means. 1932. *The Modern Corporation and Private Property*. New York: Macmillan.

Blanchard, Olivier Jean. 1992. "Restructuring in Central Europe: The Case in Poland." M.I.T., Cambridge, Mass. Mimeo.

Blanchard, Olivier Jean, and Richard Layard. 1991. "How to Privatise." Centre for Economic Performance, London School of Economics, London.

BOK. *See* Bank of Korea.

The Boston Consulting Group (BCG). 1991. *Polish Textile and Clothing*

Industry Restructuring Programme: Executive Summary for the Government of Poland and the World Bank. London: The Boston Consulting Group.

Braudel, Fernand. 1981–1984. *Civilization and Capitalism: 15th to 18th Century.* New York: Harper and Row.

Bresser Pereira, Luiz Carlos, Jose Maria Maravall, and Adam Przeworski. 1993. *Economic Reforms in New Democracies: A Social-Democratic Approach.* Cambridge: Cambridge University Press.

Broadbridge, Seymour A. 1989. "Aspects of Economic and Social Policy in Japan, 1868–1945." In Peter Mathias and Sidney Pollard, eds., *Cambridge Economic History of Europe,* vol. 8. Cambridge: Cambridge University Press.

Browne, Malcolm W. 1992. "U.S. Students Rank Fourth in Chemistry Competition." *New York Times.* July 22.

Bruno, Michael. 1993. *Crisis, Stabilization, and Economic Reform: Therapy by Consensus.* Oxford: Clarendon Press.

Brus, Włodzimierz, and Kazimierz Łaski. 1989. *From Marx to the Market: Socialism in Search of an Economic System.* Oxford: Clarendon Press.

Buchanan, J. M., Robert D. Tollison, and Gordon Tullock, eds. 1980. *Toward a Theory of the Rent-Seeking Society.* College Station: Texas University Press.

Calvo, Guillermo, and Fabrizio Coricelli. 1992. "Stagflation Effects of Stabilization Programs in Reforming Socialist Countries: Enterprise-Side and Household Factors." *World Bank Economic Review* 6: 71–90.

Carneiro, Dionisio D., and Roerio L. F. Werneck. 1993. "Brazil." In Lance Taylor, ed., *The Rocky Road to Reform.* Cambridge, Mass.: M.I.T. Press.

Chandler, Alfred. 1990. *Scale and Scope: The Dynamics of Industrial Capitalism.* Cambridge, Mass.: The Belknap Press of Harvard University Press.

Chang, Ha-Joon. 1993. "The Political Economy of Industrial Policy in Korea." *Cambridge Journal of Economics* 17: 131–157.

Chang, Ha-Joon, and Ajit Singh. 1993. "Public Enterprises in Developing Countries and Economic Efficiency." *UNCTAD Review,* no. 4: 45–82.

Charemza, Wojciech W. 1992. "Market Failure and Stagflation: Some Aspects of Privatization in Poland." *Economics of Planning* 25: 21–35.

Chenery, Hollis, Sherman Robinson, and Moshe Syrquin. 1986. *Industrialization and Growth: A Comparative Study.* New York: Oxford University Press for the World Bank.

Chirot, Daniel. 1980. "The Corporatist Model and Socialism." *Theory and Society* 9, no. 2.

Chirot, Daniel, ed. 1989. *The Origins of Backwardness in Eastern Europe: Economics and Politics from the Middle Ages until the Early Twentieth Century.* Berkeley: University of California Press.

Cho, Dong Sung. 1987. *The General Trading Company: Concept and Strategy.* Lexington, Mass.: Lexington Books.

Coase, Ronald. 1937. "The Nature of the Firm." *Economica* 4: 386–405.

Cole, David C., and Yung Chul Park. 1983. *Financial Development in Korea, 1945–1978.* Cambridge, Mass.: Harvard University Press for the Council on East Asian Studies, Harvard University.

Collins, Randall. 1980. "Webster's Last Theory of Capitalism: A Systemization." *American Sociological Review* 45: 925–942.

Corbett, Jenny, and Collin P. Mayer. 1991. "Financial Reform in Eastern Europe: Progress with the Wrong Model." *Oxford Review of Economic Policy* 7, no. 4: 57–75.

Coricelli, Fabrizio, and Ana Revenga, eds. 1992. "Policy during Transition to a Market Economy: Poland 1990–91." Discussion Paper 158. World Bank, Washington, D.C.

Crisp, Olga. 1976. *Studies in the Russian Economy before 1914.* London: Macmillan.

Crotty, James R., and Don Goldstein. 1993. "Do U.S. Financial Markets Allocate Credit Efficiently? The Case of Corporate Restructuring in the 1980s." In Gary A. Dymski, Gerald Epstein, and Robert Pollins, eds., *Transforming the U.S. Financial System.* Armonk, N.Y.: M. E. Sharpe.

Cumings, Bruce. 1988. "The Northeast Asian Political Economy under Two Hegemonies." In Edmund Burke, ed., *Global Crises and Social Movements: Artisans, Peasants, Populists, and the World Economy.* Boulder, Colo., and London: Westview Press.

Dąbrowski, Janusz M., Michał Fedorowicz, and Anthony Levitas. 1991. "Stabilization and State Enterprise Adjustment." Central Eastern European Working Paper Series, no. 6. Harvard University, Cambridge, Mass.

Donath, Ferenc. 1980. *Reform and Revolution: Transformation of Hungary's Agriculture, 1945–1970.* Budapest: Corvina Books.

Dore, Ronald. 1986. *Flexible Rigidities: Industrial Policy and Structural Adjustment in the Japanese Economy, 1970–1980.* Stanford: Stanford University Press.

Dutt, Amitava, and Bill Gibson. 1993. "Privatization and Accumulation in Mixed Economies." *Journal of Comparative Economics* 17: 1–22.

Dyba, K., and J. Svejnar. 1992. "Stabilization and Transition in Czechoslovakia." Paper presented at the National Bureau of Economic Research Conference on Transition in Eastern Europe, Cambridge, Mass. February.

Ehrlich, Eva, and Gabor Revesz. 1991. *Collapse and Systemic Change in Central-Eastern Europe.* Turin: Eunaldi.

Ellman, Michael, and Vladimir Kontorovich. 1992. "Overview." In M. Ellman and V. Kontorovich, eds., *The Disintegration of the Soviet Economic System.* London and New York: Routledge.

Evans, David. 1991. "Institutions, Sequencing, and Trade Policy Reform." Institute of Development Studies, University of Sussex. Mimeo.

Evans, Peter B. 1992. "The State as Problem and Solution: Predation, Embedded Autonomy, and Structural Change." In Stephen Haggard and

Robert R. Kaufman, eds., *The Politics of Economic Adjustment.* Princeton: Princeton University Press.

Evans, Peter B., Dietrich Rueschemeyer, and Theda Skocpol, eds. 1985. *Bringing the State Back In.* Cambridge: Cambridge University Press.

Fanelli, José María, Robert Frenkel, and Guillermo Rozenwurcel. 1990. "Growth and Structural Reform in Latin America: Where We Stand." Buenos Aires.

Fanelli, José María, Robert Frenkel, and Lance Taylor. 1993. "The World Development Report 1991: A Critical Assessment." In *International Monetary and Financial Issues for the 1990s.* New York: United Nations.

Fedorowicz, Michał, and Anthony Levitas. 1994. "Works Councils in Poland: 1944–1991." In Joel Rogers and Wolfgang Streek, eds., *Contemporary Works Council.* Forthcoming.

Freeman, Christopher. 1982. *The Economics of Industrial Innovation.* Cambridge, Mass.: M.I.T. Press.

Freeman, Richard B. 1993. "Labor Market Institutions and Policies: Help or Hindrance to Economic Development." In *Proceedings of the World Bank Annual Conference on Development Economics, 1992.* Washington, D.C.: World Bank.

Frydman, Roman, Andrzej Rapaczyński, and John S. Earle. 1993. *The Privatization Process in Central Europe.* London: Central European University Press.

Gacs, János. 1991. "Foreign Trade Liberalization (1968–1990)." In András Koves and Paul Marer, eds., *Foreign Economic Liberalization: Transformations in Socialist and Market Economies.* Boulder: Westview.

Galbraith, John Kenneth. 1967. *The New Industrial State.* London: Hamish Hamilton.

Gerschenkron, Alexander. 1952. "Economic Backwardness in Historical Perspective." In Bert Hoselitz, ed., *The Progress of Underdeveloped Countries.* Chicago: University of Chicago Press.

Gerth, Hans H., and C. Wright Mills, eds. 1947. *From Max Weber: Essays in Sociology.* New York and London: Oxford University Press.

Główny Urząd Statystyczny (GUS). 1992. *Rocznik Statystyczny 1992* [Statistical Yearbook 1992]. Warsaw: Główny Urząd Statystyczny.

——— Various months. *Statistical Bulletin.* Warsaw: Główny Urząd Statystyczny.

Glyn, Andrew. 1992. "Real Wages and Reconstruction in Eastern Europe." Institute of Economics and Statistics, University of Oxford, Oxford.

GOH. *See* Government of Hungary.

Gomulka, Stanislav. 1976. "Growth and the Import of Technology: Poland, 1971–1980." *Cambridge Journal of Economics* 2, no. 1.

GOP. *See* Government of Poland.

Government of Hungary. 1992. "Review of Industrial Export and Restructuring Project." Budapest. Mimeo.

Government of Poland. 1991. "Summary of Poland Privatization and Restructuring Project." Warsaw. Mimeo.

—— 1993. "Summary of Enterprise and Financial Sector Adjustment Project." Warsaw. Mimeo.

GUS. See Główny Urząd Statystyczny.

Haggard, Stephan. 1990. *Pathways from the Periphery: The Politics of Growth in the Newly Industrialized Countries.* Ithaca: Cornell University Press.

Hanel, Petr. 1992. "Trade Liberalization in Czechoslovakia, Hungary and Poland through 1991: A Survey." *Comparative Economic Studies* 34, nos. 3–4 (Fall–Winter).

Helleiner, G. K. 1994. "Introduction." In G. K. Helleiner, ed., *Trade Policy and Industrialization in Turbulent Times.* London: Routledge.

Hikino, Takashi, and Alice Amsden. 1994. "Staying Behind, Stumbling Back, Sneaking Up, Surging Ahead: Late Industrialization in Historical Perspective." In William Baumol, Richard Nelson, and Edward Wolff, eds., *International Convergence in Productivity: Cross-National Studies and Historical Evidence.* New York and London: Oxford University Press.

Hinds, Manuel. 1991. "Issues in the Introduction of Market Forces in Eastern Europe." IDP-0057. World Bank, Washington, D.C. April.

Hirschman, Albert. 1958. *The Strategy of Economic Development.* New Haven: Yale University Press.

—— 1970. *Exit, Voice, and Loyalty: Responses to Decline in Firms, Organizations, and States.* Cambridge, Mass.: Harvard University Press.

—— 1981. "The Rise and Decline of Development Economics." In Hirschman, *Essays in Trespassing: Economics to Politics and Beyond.* New York: Cambridge University Press.

—— 1982. *Shifting Involvements: Private Interest and Public Action.* Princeton: Princeton University Press.

Ho, Yinping, and Tzong-biau Lin. 1991. "Hong Kong: Structural Adjustment in a Free Trade Market Economy." In Hugh Patrick and Larry Meissner, eds., *Pacific Basin Industries in Distress: Structural Adjustments and Trade Policy in the Nine Industrialized Economies.* New York: Columbia University Press.

Hou, Chi Ming, and San Gee. 1993. "National Systems Supporting Technical Advance in Industry: The Case of Taiwan." In Richard R. Nelson, ed., *National Innovation Systems: A Comparative Analysis.* New York and Oxford: Oxford University Press.

Huntington, Samuel P. 1993. "The Clash of Civilizations?" *Foreign Affairs* (Summer).

IDI. *See* International Development Ireland.

ILO. *See* International Labour Organization.

IMF. *See* International Monetary Fund.

International Development Ireland (IDI). 1991a. *Final Report on UNIONTEX.* Warsaw.

—— 1991b. *Uniontex*. Ministry of Trade and Industry, Warsaw.

International Labour Organization (ILO). 1992. *Economic Transformation and Employment in Hungary*. Geneva: ILO.

International Monetary Fund (IMF). 1992. *World Economic Outlook*. Washington, D.C.

Janos, Andrew C. 1986. *Politics and Paradigms: Changing Theories of Change in Social Science*. Stanford: Stanford University Press.

Jensen, Michael. 1986. "Agency Costs of Free Cash Flow, Corporate Finances, and Takeovers." *American Economic Review* 76, no. 2: 323–329.

Jensen, Michael, and William Meckling. 1976. "Theory of the Firm: Managerial Behavior, Agency Costs, and Ownership Structure." *Journal of Financial Economics* 3: 305–360.

Johnson, Chalmers. 1982. *MITI and the Japanese Miracle: The Growth of Industrial Policy, 1925–1975*. Stanford: Stanford University Press.

—— 1987. "Political Institutions and Economic Performance: The Government-Business Relationship in Japan, South Korea, and Taiwan." In Frederic C. Deyo, ed., *The Political Economy of the New Asian Industrialism*. Ithaca: Cornell University Press.

Jones, E. L. 1981. *The European Miracle: Environments, Economies, and Geopolitics in the History of Europe and Asia*. Cambridge: Cambridge University Press.

Kaldor, Nicholas. 1956. "Alternative Theories of Distribution." *Review of Economic Studies* 23: 83–100.

—— 1957. "A Model of Economic Growth." *Economic Journal* 67: 591–624.

Kalecki, Michał. 1971. *Selected Essays on the Dynamics of the Capitalist Economy*. Cambridge: Cambridge University Press.

—— 1982. *Dzieła* [Collected Works]. Vol. 3. Warsaw: Państwowe Wydawnictwo Ekonomiczne.

Katz, Jorge M., ed. 1987. *Technology Generation in Latin American Manufacturing Industries*. Basingstoke: Macmillan.

Kemme, David M., and John L. Neufeld. 1991. "The Estimation of Technical Efficiency in Polish Industry, 1961–1986." *Economic Systems* 15, no. 1 (April).

Kim, Kwang-Suk. 1990. "Import Liberalization and Its Impact in Korea." In Jene K. Kwon, ed., *Korean Economic Development*. New York: Greenwood Press.

—— 1991. "Korea." In Demetris Papageorgiou, M. Michaely, and A. Choksi, eds., *Liberalizing Foreign Trade*. Cambridge, Mass., and Oxford: Basil Blackwell.

—— 1993. "Industrial Policy and Trade Regimes in Korea: Past, Present, and Future." In Lee-Jay Cho and Yoon-Hyung Kim, eds., *Korea's Political Economy: Past, Present, and Future*. Honolulu, Hawaii: East-West Center.

Kim, Linsu. 1993. "National System Innovations: Dynamics of Capability Building in Korea." In Richard R. Nelson, ed., *National Innovation Systems: A Comparative Analysis*. New York and Oxford: Oxford University Press.

Kim, Mahn-Je. 1992. "Korea's Successful Economic Development and the World Bank." Seoul. December 29. Mimeo.

Kochanowicz, Jacek. 1989. "The Polish Economy and the Evolution of Dependency." In Daniel Chirot, ed., *The Origins of Backwardness in Eastern Europe: Economics and Politics from the Middle Ages until the Early Twentieth Century*. Berkeley: University of California Press.

—— 1991. "Is Poland Unfit for Capitalism?" Program on Central and Eastern Europe Working Paper Series, no. 10. Harvard University, Cambridge, Mass.

—— 1993. "Transition to Market in a Comparative Perspective: A Historian's Point of View." In Kasimierz Poznański, ed., *Stabilization and Privatization in Poland: An Economic Evaluation of the Shock Therapy Program*. Boston: Kluwer Academic Publishers.

—— 1994. "Transition to Market and Democracy in Poland in the 1980s and the 1990s." In Joan Nelson, ed., *A Precarious Balance: Democracy and Economic Reform in Eastern Europe*. San Francisco: International Center for Economic Growth (ICEG).

Kocka, Jürgen. 1978. "Entrepreneurs and Managers in German Industrialization." In Peter Mathias and M. M. Postan, eds., *Cambridge Economic History of Europe*, vol. 7. Cambridge: Cambridge University Press.

Kornai, János. 1980. *Economics of Shortage*. Amsterdam: North Holland.

—— 1981. *Growth, Shortage, and Efficiency: A Macrodynamic Model of the Socialist Economy*. Oxford: Basil Blackwell.

—— 1986. "The Hungarian Reform Process: Visions, Hopes, and Reality." *Journal of Economic Literature* 24, no. 4 (December): 1687–1737.

—— 1993. "Transformation Recession: A General Phenomenon Examined through the Example of Hungary's Development." The François Perroux Lecture, delivered at the Collège de France, Paris, June 9, 1993. Harvard University, Cambridge, Mass., mimeo, and published in *Economie Applique*.

Körösényi, András. 1991. "Revival of the Past or New Beginning? The Nature of Post-Communist Politics." *Political Quarterly* 62, no. 1 (January–March).

—— 1994. "Demobilization and Gradualism: The Political Economy of the Hungarian Transition." In Joan Nelson, ed., *A Precarious Balance: Democracy and Economic Reform in Eastern Europe*. San Francisco: International Center for Economic Growth (ICEG).

Kreft, J. 1991. "Pod Lupą." *Gazeta Bankowa*, no. 46. Warsaw.

Krueger, Anne O. 1974. "The Political Economy of the Rent-Seeking Society." *American Economic Review* 64: 291–303.

Kuznetsov, Yevgeny. 1991. "Transition or Development Strategy? Structural Considerations in Elaboration of the Russian Federation's Strategy of Market Transformation." Peace Studies Program, Cornell University, Ithaca, N.Y. Mimeo.

Leff, Nathaniel H. 1979. " 'Monopoly, Capitalism,' and Public Policy in Developing Countries." *Kyklos* 4: 718–738.

Lenin, Vladimir I. 1964 [1899]. *The Development of Capitalism in Russia.* Moscow: Progress Publishers.

Levitas, Anthony, and Piotr Strzałkowski. 1990. "What Does Privatization of the Nomenklatura Really Mean?" *Journal of Communist Economics* 3 (June): 413–416.

Lipowski, Adam, and Jan Kulig. 1992. *Państwo czy rynek? Wokół "cudu gospodarczego" w Korei Południowej* [State or Market? Origins of the "Economic Miracle" of South Korea]. Warsaw: Poltext.

Lipton, David, and Jeffrey Sachs. 1990. "Creating a Market Economy in Eastern Europe: The Case of Poland." *Brookings Papers on Economic Activity* 1: 75–133.

Łuczak, Czesław. 1984. *Dzieje gospodarcze Niemiec, 1871–1945* [Economic History of Germany, 1871–1945]. Poznań: Wydawnictwo Naukowe UAM.

Luedde-Neurath, R. 1986. *Import Controls and Export-oriented Development: A Reassessment of the South Korean Case.* Boulder: Westview.

Lyashchenko, P. I. 1949. *History of the National Economy of Russia to the 1917 Revolution.* New York.

Maidique, Modesto A. 1987. "Entrepreneurs, Champions, and Technological Innovation." In Edward B. Roberts, ed., *Generating Technological Innovation.* New York and London: Oxford University Press.

Malinvaud, Edmond. 1977. *The Theory of Unemployment Reconsidered.* New York: Halstead Press.

Marglin, Stephen, and Amit Bhaduri. 1990. "Profit Squeeze and Keynesian Theory." In Stephen Marglin and Juliet Schorr, eds., *The Golden Age of Capitalism.* Oxford: Clarendon Press.

Marody, Mira. 1993. "W poszukiwaniu sensu zbiorowego" [Searching for the Common Meaning of Life]. *Polityka,* no. 42 (November 16).

Massachusetts Institute of Technology Commission on Industrial Productivity (MIT-CIP). 1989. *The Working Papers of the MIT Commission on Industrial Productivity.* Cambridge, Mass.: M.I.T. Press.

McIntyre, Robert. 1992. "The Phantom of the Transition: Privatization of Agriculture in the Former Soviet Union and Eastern Europe." *Comparative Economic Studies* 34, nos. 3–4: 81–95.

Migdal, Joel S. 1988. *Strong Societies and Weak States: State-Society Relations and State Capabilities in the Third World.* Princeton: Princeton University Press.

Miller, Rich. 1991. "Japan-U.S. Clash Looms on World Bank Strategy." *Journal of Commerce* (December 11): 1A.

Ministry of Industry and Trade (MIT), Hungary. 1991. *Hungarian Industry, 1980–1990.* Budapest.

Ministry of Trade, Industry, and Energy (MTIE), Republic of Korea. 1993. "New Economy: Its Implications for Korea's Trading Partners." MTIE, Seoul.

Minsky, Hyman. 1986. *Stabilizing an Unstable Economy.* New Haven: Yale University Press.

MIT. *See* Ministry of Industry and Trade, Hungary.

MIT-CIP. *See* Massachusetts Institute of Technology Commission on Industrial Productivity.

Miyajima, Hideaki. Forthcoming. "Privatization of Ex-Zaibatsu Stocks and Emergence of Bank-Centered Corporate Groups." In M. Aoki, ed., *Corporate Governance in Transition Economies.* Tokyo: Waseda University.

Modzelewski, Karol. 1993. *Dokąd od komunizmu?* [From Communism— Where To?]. Warsaw: Polska Oficyna Wydawnicza BGW.

MTIE. *See* Ministry of Trade, Industry, and Energy, Republic of Korea.

Nakamura, Takafusa. 1981. *The Postwar Japanese Economy: Its Development and Structure.* Tokyo: University of Tokyo Press.

Nell, Edward. 1992. "The Failure of Demand Management in Socialism." In Mark Knell and Christine Rider, eds., *Socialist Economies in Transition: Appraisals of the Market Mechanisms.* Brookfield, Vt.: Edward Elgar.

Nelson, Joan M. Forthcoming. "Labor, Business, and the State." In Joan M. Nelson, ed., *Intricate Links: Democratization and Market Reform in Latin America and Eastern Europe.* Washington, D.C.: Overseas Development Council Policy Perspectives Series.

Nikova, Ekaterina. 1994. "The Bulgarian Transition: A Difficult Beginning." In Joan Nelson, ed., *A Precarious Balance: Democracy and Economic Reform in Eastern Europe.* San Francisco: International Center for Economic Growth (ICEG).

NLK-Celpap. 1991. *Opportunities for the Polish Forest Products Industry.* Ministry of Trade and Industry, Warsaw.

North, Douglas. 1981. *Structure and Change in Economic History.* New York: W. W. Norton.

North, Douglas, and Robert P. Thomas. 1973. *The Rise of the Western World: A New Economic History.* Cambridge: Cambridge University Press.

Nuti, Mario, and Richard Portes. 1993. "Central Europe: The Way Forward." In Richard Portes, ed., *Economic Transformation in Central Europe: A Progress Report.* London: Centre for Economic Policy Research for the European Communities.

OECD. *See* Organisation for Economic Co-Operation and Development.

Ohkawa, Kazuchi, and Henry Rosovsky. 1978. "Capital Formation in Japan." In Peter Mathias and M. M. Postan, eds., *Cambridge Economic History of Europe,* vol. 7. Cambridge: Cambridge University Press.

Olson, Mancur. 1982. *The Rise and Decline of Nations*. New Haven: Yale University Press.

Organisation for Economic Co-Operation and Development. 1991a. *OECD Economic Surveys: Czech and Slovak Republic, 1991*. Paris: OECD.

—— 1991b. *OECD Economic Surveys: Hungary, 1991*. Paris: OECD.

—— 1991c. *The Transition to a Market Economy*. Paris: OECD.

—— 1992a. *Industry in Poland: Structural Adjustment Issues and Policy Options*. Paris: OECD.

—— 1992b. *OECD Economic Surveys: Poland, 1991*. Paris: OECD.

—— 1992c. "Hungary: Industrial Development and Industrial Policy— Outlines of an Industrial and Trade Policy, 1991–1994." OECD, Paris. Mimeo.

—— 1993. "Investment Patterns of Companies from OECD Member Countries into Central and Eastern Europe and the Newly Independent States: A Study Prepared for the OECD by Arthur Andersen." OECD, Paris. Mimeo.

Ost, David. 1989. "Towards a Corporatist Solution in Eastern Europe: The Case of Poland." *Eastern European Politics and Societies* 3, no. 1.

—— 1990. *Solidarity and the Politics of Anti-Politics*. Philadelphia: Temple University Press.

Pasinetti, Luigi L. 1962. "Rate of Profit and Income Distribution in Relation to the Rate of Economic Growth." *Review of Economic Studies* 29: 267–279.

Passell, Peter. 1993. "Russia Is Quietly Dismantling Socialism at a Remarkable Pace." *New York Times*. November 11, p. D2.

Patrick, Hugh, and Larry Meisner, eds. 1991. *Pacific Basin Industries in Distress: Structural Adjustment and Trade Policy in the Nine Industrialized Economies*. New York: Columbia University Press.

Pinto, Brian. 1992. "Incomes Policy and Wage Setting Behavior: Evidence from Polish SOEs during the Economic Transition Program." In Fabrizio Coricelli and Ana Revenga, eds., *Policy during the Transition to a Market Economy, Poland 1990–91*. Discussion Paper 158. World Bank, Washington, D.C.

Pinto, Brian, Marek Belka, and Stefan Krajewski. 1992. "Microeconomics of Transition in Poland: A Survey of State Enterprise Responses." WPS 982, Country Economics Department, World Bank, Washington, D.C. September.

—— 1993. "Transforming State Enterprises in Poland: Evidence on Adjustment by Manufacturing Firms." *Brookings Papers on Economic Activity* 1: 213–261.

Poggi, Gianfranco. 1978. *The Development of the Modern State: A Sociological Introduction*. Stanford: Stanford University Press.

—— 1990. *The State: Its Nature, Development, and Prospects*. Stanford: Stanford University Press.

Polanyi, Karl. 1944. *The Great Transformation: The Political and Economic Origins of Our Times.* New York: Rinehart.

Polanyi, Karl, Conrad M. Arensberg, and Harry W. Pearson, eds. 1957. *Trade and Market in Early Empires.* Glencoe, Ill.: Free Press.

Poznański, Kazmierz. 1987. *Technology, Competition, and the Soviet Bloc in the World Market.* Berkeley: Institute of International Studies, University of California.

Pryor, Frederic. 1992. *The Red and the Green: The Rise and Fall of Collectivized Agriculture in Marxist Regimes.* Princeton: Princeton University Press.

Przeworski, Adam. 1992. "The Neoliberal Fallacy." *Journal of Democracy* 3, no. 3 (July): 45–49.

Rao, J. Mohan, and José María Caballero. 1990. "Agricultural Performance and Development Strategy: Retrospect and Prospect." *World Development* 18: 899–913.

Rhee, Yung-Whee, Bruce Ross-Larson, and Garry Pursell. 1984. *Korea's Competitive Edge: Managing the Entry into World Markets.* Baltimore: Johns Hopkins University Press.

Richter, Sandor. 1992. "Hungary." *Wiener Institut für Wirtschaftsvergleiche Quarterly Report.* June.

Rodrick, Dani. 1992a. "Closing the Productivity Gap: Does Trade Liberalization Really Help?" In G. K. Helleiner, ed., *Trade Policy, Liberalization, and Development: New Perspectives.* Oxford: Clarendon Press.

——— 1992b. "Foreign Trade in Eastern Europe's Transition: Early Results." Working Paper Series. National Bureau of Economic Research, Cambridge, Mass.

Roskin, Michael G. 1992. "The Emerging Party Systems of Central and Eastern Europe." *East European Quarterly* 27, no. 1 (March).

Rothschild, Joseph. 1989. *Return to Diversity: A Political History of East Central Europe since World War II.* New York and London: Oxford University Press.

Rychard, Andrzej. 1987. *Władza i interes w gospodarce* [Power and Interests in the Economy]. Warsaw: University of Warsaw.

Sachs, Jeffrey. 1993a. *Poland's Jump to the Market Economy.* Cambridge, Mass.: M.I.T. Press.

——— 1993b. "Reply to Jan Adam." *Economics of Planning* 26: 185–189.

Schaffer, Mark E. 1990. "State-Owned Enterprises in Poland: Taxation, Subsidation, and Competition Policies." *European Economy* 43 (March).

——— 1991. "A Note on the Polish State-Owned Enterprise Sector in 1990." Research Paper Series, no. 9. Center for Economic Performance, London School of Economics, London. April.

——— 1992. "The Polish State-Owned Enterprise Sector and the Recession in 1990." *Comparative Economic Studies* 34, no. 4 (Spring): 58–85.

Scherer, F. M., and David Ross. 1990. *Industrial Market Structure and Economic Performance.* 3rd ed. Boston: Houghton Mifflin.

Schneider, Ben Ross. 1991. *Politics within the State: Elite Bureaucrats and Industrial Policy in Authoritarian Brazil.* Pittsburgh: University of Pittsburgh Press.

Schremmer, D. E. 1978. "Taxation and Public Finance: Britain, France and Germany." In Peter Mathias and M. M. Postan, eds., *Cambridge Economic History of Europe,* vol. 7. Cambridge: Cambridge University Press.

Schumpeter, Joseph A. 1943. "Capitalism in the Post-War World." In Seymour E. Harris, ed., *Post-War Economic Problems.* New York: McGraw Hill.

────── 1950. *Capitalism, Socialism, and Democracy.* New York: Harper and Brothers.

Shanin, Teodore. 1986. *The Roots of Otherness: Russia's Turn of the Century.* Vol. 2. New Haven: Yale University Press.

Shapiro, Helen. 1991. "The Public-Private Interface: Brazil's Business-Government Relations in Historical Perspective, 1950–1990." Harvard Business School, Cambridge, Mass.

Shapiro, Helen, and Lance Taylor. 1990. "The State and Industrial Strategy." *World Development* 18: 861–878.

Sikkink, Kathryn. 1991. *Ideas and Institutions: Developmentalism in Brazil and Argentina.* Ithaca: Cornell University Press.

Singh, Ajit. 1993. "The Plan, the Market, and Evolutionary Economic Reform in China." Faculty of Economics, University of Cambridge, Cambridge.

Skilling, H. Gordon. 1989. *Samizdat and an Independent Society in Central and Eastern Europe.* Columbus: Ohio State University Press.

Slay, Ben, ed. 1993. "Roundtable: Privatization in Eastern Europe." *RFE/RL Research Report* 32, no. 2: 47–57.

Solimano, Andrés. 1991. "On the Economic Transformation in East-Central Europe: A Historical and Institutional Perspective." Country Economics Department, World Bank, Washington, D.C. Mimeo.

────── 1993. "The Post-Socialist Transition in Comparative Perspective: Issues and Recent Experience." *World Development* (November).

────── 1994. "After Socialism and Dirigisme: Which Way Now?" In Andrés Solimano, Osvaldo Sunkel, and Mario Blejer, eds., *Rebuilding Capitalism: Alternative Roads after Socialism and Dirigisme.* Ann Arbor: University of Michigan Press.

Stark, David, and Victor Nee. 1989. "Toward an Institutional Analysis of State Socialism." In Victor Nee and David Stark, eds., *Remaking the Institutions of Socialism: China and Eastern Europe.* Stanford: Stanford University Press.

Stolper, Gustav. 1967. *The German Economy to the Present.* New York: Harcourt, Brace and World.

Sulieman, Ezra N. 1974. *Politics, Power, and Bureaucracy in France: The Administrative Elite.* Princeton: Princeton University Press.

Summers, Lawrence H. 1992. "Keynote Address: Knowledge for Effective Action." *Proceedings of the World Bank Annual Conference on Development Economics, 1991.* Washington, D.C.

Szacki, Jerzy. 1993. "Liberalizm po komunizmie" [Liberalism after Communism]. *Res Publica Nowa,* no. 11 (November).

Szelenyi, Ivan. 1988. *Socialist Entrepreneurs: Embourgeoisement in Rural Hungary.* Madison: University of Wisconsin Press.

Szlajfer, Henryk, ed. 1990. *Economic Nationalism in East-Central Europe and South America.* Geneve: Libraire Droz.

Szlek Miller, Stefania. 1992. "Post-Communist Poland: The End of the 'Third Way'?" *Canadian Slavonic Papers* 34, nos. 1–2 (March–June).

Taylor, Lance. 1988. *Varieties of Stabilization Experience.* Oxford: Clarendon Press.

—— 1991. *Income Distribution, Inflation, and Growth: Lectures on Structuralist Macroeconomic Theory.* Cambridge, Mass.: M.I.T. Press.

—— ed. 1993. *The Rocky Road to Reform.* Cambridge, Mass.: M.I.T. Press.

—— 1994. "The Post-Socialist Tradition from a Development Economics Point of View." In Andrés Solimano, Osvaldo Sunkel, and Mario Blejer, eds., *Rebuilding Capitalism: Alternative Roads after Socialism and Dirigisme.* Ann Arbor: University of Michigan Press.

Teichova, Alice. 1995. "The Czechoslovak Case: The Halting Pace to Scope and Scale." In A. Chandler, Jr., F. Amatore, and T. Hikino, eds., *Global Enterprise.* Cambridge: Cambridge University Press. Forthcoming.

Tewari, Meenu. 1991. "The State, Intersectoral Linkages, and the Historical Conditions of Accumulation in Ludiana's Industrial Regime." Department of Urban Studies and Planning, Massachusetts Institute of Technology, Cambridge, Mass.

Tirole, Jean. 1991. "Privatization in Eastern Europe: Incentives and the Economics of Transition." Department of Economics, Massachusetts Institute of Technology, Cambridge, Mass.

Udis, Bernard. 1987. *The Challenge of European Industrial Policy.* Ithaca: Cornell University Press.

UNDP. *See* United Nations Development Program.

UNECE. *See* United Nations Economic Commission for Europe.

UNIDO. *See* United Nations Industrial Development Organization.

United Nations Development Program (UNDP). 1992. *Human Development Report, 1992.* New York: United Nations.

United Nations Economic Commission for Europe (UNECE). 1992. *Economic Survey of Europe in 1991–1992.* New York: United Nations.

—— 1993. *Economic Survey of Europe in 1992–1993.* New York: United Nations.

United Nations Industrial Development Organization (UNIDO). 1991. *Industry Development Global Report 1991/92.* Vienna.

—— 1992. *Industry Development Global Report 1992/93.* Vienna.

U.S. Bureau of the Census. 1986. "Concentration Ratios in U.S. Manufacturing." In *1982 Census of Manufacturers*. MC82-S-7, 5–7. Washington, D.C.: U.S. Government Printing Office, April.

Van der Vee, Herman. 1986. *Prosperity and Upheaval: The World Economy, 1945–1980*. Harmondsworth: Viking.

Verdery, Katherine. 1991. *National Ideology under Socialism: Identity and Cultural Politics in Ceausescu's Romania*. Berkeley: University of California Press.

Vogel, Ezra F. 1991. *The Four Little Dragons: The Spread of Industrialization in East Asia*. Cambridge, Mass.: Harvard University Press.

von Hayek, Friedrich. 1944. *The Road to Serfdom*. Chicago: University of Chicago Press.

——— 1945. "The Use of Knowledge in Society." *American Economic Review* 35 (September).

——— 1949. *Individualism and Economic Order*. London: Routledge and Kegan Paul.

——— 1960. *The Constitution of Liberty*. London: Routledge and Kegan Paul.

von Laue, Theodore H. 1963. *Sergei Witte and the Industrialization of Russia*. New York: Columbia University Press.

von Mises, Ludwig. 1935. "Economic Calculation in the Socialist Commonwealth." In Friedrich von Hayek, ed., *Collectivist Economic Planning*. London: Routledge and Kegan Paul.

Vorobyov, Alexander Yu. 1993. "Production Aspects of Russian Transition." World Institute for Development Economics Research, Helsinki.

Wade, Robert. 1990. *Governing the Market: Economic Theory and the Role of Government in East Asian Industrialization*. Princeton: Princeton University Press.

Weber, Max. 1968. *Economy and Society*. Ed. Guenther Roth and Claus Wittich. New York: Bedminster Press.

Webster, Leila M. 1993a. "The Emergence of Private Sector Manufacturing in Hungary: A Survey of Firms." Technical Paper no. 229. World Bank, Washington, D.C.

——— 1993b. "The Emergence of Private Sector Manufacturing in Poland: A Survey of Firms." Technical Paper no. 237. World Bank, Washington, D.C.

Webster, Leila, and Dan Swanson. 1993. "The Emergence of Private Sector Manufacturing in the Former Czech and Slovak Federal Republic: A Survey of Firms." Technical Paper no. 230. World Bank, Washington, D.C.

Westphal, Larry E., Linsu Kim, and Carl Dahlman. 1985. "Reflections on the Republic of Korea's Acquisition of Technological Capability." In Nathan Rosenberg and C. Frischtak, eds., *International Technology Transfer: Concepts, Measures, and Comparisons*. New York: Praeger.

Williamson, John. 1990. "What Washington Means by Policy Reform." In

John Williamson, ed., *Latin American Adjustment: How Much Has Happened?* Washington, D.C.: Institute for International Economics.

Williamson, Olivier. 1975. *The Economic Institutions of Capitalism.* New York: Free Press.

Winiecki, Jan. 1991a. "The Inevitability of a Fall in Output in the Early Stages of Transition to the Market." *Soviet Studies* 43: 669–676.

—— 1991b. "Theoretical Underpinnings of the Privatization of State-Owned Enterprises in Post-Soviet-type Economies." *Communist Economies and Economic Transformations* 3: 397–416.

World Bank. N.d. "Industrial Restructuring in Poland—Some Case Studies." World Bank, Washington, D.C. Mimeo.

—— 1984. "Hungary: Economic Developments and Reforms." World Bank, Washington, D.C.

—— 1986. *Hungary: Industrial Policy, Performance, and Prospects for Adjustment.* World Bank, Washington, D.C.

—— 1991. *World Development Report, 1991.* New York and Oxford: Oxford University Press.

—— 1992a. "Poland: Economic Transformation at a Crossroads." World Bank, Washington, D.C. Mimeo.

—— 1992b. *Statistical Handbook: States of the Former USSR.* Washington, D.C.: World Bank.

—— 1993. *The East Asian Miracle: Economic Growth and Public Policy.* Policy Research Department. Washington, D.C.: World Bank.

World Bank–OED. *See* World Bank–Operations Evaluation Division.

World Bank–Operations Evaluation Division. 1992. *World Bank Support for Industrialization in Korea, India, and Indonesia.* Washington, D.C.: World Bank.

World Development. 1994. "Symposium on the East Asian Miracle." 22, 4: 615–670.

Yamamura, Kozo. 1978. "Entrepreneurship, Ownership and Management in Japan." In Peter Mathias and M. M. Postan, eds., *Cambridge Economic History of Europe,* vol. 7. Cambridge: Cambridge University Press.

Yavlinsky, Grigory, and Serguey Braguinsky. 1994. "The Inefficiency of Laissez-Faire in Russia: Hysteresis Effects and the Need for Policy-Led Transformation." *Journal of Comparative Economics* 18 (August).

Yudanov, Andrei Yu. 1995. "Large Enterprises in the USSR: The Functional Disorder." In A. Chandler, Jr., F. Amatore, and T. Hikino, eds., *Global Enterprise: Big Business and the Wealth of Nations.* Cambridge: Cambridge University Press. Forthcoming.

Zhukov, Stanislav V. 1993. "Monetary Aspects of Russian Transition." World Institute for Development Economics Research, Helsinki.

Zhukov, Stanislav V., and Alexander Yu. Vorobyov. 1991. "Reforming the Soviet Union: Lessons from Structural Experience." Institute of World

Economy and International Relations, Soviet Academy of Sciences, Moscow.

Żukowski, Tomasz. 1988. "Fabryki-urzędy i ich ewolucja: Rozważania o ładzie społeczno-gospodarczym w polskich zakładach przemysłowych" [Plants-Offices and Their Evolution: Considerations on the Socioeconomic Order in Polish Industrial Plants]. In Witold Morawski and Wiesława Kozak, eds., *Załamanie porządku etatystycznego* [The Breakdown of the Statist Order]. Warsaw: Institute of Sociology, University of Warsaw.

INDEX

Absolutist systems, 187
Administrative systems, 180, 192, 193
Africa, 25
Agriculture, 5, 131, 170, 196, 198, 203;
    market, 130, 146, 171; reform, 136,
    150–151; as financial asset, 142–143
Allocation of resources, 4, 20, 132, 151
Anglo-American institutional model,
    141–142
Anti-Semitism, 161, 165
Armaments industry, 174
Assets, financial, 142–143
Austerity, 47, 207
Austria, 131
Authoritarianism, 183, 185, 188–189,
    202, 203, 204, 205
Autokonszern, 74
Automobile industry, 72

Bain and Company, 53
Balance of payments, 7, 99, 104, 208. *See
    also* Debt and indebtedness
Balcerowicz, Leszek, 165, 168
Bangladesh, 49
Bankruptcy, 9, 69, 81
Banks and banking systems, 21, 31, 70,
    73, 174; state-owned, 14, 114, 123–124,
    134, 146, 173; central, 20, 45; invest-
    ment, 22, 73; industry loans, 63–66;
    development, 120–123, 126, 130, 135,
    146, 204, 208; commercial, 121,
    122–123, 146, 173; private, 121,
    122–123; assets, 139; credits, 146, 147.
    See also World Bank
Barclays de Zoete Wedd, 73
Belgium, 72
Big bangs, 6, 23, 26, 34, 44, 80

Big business, 96–98. *See also* Enter-
    prise(s); Firm(s)
Bobrowski, Czesław, 165
Bonds, 121
Boston Consulting Group, 53, 56, 60–63,
    122
Braudel, Fernand, 13, 117
Brazil, 11, 60, 97, 149, 207
Bretton Woods institutions, 5, 12, 13, 18,
    42, 47, 141, 144, 152, 193, 202; condi-
    tions on loans, 116; East Asia and,
    124–128; recommendations, 147, 148.
    See also International Monetary Fund;
    World Bank
Brezhnev, Leonid, 19
Bulgaria, 31, 34, 81, 103, 164, 202
Bureaucracies, 119, 120, 169, 180,
    184–185, 202, 204, 206, 210; elite, 185;
    East European, 187; inefficiency of,
    191, 193
Bush, George, 18, 126

Calculation debate, 132–133
Camdessus, Michael, 171
Capital: formation, 6, 11, 27, 38, 48, 136,
    141; market, 22, 139; accumulation,
    174, 180; human, 174, 210
Capitalism: post-socialist transition to,
    1–3, 151–152, 158–161, 164, 170–171;
    venture, 22, 133, 147; monopoly, 123;
    progressive, 145; development of,
    170–176; state, 175; unregulated, 197;
    modern, 206; corporatist, 210
Cartels, 173, 210
Catholicism, 161. *See also* Church and
    religion
Ceaușescu, Nicolae, 161

Chaebols. See South Korea

Chemical industry, 79

Chile, 29, 42, 48, 139, 140, 145, 152, 209

China, 23, 171, 215n8; economy, 3, 19, 147, 207; foreign investments in, 11; output growth, 29; banking system, 120

Church and religion, 197, 200

Civil services, 193–194, 204

Civil society, 184

Class conflict, 199. *See also* Middle class

CMEA (socialist trade-clearing authority), 27, 31, 39–41

Coal industry, 117

Coalitions, political, 182

COMECON, 160

Commodities, 21, 24

Commonwealth of Independent States (CIS), 45. *See also* Russia

Communism, 161, 162, 189, 190, 194, 196; collapse of, 167; social structures and, 197–198

Communist Party, 19, 119

Competition: subsidies, 55; textile market, 59–60, 69–70; in global markets, 79, 87, 95–96; atomistic, 98; SOE, 141–142

Concentration ratios, 218n2

Constraints: "soft" budget, 6, 24, 133, 134, 141, 208; on product quality, 57, 58, 69–70; "hard" budget, 147

Consumer goods, 38, 102–103, 179

Consumer price index, 44

Consumption, 23, 24, 38–39

Coopers & Lybrand Deloitte, 73

Corporatism, 223n2

Credit, 76, 103, 208

Crowding in: on capital formation, 48, 143; on private sector activities, 135; of public investments, 151

Crowding out, 20, 129, 134, 220n6

Czechoslovakia/Czech Republic/CSFR, 31, 103, 130, 140, 160, 161, 162, 170, 188; foreign investments in, 11; GDP, 17; prices, 34; exports, 39, 105; technology, 56; industries, 94–95, 96; imports, 102; subsidies to, 116; politics, 164, 201–202; communism, 190, 192; economy, 207

Debt and indebtedness, 7, 70, 160, 174, 218n2; crises, 29, 163, 175; overhang, 114; for equity exchange, 122, 123, 124; short-term, 139; public, 172. *See also* Balance of payments; Loans

Deficits, 99; fiscal, 38, 39, 46, 134; trade, 46, 49, 80, 102–104

Demand, 27, 58; /real income ratio, 6–7, 9; aggregate, 24, 26, 38, 40; leakages, 24, 39; contraction, 39; expansion, 48

Democracy, 2, 179, 187, 194, 203, 204, 210; capitalism and, 183. *See also* Social democracy/Social Democrats

Demonstration effect, 178, 179

Detergent industry, 95

Developmental state. *See* State(s)

Development economies, 18, 162–163, 165, 171, 183

Directly unproductive profit seeking (DUP), 148, 149, 150

Distribution, 207; of wealth, 25, 185, 215n7; income, 24, 25, 38, 46, 47, 125, 130. *See also* Redistribution

Dodge Plan, 125

Dubček, Alexander, 161

Dumping practice, 109, 148

East Asia, 7, 175–176; economy, 4, 144, 204; industrialization, 4, 5, 15–16, 76, 77; market mechanism, 4, 166; growth and development, 15, 184; restructuring, 77, 202; imports, 98–99, 101; exports, 100–101, 106; Bretton Woods institutions and, 124–128

Eastern Europe, 4, 10–11, post-socialist transition to capitalism, 1–5, 13, 16, 17, 30–42, 83, 111, 147; privatization of, 3, 7, 10–11, 13–14, 16, 52; industries and industrial policies, 4–5, 7–10, 14–16, 19–23, 52, 76; education levels, 7–8, 13; macroeconomic policies, 23–30; inflation, 35; wages, 36; economy, 41, 150, 164, 176; employment levels, 83, 89; imports, 98, 99, 100; exports, 104, 106; debt, 118; market, 159; state traditions, 187–191; communism, 192; social structure and politics, 199–202

Economies of scale, 137, 141, 149, 209

Education, 7–8, 13, 159, 174–176, 185, 194, 196–197, 207

Egalitarianism, 204–205

Elite(s), 179, 181, 189; social, 22–23; intellectual, 158, 161, 164, 165, 167, 169,

205; political, 158, 186, 192, 201, 205; bureaucratic, 185

Embedding: of enterprise structures, 130; of capitalism, 145; in transition to capitalism, 151–152; of public/private collaboration, 210

Employee-owned companies, 223n5

Employees' councils, 73, 82, 118, 167–168, 217nn4,5

Employment, 81–88, 137. *See also* Unemployment

England, 2, 14, 49, 95, 130, 137, 145

Enterprise(s), 21, 23, 129–130; restructuring, 53, 111; post-socialist, 77, 79; size, 92–96; public, 129; theories, 131–133; conglomerate, 140. *See also* Privately owned enterprises; State-owned enterprises

Enterprise and Bank Restructuring and Privatization Program (EBRP), 114

Enterprise and Financial Sector Adjustment Loan, 123

Entry barriers, 14

Environmental issues, 109, 160

Estonia, 9, 49

Ethnic differences, 200. *See also* Anti-Semitism

European Commission (United Nations), 12

European Community (EC), 160, 203; Common Agriculture Policy, 151

Excess capacity, 79

Exchange rate(s), 30, 34, 35, 40–41, 47, 98, 100; /price ratio, 36–38; in Soviet Union, 44–45

Eximtrade GmbH, 74

Export(s), 7, 24, 38–39, 100–102, 106, 176, 179; technology and, 22; elasticity of, 30; decline, 39–40; market, 39, 53, 58, 106–108, 141; growth, 41, 149, 208; industrial, 52, 107; machinery, 70–71; hard currency, 72–73; subsidies, 80, 98, 113; duties, 98; incentives, 101, 208; SOE, 104–106; product composition, 106–108; /import ratio, 110

Export Development Bank (Poland), 100, 104

Festo, 72, 74

Finance, speculative, 220n10

Finland, 72

Firm(s): levels and size, 5, 10, 86, 91, 92–96, 97, 131; multinational, 92; equity of, 142. *See also* Enterprises(s)

Flow: transfers, 130, 143; of funds, 142; information, 150

Food processing industry, 79

Foreign Investment Act (Hungary), 73–74

France, 102, 160, 187, 204

Free-rider problem, 138, 139, 140, 144

Galbraith, John Kenneth, 138, 178

Germany, 2, 9, 130, 160, 178; exports, 72; economy, 172; banking system, 173, 221n12; political system, 204

Gerschenkron, Alexander, 14, 172

Gorbachev, Mikhail, 43

Gosplan, 19, 20, 45. *See also* Soviet Union

Gossnab, 27, 45. *See also* Soviet Union

Gross domestic product (GDP), 135, 136, 141

Heckscher-Ohlin model, 148

Holding companies, 145

Holding entities, 144

Hong Kong, 97

Housing, 136

Human capital, 174, 210

Hungary, 161, 162, 188, 196; transition to capitalism, 1, 4, 160; foreign investment in, 11; exports, 22, 39, 105, 107; prices, 23, 34; imports, 27, 98; market reform, 29; debt, 31, 115, 116–117, 118, 127; privatization policies, 73–74; enterprises, 81, 92; inflation, 89; monopolies, 89; consumer goods, 103; economy, 116, 170, 207; subsidies to, 116; politics and political reform, 164, 201–202; communism, 190, 192. *See also* MMG Automatika Muvek

Huta Katowice Steel Company, 85, 109, 110

Import(s), 8, 11, 87, 179; decline, 39–40; trade credits for, 80; -led economies, 98–104; liberalization, 98, 101, 110–111; contractions, 99; policy bias, 99–100, 103; /export ratio, 110; substitution, 149, 175

Incentives, 101, 141; capital market, 22; enterprise, 23, 184; export, 101, 208; price, 151

Income, 15, 17, 31; distribution, 24, 25, 38, 46, 47, 125, 130
India, 60, 98–99, 149
Industrial concentration, 106–107
Industrial Development Agency (IDA) (Poland), 117–118, 122
Industrial Development Bureau (Taiwan), 118
Industrialization, 2, 9, 14–16, 189
Industrial policies, 146–147, 159, 168, 174, 198, 202
Industrial Restructuring Fund (Poland), 117
Industrial Sector Adjustment Loan, 116
Inflation, 23, 24–25, 47, 206; wage/price, 7, 25, 27; rates, 9, 27, 38, 43; repressed, 24; tax, 25, 27; hyperinflation, 34, 176, 215n12; estimates, 35; stabilization, 40; acceleration, 45; -reducing policies, 48–49; monopolies and, 80; average, 100
Input, 26, 53, 70, 214n4
Insider speculation, 139
Institutions, 3–4, 7, 13, 146–151. *See also* Bretton Woods institutions
Intellectuals. *See* Elite(s): intellectual
Interest rates, 7, 26, 41, 63–66, 100
Intermediaries, financial, 145, 146
International Development Ireland (IDI), 58
International Finance Corporation, 119
International Monetary Fund (IMF), 5, 18, 29, 35, 47, 65. *See also* Bretton Woods institutions
Investment, 1, 11–12, 21, 23, 24, 169; long-term, 13, 174; banks, 22, 73; fixed, 27; -led economies, 27; infrastructure, 38, 159, 160; private, 143, 146, 173; public, 146, 173; human capital, 174, 210; research, 174
Italy, 2, 72

Japan, 2, 118, 125, 130, 138–139, 183, 209; exports, 106–107, 141; banking system, 173–174; technology, 175, 178; political system, 204
Joint stock companies, 67, 70, 73
Joint ventures, 55, 68, 73–74, 77

Kalecki, Michał, 24, 165
Kim, Mahn-Je, 125, 126
Korea. *See* South Korea

Korea Development Bank (KDB), 120–121
Korea Development Institute, 125
Kornai, János, 13, 18, 133, 166
Kulig, Jan, 166
Kuznetsov, Yevgeny, 28
Kwiatkowski, Eugeniusz, 185

Labor: policy, 81–88; costs, 11. *See also* Employment
Laissez-faire policy, 2, 15, 132; macroeconomic, 7–10; in Poland, 58, 109; restructuring and, 120, 127
Land: reform, 125; transfers, 143. *See also* Agriculture
Lange, Oskar, 164, 165
Late-industrializing model, 14–16
Latin America, 7, 25, 98, 118, 175, 179, 186
Leninism, 19, 22, 151
Licensing, foreign, 72, 76
Lipowski, Adam, 166
Loans, 122, 124. *See also* Banks and banking systems; International Monetary Fund; World Bank; *specific countries*
Lobbies, 165–166

Machine engineering industry, 95, 70–71. *See also* MMG Automatika Muvek
Macroeconomics, 2, 5, 6–7, 16, 23–30, 166, 207; laissez-faire policies and, 7–10; transition, 17, 18, 25–26, 158
Malaysia, 11
Management, 22, 145, 175, 208–209; supply inertia and, 53–55; restructuring, 69; corporate, 132; discipline, 138, 139; of SOEs, 192–193
Market(s), 4–6, 170; transition to capitalism and, 1, 92, 158–159, 166; free, 3, 17–18, 52, 54, 63, 79, 115, 160, 162, 202, 209; forces, 7, 10; reform, 16, 58, 63, 115, 165, 168, 169; invisible hand, 18, 29, 69, 114; black, 20, 133, 170, 208; commodity, 21, 24; failures, 21, 133; capital, 22, 139; export, 39, 53, 58, 106–108, 141; regulation, 49, 159, 163; restructuring and, 78, 79; liberalization, 79, 81, 130, 146, 148, 160; world, 79; export, 106–108, 141; economy, 132, 177; financial, 143, 145; private, 151; foreign, 176, 179

Marketing, 67–68, 74

Marxism, 151–152, 161, 164, 165, 170

Mass society, 199

Matsushita Electronics, 76

Media, 168, 169

Meiji bureaucracy, 172–173

Mergers, acquisitions, and takeovers, 138, 142, 144, 220n10

Metalworking industry, 54. *See also* MMG Automatika Muvek

Mexico, 29, 42, 49

Microeconomics, 163, 166

Middle class, 163, 189, 190, 194–195, 199, 201

Military-industrial complex, 22, 23, 147, 202

Ministries of industry, 52, 117, 118–120, 204

Ministries of privatization, 119, 120

Ministry of Finance (Poland), 63

Ministry of Industry and Trade (Hungary), 119

Ministry of International Trade and Industry (MITI) (Japan), 118

Ministry of Labor (Hungary), 81

Ministry of Ownership Change (Poland), 119

MMG Automatika Muvek (Hungary), 70, 79; restructuring, 71, 73–76; technology, 71–73, 76–77; marketing, 74; cost and efficiency, 75; employment levels, 85–86

Modernization, 177–178, 181–183, 186, 189, 190

Modzelewski, Karol, 169

Money: overhang, 30, 31, 34, 43; supply, 41, 45, 47, 177; illusion, 100

Monopolies, 29, 125, 140, 171; antimonopoly legislation, 79, 80, 111, 116, 125; inflation and, 80; power, 88–98; natural, 141; of information, 165–166, 191

Moscow International Currency Exchange (MICE), 44

Multifaceted price system (MPS), 29

Mutual funds, 144, 145

Nationalism, 172, 188, 197

Neoclassicism, 163–164, 166, 167, 172

Neoliberalism, 161–170

Nomenklatura, 52, 119–120, 133, 170, 189, 193, 199, 201

Obsolescence, 117. *See also* Technology: obsolete

Output, 26, 48, 134, 206; decline in, 17, 24, 38–39, 43, 81; growth, 18, 19, 24, 29, 47, 130, 207, 210; real wages and, 27, 30; shocks, 38; manufacturing, 53, 83; contraction, 88, 214n3; distribution, 89–91

Ownership concept, 137–138, 164

Patterns of politics, 200–201

Peasant Party (Poland), 198–199

Pension system, 145, 191, 194, 195, 198

Piłsudski, Marshal, 184, 185

Planning, 210; administrative, 19–23, 43; central, 52, 111, 165–166, 190–191; state, 148; development, 162; economies, 166

Poland, 48, 160, 161, 162, 184, 188; textile industry, 9, 55, 68, 69–70, 101; foreign investment in, 11; GDP growth rates, 17; exports, 22, 39, 105, 108, 110; prices, 23, 29, 34, 41; imports, 27, 98; inflation, 27, 176; debt, 31, 119, 127, 218n1; domestic competition, 57, 69–70; economy, 58, 119, 170; tax policies, 65–66; enterprises, 81, 92–94, 167; monopolies, 89; output distribution, 98–91; industries, 92–96, 100, 107–108; steel industry, 94–95, 108–111; banking system, 100, 104, 117, 121, 122, 123; consumer goods, 102–103; privatization, 113; subsidies to, 116; agriculture, 131; politics and political reform, 164, 165, 168, 201–202, 206; history, 187–188; communism, 190, 192; social structure and politics, 197–199; living standards, 216n15. *See also* Uniontex Company

Polanyi, Karl, 16, 151, 152

Polish Development Bank (PDB), 117, 121, 123

Ponzi schemes, 140, 145

Post-socialism, 52, 169, 178, 190–201, 206, 210; in Eastern Europe, 1–5, 13, 16, 17, 30–42, 83, 111, 147; political instability and, 70; enterprises, 77; restructuring, 80–81; financial backing, 118; SOEs, 134; role of state in, 158–161; state, 191–194

Price(s), 17, 20, 111; increases, 6–7, 25, 26–27, 43–44, 45; subsidies, 20–21; relative, 23; input, 26; inflation, 30; /exchange rate ratio, 36–38; controls, 47; dumping, 109, 148; linkages, 132; policy, 137; wars/competition, 141, 209
Principal/agent model of socialist enterprise, 133, 144, 208
Privately owned enterprises (SOEs), 49, 53, 97, 144, 146; transition to, 81–82; /SOE linkages, 128, 129–130, 131, 133–136, 153–157
Private sector, 77, 126, 135–142, 176–177, 193, 209
Privatization, 130, 136, 195, 206; restructuring before, 12, 13–14, 70; enterprise, 23; failure, 77; POE/SOE linkages and, 129–130; schemes and modes, 130, 140, 142–146; vouchers, 130, 140; agencies, 136, 142; role of state in, 158–161; investment funds, 221n6. See also Pseudo-privatization
Product: quality, 9, 53–69, 80; innovation, 55; restructuring, 69
Production, 7, 9, 22, 24, 206; technology and, 21–22, 178; consolidation, 69; economies of scale, 149; role of state in, 162, 173; concentration of, 173; taxation and, 174; mass, 178
Productivity, 81, 88
Profit(s), 134; -led economies, 28, 29, 30
Property, 74, 83, 195; rights, 4, 5, 158, 172
Prussia, 172–173, 174, 187, 188
Przeworski, Adam, 47
Pseudo-capitalism, 2, 13
Pseudo-privatization, 12–14, 54–55, 123–124, 127, 144, 177
Pseudo-socialism, 1, 4–5, 11, 159, 165, 178, 189, 191–192, 195; in Russia, 4, 200–201; collapse of, 161–170
Public enterprise sector, 135–142
Public ownership, 140
Public sector, 9–10, 80, 127, 143
Pulp and paper industry, 85–86, 95–96

Quotas, 11, 101, 209, 221n13; rents, 148, 150

Reagan, Ronald, 18, 39, 126, 163
Real wages, 26, 138, 208; declines and

cuts in, 6, 9, 24, 25, 27, 40, 45, 54, 80, 81, 87–88, 111; output and, 27, 30; collapse of, 152
Recession, 177, 198
Redistribution, 167, 171, 172, 195, 198, 203; models, 214n6
Reform programs, 2, 152; market, 16, 58, 63, 115, 165, 168, 169. See also specific countries
Re-industrialization, 2, 5, 9, 177, 179–180
Rental arrangements, 142
Rent-seeking activities, 140, 150, 163, 166, 180, 183, 221n13
Research and development, 77, 97, 147, 159, 174, 178, 194; institutes, 52
Resource allocation, 4, 20, 132, 151
Restructuring, 69, 210; financing of, 63, 68–69; autonomous, 67–68, 70, 73–75, 77; management, 69, 209; barriers to, 75–76, 79; time intervals for, 76; post-socialist, 81; privatization and, 85; of the state, 202–205
Reverse engineering, 178
Romania, 31, 34, 41, 81, 95, 145, 161, 188, 202; transition to capitalism, 192; economy, 207
Rule of law, 198, 200
Russia, 10, 36, 49, 175; pseudo-socialism in, 4, 200–201; macroeconomic policy, 23–30; prices, 27, 47, 91; economy, 41, 150, 172, 173, 208; transition to capitalism, 42–46, 147, 161; labor policy, 81; monopolies, 91; industries, 96–97, 174, 183–184; Poland and, 162; military strength, 201; political reform, 206–207. See also Soviet Union

Samsung Electronics, 76
Saving, 173; forced, 24–25, 26, 27, 48, 214n6, 215n7; private, 143
Say's Law, 6
Service sector, 131, 141, 142
Shock economic reform therapy, 4, 16, 168, 170, 176, 177, 206; global, 6, 23, 26; external, 12, 39; to output, 38; policy and programs, 40, 43, 132; effect on restructuring efforts, 58; consumerism and, 87; liberalization, 150; in political transition, 192, 194
Singapore, 97
Slovak Federal Republic, 105, 162

Slovenia, 49
Social democracy/Social Democrats, 162, 169, 196, 198–199
Social discipline, 186–187, 204
Social groups and structures, 181, 182, 197–199
Socialism, 1–3, 131–132, 209; planning systems, 19, 23; elite, 22–23; municipal, 147; market, 164; bureaucratic, 169. *See also* Post-socialism; Pseudo-socialism
Social policies, 158, 161
Social services, 86–87, 141, 195
Solidarity, 119, 167, 168, 169, 197. *See also* Poland
South Korea, 3, 22, 30, 60, 101; output growth, 29; *chaebols* (trading/industrial companies), 30, 49, 140, 145, 150; industrialization, 76, 97, 209; debt, 99, 103; exports, 103–104, 141, 149; banking system, 120, 121–122; World Bank and, 125–126; reform programs, 152; economy, 166, 176, 207, 208; government, 184, 185
Soviet Union, 7, 21, 44–45, 161; transition to capitalism, 17, 179; economy, 19, 20, 42–43; planning system (Gosplan), 19, 20, 45; Gossnab, 27, 45; Poland and, 162; Marxism, 164; communism, 190. *See also* Russia
Spain, 152
Stakeholders in enterprises, 138, 139, 141, 142, 147
Stalinism, 161, 179, 189
Star Truck Company, 122
State(s), 162; role in transition to capitalism, 158–161, 162–163, 164, 173, 180; interventionism, 168–169; protection of industries, 174; capitalism, 175; private sector, 176; role in development, 181, 182–187, 219n3; predatory, 183; modern, 188; revenues, 194; restructuring, 202–205
State-owned enterprises (SOEs), 7, 12, 21, 53, 80, 128, 146, 169, 177, 195, 198; restructuring, 10–11, 52, 54, 77–78, 95–96, 114–115, 123, 124, 126, 127, 217n6; taxes on, 24, 38, 63, 134; tax revenues, 24, 38; prices, 35; privatization and, 63, 76, 160; debt, 64; employment and wage levels, 68, 87; exports, 104–106; World Bank and, 118; bottlenecks, 124; /POE linkages, 128, 129–130, 131, 133–136, 153–157; inefficiency of, 133, 140; post-socialist, 134; subsidies, 134; asset values, 136; shares of production, 136; competition, 141–142; goals, 141; management structure, 192–193. *See also* Uniontex Company
State Property Agency (SPA), 73, 74, 76
Statism, 161–163, 169, 172, 180, 184, 189–190, 192
Steel and iron industry, 79, 94–95, 117
Stocks and stock markets, 121, 130, 132, 137–138, 139; transfers, 144
Subsidies, 31, 148, 169; price, 20–21; precompetition, 55; for restructuring, 70, 127–128, withdrawal or curtailment of, 79, 95, 115–118, 219n4; export, 80, 98, 113, 150; to SOEs, 134; public sector, 140; consumer, 177
Subsidized credit, 87
Supply, 26, 27, 218n5; inertia, 53–55, 58, 70, 77;–side growth, 80–81
Suzuki Hungary, 74
Sweden, 9, 14, 72, 85
Taiwan, 3, 22, 76, 97, 103, 136, 138–139, 166, 184; debt, 103; reform programs, 152; economy, 176; government, 184, 185
Tariffs, 11, 101, 150, 169, 173, 177, 209
Tax(es), 21, 172, 174; on SOEs, 24, 38, 63, 134; inflation, 25, 26, 215n7; on assets, 63–64; on joint ventures, 73–74; value-added, 74, 127; penalties, 77; income, 127; export, 148; wage, 169; arrears, 218n2
Technology, 53, 175, 209; obsolete, 9, 10, 21–22, 54, 56, 71–73, 76, 77, 80; innovations, 21–22, 55; bottlenecks, 54, 70–78; transfers, 72; upgrades, 75; acquisition, 76–77, 144, 149, 178–179, 209; borrowed, 111; production, 116; war, 172; hard, 182
Textile industry, 60, 101, 103, 106–107. *See also* Uniontex Company
Thatcher, Margaret, 137, 163
Third World/developing countries, 18, 162, 165, 183

Trade, 176, 202; credits and deficits, 46, 49, 80, 102–104, 148; liberalization, 101–102, 116, 147; external, 147
Trade unions. *See* Unions
Transnational corporations, 149
Turkey, 29, 60, 152, 161, 184

Unemployment, 7, 42, 80, 81–88, 177, 195; in defense industries, 10; laid-off workers, 58–59, 85
Unions, 12, 73, 167, 168, 194
Uniontex Company (Poland), 56–58, 79; labor costs and product quality, 58–63, 66–67; indebtedness, 63–66, 70, 123; penalty interest rates, 63–66; restructuring attempts, 67–69, 71, 76; marketing, 67–68; product constraints on, 69–70; employment levels, 85–86
United States: economy, 14, 138, 173; fiscal deficit, 39; foreign licensing agreements, 72; steel imports, 109; financial system, 137; output distribution, 89–91; ownership structure, 130; technology, 178
USAID, 125, 126

Vietnam, 3
Voluntary associations, 159
Von Hayek, Friedrich, 132, 151, 159, 167, 212n2
Von Mises, Ludwig, 131–32, 151, 213n2

Wage(s), 20, 47, 193; -led economies, 24, 26, 29, 30–31; index, 25, 31, 35, 80; cuts, 26, 41–42, 58; restraints/controls, 27, 31, 220n6; /output linkages, 30; freezes and caps, 34, 74, 80; contraction, 40; increases, 48, 63–64; /labor costs ratio, 58–63; social, 86–87; regulation, 87, 208; tax, 169
Wałesa, Lech, 182
Washington consensus on economic reform, 46–47, 147, 150, 209
Wealth distribution, 25, 185, 215n7; transfers, 140
Weber, Max, 151, 152
Welfare, 159–160, 162; state, 191, 193, 194, 197, 200, 209
Workers' organizations, 125. *See also* Employees' councils; Unions
World Bank, 5, 29, 47, 53; loans, 11, 119, 123, 218n1; economic reform and, 18, 113–114; Warsaw Mission, 89; export policy, 101; role in restructuring of Eastern Europe, 113, 114, 124, 126, 162; SOEs and, 114–115; conditions and restrictions, 115–117, 120, 121, 126, 128; private financial institutions and, 122–123; ban on development banking, 146. *See also* Bretton Woods institutions

Yeltsin, Boris, 46
Yugoslavia (former), 3, 31, 34, 49, 152, 207, 208